The Story of Exeter's
St James' Park

Commemorating the 125th anniversary of the first association-football match ever played at St James' Park

The Story of Exeter's
St James' Park
Land of Grecian Glory

Aidan Hamilton
Exeter City Supporters' Trust

HALSGROVE

First published in Great Britain in 2019

Copyright © Exeter City Supporters' Trust

All rights reserved. No part of this publication may be reproduced,
stored in a retrieval system, or transmitted in any form or by any
means without the prior permission of the copyright holder.

British Library Cataloguing-in-Publication Data
A CIP record for this title is available from the British Library

ISBN 978 0 85704 342 9

Halsgrove
Halsgrove House,
Ryelands Business Park,
Bagley Road, Wellington,
Somerset TA21 9PZ
Tel: 01823 653777
Fax: 01823 216796
email: sales@halsgrove.com

Part of the Halsgrove group of companies
Information on all Halsgrove titles is available at: www.halsgrove.com

Printed and bound in India by Parksons Graphics Pvt Ltd

Contents

Acknowledgements 7

Foreword 8

Introduction. 9

1. The Parish Field 11

2. Bradford's Field 15

3. Clown cricketers 19

4. Steadily gaining favour 23

5. At St James' Field 27

6. A scientific game 31

7. 'Who are the leaders?'. 36

8. Oddities of the pitch 41

9. In the very heart of the city 45

10. 'Up Grecians!'. 49

11. Uncle Tom Cobley 54

12. Strangely different 59

13. Unparalleled happenings 64

14. Record day 69

15. A flourishing example. 75

16. A deserted scene. 80

17. Serious losses 85

18. Turnstiles clicked 90

19. Burning to ashes 94

20. 'Dido's Day!' 99

21. Under cover. 105

22. Gaping wounds 110

23. Tidy terraces 115

24. By ticket only 119

25. Under the lights. 124

26. The European champions. 130

27. Keep off the pitch. 135

28. Fortress St James' Park 140

29. Saved!. 145

30. A community club 150

Bibliography. 156

Index 157

Subscribers 159

In memory of the Tucker family
who lived in Alphington Street *c.*1891,
one of whom was my grandmother Dora.

Acknowledgements

THE idea for this book came out of the 'History of St James Park' project in 2016. Since the go-ahead was given by the Exeter City Supporters' Trust and its History Group, I've worked on the book with Sarah Willis and Martin Weiler. I'm hugely indebted to both of them for their assistance: Sarah for managing the project, doing the copy-editing and liaising with the publishers; Martin for providing constant feedback throughout the writing process, helping to locate material and suggesting topics. A big thanks also to: Paul Farley for helping out with City-related publications and giving me tours of the Park on matchdays; Will Barrett for helping with images; Alison Styles for filling gaps in the research and discovering the oldest images we have of St James' Park, the two which date from the 1890s; Gabriella Giannachi from the University of Exeter, who has done much to shape and drive Exeter City's heritage work; Alan Banks for sharing with me his memories of St James' Park; Brian Carpenter at the Devon Heritage Centre for checking sources and providing access to the Dave Fisher Collection; Brian's colleagues, especially John Booker who produced a transcript of the seventeenth-century Bill of Complaint; Norman Shiel for offering access to his programme collection; Lewis Jones regarding his collection; Chris Vickery for doing the scanning of the City programmes on the Grecian Archive; staff at the Devon & Exeter Institution; Andy Gillard, Simon Larkins and Scott Palfrey at ECFC; Jo Smith (archivist) at the Southampton City Archive; staff at the National Archives and the British Library; Gillian Lonergan (librarian) and Sophie McCulloch (archivist) at the National Co-operative Archive; my brother Nick Hamilton, Dave Juson and Jim Knight for reading sections of the manuscript and giving feedback; staff at Ciao's bakery-cum-café on Minglun Street in Kaifeng, where a good part of the writing was done; and those who've helped out with accommodation: my brother Nick, Sarah Lawson, Boucar Ngom, Dave Juson and John Dye. And finally, thank you to the Supporters' Trust for funding the book and to everyone at Halsgrove. Sincere apologies to anyone I have failed to mention.

We have endeavoured to trace all photographers but due to the age of many of the photos and the donation of many images from unknown photographers to the Grecian Archive, this has not always been possible. Any information can be sent to the ECFC History Group and will be rectified in any future editions.

Specific thanks regarding image copyright go to: Skyscan.co.uk for the aerial photograph on the front cover; the National Portrait Gallery for the painting of Lady Anne Clifford; Georgia Shorrock for permission to reprint the Stil cartoons drawn by her late father; the *Express & Echo* for permission to use its photos and articles and those of its sister titles; Hazel Harvey for allowing the use of a photograph of the old St James' church from her excellent book *The Story of Exeter*, and to Bob and Betty Youngson who provided the photograph; David Cornforth at Exeter Memories website for his help with images; QPR for use of its 1914 matchday programme; John Fox for the St James' Park redevelopment photograph.

Lastly, thank you to all the subscribers and Grecian Groups including the Supporters' Club, the Senior Reds, Grecian Goal, the Yorkshire Grecians, the East Devon Grecians and *Some Sunny Day*.

Aidan Hamilton

June 2019

Foreword

ST James' Park is special for me, as I am always warmly greeted whenever I am there, and I love arriving at the ground and seeing all the faces I have seen for many years. There is always a good atmosphere at the Park and the development has not changed this. Of course, it heightens when it is a Cup match or a possible promotion game then the place starts buzzing. When we played the match against Manchester United in 1969, the place was jumping and the atmosphere was electric. In fact, during the week leading up to the game, the whole city was buzzing. Of course, this was repeated when Liverpool were here in 2016.

I had some of the best times of my life in those changing rooms, having the mickey taken out of you by great characters every day and giving as much as you got with the walls rocking with laughter. It was a golden time of life. We had one small bath, one shower and one toilet.

I think the location of St James' Park is excellent, mainly because it is accessible to all the fans by using public transport and being where it is feels part of the city. The heritage displays around the ground are amazing, both down at pitch level and indoors, namely the Heritage Lounge and the approaching passageway, also the museum display. I am a great admirer of the work being done by the History Group and I consider the club have done me an honour naming a box after me.

Alan Banks
April 2019

Introduction

THE 125th anniversary of the first-known football match at St James' Park on 6 October 1894 was too good an opportunity to miss. It was time for the first-ever comprehensive history of the ground to be written.

The focus on the stadium had been growing, especially in light of the demolition of the 90-year-old grandstand in 2017. A Heritage Lottery Fund (HLF)-backed 'History of St James Park' project took place during 2016–17 and the results of this can still be accessed on the Grecian Archive (http://grecianarchive.exeter.ac.uk/).

This was followed by a further HLF-supported project to set up and develop an Exeter City Football Club Museum. This was undertaken over 2018–19 and contributed greatly to the look and feel of the redevelopment of the ground.

With a newly developed stadium having heritage at its heart, now was the perfect moment for a considered history of the space we Grecians call home. And it is no accident that all these things came together. The Supporters' Trust, owners of our club, has long wished to safeguard and promote our heritage. In 2015, the Trust set up the Exeter City History Group to drive this work forward.

Thanks, in particular, to the wonderful support of the University of Exeter, the two HLF projects followed, culminating in the establishment of a new charity, the Exeter City Football Club Museum Trust.

The History Group was really keen to underline all this work with a detailed book on St James' Park. We approached Aidan Hamilton, who had successfully marked the centenary of our legendary game as Brazil's first-ever opponents in 1914 with his seminal book *Have You Ever Played Brazil? The Story of Exeter City's 1914 Tour to South America* and were delighted he accepted the challenge.

The Supporters' Trust agreed to back and underwrite the book and we were very lucky that Sarah Willis, a member of the History Group Committee with publishing skills, agreed to manage the project. As always, brilliant volunteers make things happen at Exeter City.

We are absolutely delighted with the result. We were conscious that much of the recent past is already covered by other books and sources such as the Internet. So with this in mind, we asked Aidan to give more weight to the older and lesser-known history. And not just of the field as a football ground, but its earlier and other uses – a real contribution to Exeter local and community history.

Aidan's research has been meticulous, and on the way he has uncovered much about the early days of football in Exeter and the emergence of Exeter City Football Club. Aidan would like to acknowledge a series of great local newspaper football reporters whose eye-witness accounts of key events provide a thread throughout the book. In particular, we are grateful for the writing of three great *Football Express* correspondents – 'Rover', 'The Chiel' and 'Nomad'.

Football fans love a debate and one we had on the publication team was how to spell the name of our stadium. Over the years, it has been variously referred to as St James's Park, St James' Park and, latterly, St James Park. So there isn't a right or wrong, but we have gone for St James' Park as this is most prevalent historically.

We commend the book to you and thank everyone involved in its publication especially the indefatigable Aidan. We are so proud of our supporter-owned club, its ground and history. Now we have a first-class book bringing everything together.

Come on the Grecians!

Up the City!

Paul Farley and Martin Weiler
Exeter City Supporters' Trust
History Group
April 2019

1

The Parish Field

THE story of St James' Park can be divided into two parts: before and after 1908. In that year, Exeter City Football Club took out a 21-year lease on the ground they'd been playing on since 1903. The club needed a secure home after becoming a limited liability company and getting elected to the Southern League. Consequently, by the start of the 1908–09 season, St James' Park was completely transformed. The layout of the land became much as it is today in terms of the relation of the pitch to the areas where spectators sit or stand.

The 1908 lease document states that the tenants would 'level the land and premises' at their own expense. Embanking and the putting up of stands would 'fit the same for a Football and Athletic Ground in accordance with Plans submitted by the Tenants to the Lessors'. What was being leased is described in the indenture text as follows:

> [T]hat field or close of land with the appurtenances containing about Two acres two roods and twenty-eight perches called the Parish Field situate adjoining Saint James Road in the Parish of Saint Sidwell in the County of the City of Exeter.

The name 'Parish Field' is misleading; there's no connection to St Sidwell's church. On a late eighteenth-century map, the field is labelled as 'belonging to the poor of the Parish of St Stephen'. It's at St Stephen's, in the centre of Exeter, that the story begins.

The Parish Field was being leased out by a Trust that had been established after a charitable donation to St Stephen's church. The donor, as it happened, was one of the most significant women of the seventeenth century. Lady Anne Clifford, Countess Dowager of Pembroke, Dorset and Montgomery – Lady Anne, as she was affectionately known – bought the land from a former Mayor of Exeter, Simon Snow, in 1654.

The Trust she set up was in memory of her mother, Lady Margaret Russell, who was baptised at St Stephen's.

Andrew Jenkins' early nineteenth-century history of Exeter refers to the original indenture document. Rent from the field was to be used in a particular way:

> [F]or the putting out and placing (in the way of an Apprentice, in some honest trade or course of living) yearly to the World's end, one poor Child, Boy or Girl, born and residing within the said Parish of St. Stephen's (being such a one as shall be found to be destitute of other means of Worldly preferment, and to stand most in need of a charitable provision).

Originally, there were 13 Trustees or Feoffees: one of Lady Anne's heirs, the Mayor of Exeter, and 11 'persons of good worth and reputation inhabiting within Devon and Exeter'. The minister and churchwardens of St Stephen's were the ones who recommended a child for apprenticeship. Over time, the charity's objectives became more flexible.

Lady Margaret Russell was born at Bedford House in Exeter in 1560, the granddaughter of Lord John Russell, Earl of Bedford, an advisor to Henry VIII. It was he who had Bedford House built, a conversion from a Dominican friary, which he'd been granted by the Crown in 1539. A plaque of 1897 that marks the site today – on a wall outside Debenhams in Bedford Street – reveals that it was where Charles I's daughter Princess Henrietta was born. There was a royal connection too through Lady Anne's father George Clifford, Third Earl of Cumberland. He was a favourite courtier of Elizabeth I.

When George died in 1605, 15-year-old Anne should have inherited the Clifford family's extensive estates in Cumbria and Yorkshire. Her two elder brothers had died in infancy, so the closest direct heir, whether male or female, had to inherit; it was a condition under which the land had been granted in the reign of Edward II. In fact, the estates passed to George's brother, with Anne receiving £15,000 in compensation. From that moment, she resolved to win back what was rightfully hers. With the help of her mother, who initiated claims on her behalf, and after a determined fight, Anne succeeded in regaining her inheritance only in 1643 when the last of her male relatives died without issue.

Lady Anne's struggle for equal land rights has been seen as a milestone in feminism. Her aims were achieved single-handedly after the death of her mother, her one ally, in 1616 and in spite of opposition from James I, Oliver Cromwell and her own husbands. During the early stages of her Trust in Exeter, she learnt that the charitable use of the land was being neglected. So, the Trustees, and a Thomas Shapcott, who had got possession of the land, were cited by her in a Bill of Complaint to the Lord Chancellor. The fact that this Trust survived her – she died at Brougham in 1676 – is testament to her tenacity in overcoming obstacles.

An example of the Clifford Trust's indentured apprenticeships is the one made on 25 February 1765 between the rector and wardens of St Stephen's church, Elizabeth Ellis (daughter of a widow in the neighbouring parish of St Mary Major) and carpenter Avery Hodge and his wife, Sarah, a glover, of St Mary's. During a seven-year term, the Hodges were to 'Teach and Instruct … Elizabeth Ellis … in the Art, Trade or Mistery of a Glover or Glove maker'. They were given a first annual instalment of 'Eight Pounds'.

(Bottom, right) St Stephen's church
Source: © Aidan Hamilton, 2018

Lady Anne Clifford, Countess of Pembroke (1590–1676), painted by William Larkin, *c.*1618
Source: © National Portrait Gallery, London

Formally bound to the Hodges, Elizabeth Ellis was forbidden to play 'Cards, Dice or Tables', to frequent 'Taverns and Ale houses' and to marry. She received full board and lodgings, 'Apparel of all sorts', and at the end of the term was given 'two Decent suits of cloaths from Head to foot, the one for Sundays, the other for working days, fit and convenient for such an Apprentice'. This type of apprenticeship remained in place until changes to the law on practising a trade in the early nineteenth century.

When the Clifford Trust was set up, the yearly value of renting the land was about 12 pounds, the sum of 10 pounds going towards the apprenticeship scheme. Any surplus rent was to be equally distributed amongst as many of the poorest in the parish of St Stephen's as possible. But, as Jenkins' history illustrates, in the early 1800s the rent was inadequate:

This Charitable donation is now invested in the power of the Parish Feoffees, and the field is at present held by lease by Mr. Carter, Upholsterer of the said Parish [of St Stephen's], at more than double its former rent; yet notwithstanding the great enhancement of the value of the Land, and the care of the present Trustees; by the great advances in the Taxes, Poor Rate, and Tithes, the neat income is not sufficient to fulfil the pious intention of the Donor; this present year, the Trustees caused a number of large Elms which grew in the hedges surrounding this field, to be felled, and sold, which produced a considerable sum of money; this they intended to apply to the use of the charity, and to plant a number of others in their room.

Several months before Carter's term ended, in midsummer 1808, an auction for a fresh lease was advertised in the local press. Bidding would start at 5 p.m. at the Half Moon Inn in Exeter on Wednesday 20 April. On this occasion, the Trustees made it clear they would consider terms of more than seven years, provided the land was put to use as a garden or a nursery. The offer of an extension was not taken up.

In 1808, the land was still on the periphery of Exeter. There were buildings on 'St Sidwell Street' up to the junction of Old Tiverton Road and Blackboy Road. Right on the fork stood St Anne's Chapel – just as it does today – as a reference point for the 'Parish Field'. Then, the field contained about four acres and a half, which extended to Old Tiverton Road. There was access, called Cake Lane, where the present-day St James Road is; and opposite the field, on the town side, land that was marked 'Ammunition Ground' on an 1805 map.

Gradually, as St Sidwell's became a thickly populated and widely extending parish, there was the need for a Chapel of Ease to support the mission of St Sidwell's church, which had been rebuilt in 1812. As early as 1830, the preferred location was on the site of St Anne's Chapel. The problem was where to rehouse the almshouses on that site. While subscriptions began to raise money for the new building, the almshouses issue remained unresolved. Eventually, an alternative site was obtained – on the Clifford Trust land.

A FIELD,
In *St. SIDWELL's, EXETER.*
TO be LET, for a term of 7 years, from Midsummer next, at a yearly rent, a FIELD, or CLOSE of LAND, called the
PARISH FIELD,
Situate in St. Sidwell's, Exeter, near St. Ann's Chapel, containing about four acres, now in possession of Mr. Morgan, whose term will expire at Midsummer next.
An Auction will be held for letting the same, on TUESDAY, the 24th day of MARCH instant, at two o'clock in the afternoon, at the HALF MOON INN, in Exeter.
For further particulars, apply to Mr. CAMPION, Attorney-at-Law, Exeter.—*Exeter, 19th March, 1829.*

The letting of the Parish Field
Source: © *Exeter & Plymouth Gazette*, 21 March 1829

But that wasn't the end of it. As building work was about to begin, there were calls for the St Anne's Chapel site to be looked at again. In March 1835, the *Exeter & Plymouth Gazette* galvanised support for this site and soon a meeting of St Sidwell's church parishioners agreed to revive the St Anne's site project. Several months later, however, it was clear the increased funding that was needed was unavailable. Expressing regret, the editor of the *Gazette* made one last attempt, desperate and vindictive, to appeal for support:

Whatever may be the result, after the almost unanimous opinion of the Parishioners, and the inhabitants of Exeter generally, it would be the height of folly and madness to proceed with the building upon the obscure and most ineligible site of Lady Clifford's Charity Field, as at first intended: indeed, we should say, that without the individual consent and approbation of every person who subscribed money, or giving the subscribers an opportunity of withdrawing it, should they think proper, no Committee would be bold enough to expend the subscriptions upon work so generally disapproved.

That was in July 1835. One month later, building work began on a site in the Parish Field. On 29 August, the *Western Times* reported: 'The foundation stone of an episcopal chapel for the use of parishioners of St. Sidwell, was laid on the 19th inst. in Lady Clifford's charity field, by the Rev. Chancellor Pott.' It took just over a year for the work to be completed. Apart from a grant of £500 from the Church Building Society, the cost was met by voluntary subscriptions.

In late November 1836, the consecration service was held. The new structure was designated St James' church. Over 1,000 people were present, including 300 children. Described as a 'highly

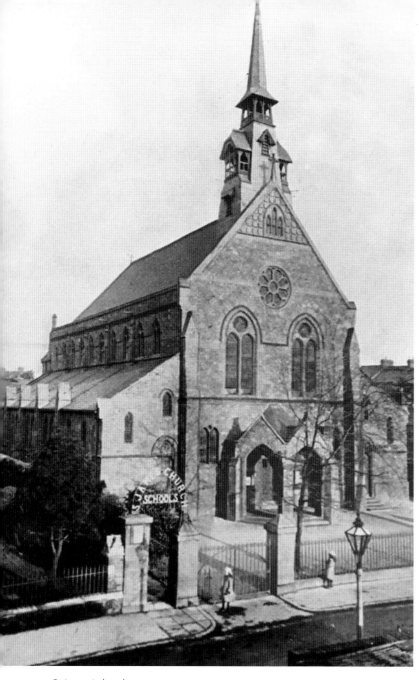

St James' church
– the rebuilt
nineteenth-century
building
Source: H. Harvey, *The Story
of Exeter*/Bob and Betty
Youngson

(Right)
Announcement of
a possible name
change for Lion's
Holt railway halt
Source: *Devon & Exeter
Gazette*, 26 July 1946

Renaming Of Halt?

Exeter City Football Club directors have suggested that Lion's Holt Halt, Exeter, on the Southern Railway, outside St. James's Park football ground, be known as St. James's Park Halt.

respectable assemblage', the gathering was led by the Bishop of Exeter. After the usual readings and psalms, there was a sermon from the bishop, 'a master-piece of pulpit eloquence', lasting an hour. This consecration was seen as proof of 'the wide-spreading influence of true religion'.

The report of the consecration, in the *Exeter & Plymouth Gazette*, included a description of the building:

> The new Church is a handsome spacious structure, 96 feet long, and 52 wide, within the walls, and is calculated to hold 1,200 sittings, 600 of which are free. There are two aisles, and spacious galleries running along each side till they join another large gallery at the West. The interior is fitted up in a remarkably neat, simple, and unobtrusive manner. The handsomely carved oak pulpit was presented by the Dean and Chapter; the reading desk is opposite to the pulpit, of plain wainscot, and there is no other ornament whatever in the church, except a small but very handsome King's Arms in the front of the Western Gallery, presented by Mr. W. Bond.

Forty years later, with the parish population having doubled to 6,000, the church needed to be rebuilt. In 1876, a notice appealing for funds described it as being 'inconveniently arranged, of the meanest character architecturally, and also in a bad state of repair'. The work was done in three stages and was completed in 1885.

Not long after it was first built, St James' church would lend its name to the field it abutted, to a road and to a school. And many years later – in 1946 – the name of Lion's Holt railway halt was changed to 'St James's Park Halt'. It followed a suggestion by the directors of the football club whose supporters were the ones who used the place most. But, by then, the church was no longer standing. It was destroyed in the Exeter Blitz in 1942.

2

Bradford's Field

I N the indenture made between the Clifford Charity and Exeter City AFC in 1908, there's one clause that stands out. It refers to the colourful and sometimes controversial history of the land:

> That the Tenants shall not nor will use or occupy or permit or suffer the demised premises or any part thereof to be used or occupied for any Meetings Shows or Exhibitions of a noisy or objectionable character or for any Menagerie or Circus or for Steam Roundabouts or erections of that description nor do nor suffer to be done anything thereon which shall be or become a nuisance or annoyance to the Residents in the neighbourhood.

St James' Park had been receiving these mid-year spectaculars – circuses and menageries – for over 50 years. For some time, local residents had been making complaints. So, when the lease changed hands in 1904, it was on the understanding that the exhibitions would be discontinued. That was not the case – hence the emphatic requirement in the lease contract when the football club took over the tenancy.

By the late 1840s, the Parish Field was hosting travelling shows. It replaced the site on which Queen Street station had been built. The name of the tenant would be used in the advertising. So, in 1847, for example, for two days – 31 May and 1 June – a 'pavilion' was put up in 'Mr Heal's Field' in St James Road. The Hughes' Royal Oriental and Grand Mammoth Equestrian Establishment was on a tour of the West Country. One month before, at the Theatre Royal Drury Lane, there had been a special performance for Queen Victoria and her family.

It was billed as 'the most magnificent Cavalcade ever exhibited in Europe'. On entering Exeter, the company's 21 richly decorated carriages processed through the streets. There were 50 horses, 15 Egyptian camels, a group of fairy ponies and two 'stupendous' elephants. Their trainers were an international cast of artistes. On each day, there was a matinee and an evening performance; the paying public had the choice of a seat in the arena or in one of two boxes. Shows such as these would become annual events.

As for the tenancy of the Clifford Trust land, in the 1850s local butcher Thomas Bradford and his wife Elizabeth took it on for a period that would extend until 1904. They had a shop at the corner of Sidwell Street and Summerland Street. Midway through their tenancy, the Exeter School Board approached the Trustees with a view to buying one-third of an acre of the field as the site for an infants' school.

In February 1873, therefore, a notice of sale was published in Devon by the Board of Charity Commissioners for England and Wales. It related to the Clifford Trust's negotiations with the Exeter School Board. The property being sold was described as follows:

Advert for the Bradfords' business
Source: © *Western Times*, 21 December 1877

A Piece of Land having a frontage to James's-road of 80 feet and 268 feet in length on the north side, and 250 feet in length on the south side, being part of a field or close of land called 'The Parish Field,' in the parish of St Sidwell, in the city of Exeter, in the occupation of Thomas Combe Bradford and Elizabeth Combe Bradford.

And also a Piece of Land adjoining the land last described, also in the occupation of the said Thomas Combe Bradford and Elizabeth Combe Bradford, which two pieces of land together contain by admeasurement two roods and seventeen perches, the first described piece of land being freehold of inheritance, and the secondly described piece of land being held for all the residue of a term of 500 years from 1781, are proposed to be sold by the Trustees thereof by private contract for the sum of £300, unless some sufficient objection to such sale, whether having reference to the sufficiency of the purchase money or to any other reasons, shall be made known to the said Commissioners within twenty-one days from the first publication of this notice.

The St James' School building, which dates from 1907
Source: © Aidan Hamilton, 2018

(Right) The building at the back of the car park at St James' Park dates from the nineteenth century. It was built as a school, and it replaced an earlier school building erected in 1844
Source: © Aidan Hamilton, 2018

The site is occupied today by the St James' School building, put up, as the inscription says, in 1907. On land adjoining this, at the back of the car park, a voluntary school was built in 1844. The ownership of a successor building was transferred by Devon County Council to Exeter City's Football in the Community charity – now the City Community Trust – in 2013. It's known as the Fountain Centre.

The Clifford Trust may have come in for criticism in 1881 about the way in which funds were being used – 'to bestow scholarships at a private school' – but the fact was the terms of the original indenture, as framed by Lady Anne, had widened. In the mid-1880s, besides apprenticeships, there was another way in which poor children benefitted from the grants:

[B]y enabling them to continue at school beyond the age of 12 years, whereby they may obtain the benefit of higher education in secondary or other schools, or to attend Science or Art Classes, or classes for technical instruction, or otherwise for aiding their advancement in life.

Application forms and particulars could be obtained at the office of the Trust's solicitor, a Mr Lambert, in Wonford Road, Exeter. Clearly, at this point in time, annual rent from the Bradfords' tenancy of St James' Park was adequate to fulfil the charity's original intentions.

The 1908 indenture document also prohibited the field from being used for 'Meetings'. Back in October 1884, a political demonstration culminated in a mass meeting at the field 'at St. James's'.

One of many nationwide, they had been organised by the Liberal Party after its measure for extending the franchise had been rejected by the Tory Lords. The demonstration in Exeter was carried out 'on business principles':

[I]t was – as intended – a serious and significant protest against the suppression of a measure of justice in order to meet party purposes. And the day's work was worthy of the County and the cause. With the whole proceeding there was abundance of spirit.

Protestors came from all parts of Devon, and with banners and to the music of 12 bands they marched from St David's Station to St James' Field. Yours truly's great-grandfather may well have been among them: a 'J Tucker' turned out with the contingent from the St Thomas Liberal Association.

According to the *Western Times*, 'over 12,000 persons marched into the field near St James' Church'. The rain, which had been falling all week, had stopped, and 'made the turf springy and pleasant to walk upon'. There were speeches from four platforms – the central one, and one for each of Devon's three parliamentary divisions. Two resolutions were proposed from each platform:

> 1st – That this meeting emphatically approves of the Franchise Bill passed in the last Session of Parliament by the representative Chamber, and strongly condemns the action of the majority of the hereditary portion of the Legislature in having refused to pass the measure, and thereby excluded from their just rights two millions of Englishmen. 2nd – That this meeting expresses its continued and unabated confidence in her Majesty's present Government.

Over 50 years later, 71-year-old Isaac Yeo, a former Exeter postal worker, recalled the demonstration in an interview for the *Western Times*: 'That was my first experience of politics. I had a rare "do" on that occasion, I can tell you.'

In the 1880s, a feature of the circuses in Bradford's Field was the 'Conundrum Nights'. These were competitions arranged by the circus proprietors 'with the object of giving a bit of local colour to the bill of fare'. In February 1885, *The London Journal* reported on one of them:

> A few nights ago, the Exeter circus was filled with a respectable assemblage, it having been announced that upon that occasion a silver goblet would be presented to the author of the best original conundrum [joke]. Shortly before ten o'clock, a platform was introduced for the literary part of the entertainment, which young Hengler [the proprietor] mounted, having a bundle of conundrums in his hand. With the conundrums was a variety of enigmas and charades, but these were laid aside. The audience were to decide the merits of the different conundrums, and, in order that their task might be as easy as possible, young Hengler divided the conundrums into what he considered 'bad' and 'good'.

A bad one? 'Why is a tradesman who allows long credit like a town in Devonshire? – Because it's Credit on.' Among the good ones? 'If a person falls into the water at Cowley Bridge, how wet would he be? – Wet in the Exe-stream.' The cup went to a conundrum that alluded to the Crimean War: 'Why is a weary night traveller in Gloucestershire like the wounded soldiers in Scutari? – Because he is cheered by the presence of a "Nightingale".' It wasn't long before shows such as Wilson's Great World Circus were performing at the Victoria Hall, after the conversion of its circular auditorium, but this venue in Queen Street could never replicate the familiar atmosphere of the big top.

In May 1887, a hearing at the Guildhall attracted particular attention. Earlier in the year, the body of a male child was discovered 'lying against the gate of Mr. Bradford's field'. A 20-year-

Isaac Yeo
Source: © *Western Times*, 15 May 1936

FIREWORKS!
FIREWORKS!!
JUNE 8TH, AND 10TH,
In the
CIRCUS FIELD, ST. JAMES'S-ROAD,
Under the patronage of the Right Worshipful the Mayor (William Peters, Esq.), and the Sheriff (W. W. Tremlett, Esq.). At 9.15 p.m.,
9.15 GRAND 9.15
FIREWORK
DISPLAY
By Messrs. Jas. Pain and Sons, of London and New York, in conjunction with Mr. G. Dunsford, of Paris-street, Exeter.
Brilliant Illuminations and Magnificent Set Picture, Destruction of the
SPANISH ARMADA.
MONSTER SHELLS! FOREST OF FIRE!
MAMMOTH SILVER FIRE WHEELS!
MAGNESIUM BALLOONS!
COLOURED ROCKETS AND MAGNIFICENT
PRISMATIC CASCADE,
Thousands of Prismatic Lamps, Chinese and Japanese Lanterns, &c., preceded at 7 o'clock by a
GRAND
MILITARY ORCHESTRAL
PROMENADE CONCERT.
THIS DAY (SATURDAY) BY THE
ROYAL ITALIAN BAND,
And on MONDAY by the
BAND OF THE 1ST DEVON REGT.
(Under the direction of Bandmaster W. M. Moody.)
Admission 6d, or to a specially Reserved Lawn 1s Separate entrance to which will be at Ivy Cottage, Tiverton-road.
Address, G. Dunsford, 2, Paris-street, or 7, North-street.

Advert for a firework display at the Circus Field
Source: © *Devon & Exeter Daily Gazette*, 8 June 1889

old domestic servant was charged with murdering her newborn son. The body had been found wrapped in a parcel by a young lad on the evening of Sunday 9 January. The scene was described as follows: 'There were two gaslights burning within a moderate distance from where he found the body. It was just before seven o'clock, as shortly after St. James' Church bell ceased ringing. Not many persons were passing at the time.' According to the post-mortem, the likely cause of death was suffocation. The hearing ended with the woman on remand being committed for trial.

Apart from the shows and meetings at the Parish Field, another cause for complaint were the animals that were kept there. The Bradfords reared pigs, and also rented out stables. In July 1886, at a meeting of the City Council's Market Committee, 'Mr. Bradford's Field' was singled out in a report by the Inspector of Nuisances. It was one of several locations at which swine were being kept near dwellings. The Inspector was instructed to take action 'in default of compliance, in any case in which he found that swine were kept so as to be a nuisance'. Poor old Tom Bradford was eventually forced to give up his holding by a 'Syndicate of citizens' who offered to pay the Clifford Trust £5 more in annual rent. But now it wasn't *his* animals that were the problem.

What angered Tom Bradford was the fact that the new lessees continued to organise shows at St James' Field. As he explained later in June 1906 in a letter to the editor of the *Devon & Exeter Gazette* entitled 'St. James' Field':

> They bombarded me for 15 years because the shows were an intolerable nuisance. But they had not had possession of the ground one fortnight before they commenced having shows there again, and have been having them ever since, notwithstanding that my having shows there was the lever used against me whereby I lost my holding.

Two years before, the issue had been referred to in the *Daily Gazette* correspondence section under the heading 'St. James's Field and Exhibitions'. It was signed 'One Interested'. It appears that conditions laid down by the Clifford Trustees in 1904 were being breached. Bradford had had to have his stables pulled down, and yet temporary ones for shows were being put up. The letter reads as follows:

> In the interests of the inhabitants of that part of Well-street opposite the St. James's Field, I think it right that attention should be drawn to what I consider a public nuisance, viz. allowing various shows to occupy the field.
>
> There was considerable trouble caused some time ago, when Mr. Bradford was the lessee, as regards letting the field to Mr. Hancock, and some of the members of the syndicate who now rent the field were the first to 'kick' against it, and obtained a petition from the inhabitants of the immediate neighbourhood, with the view of suppressing the exhibitions.
>
> I am more than surprised to find that the syndicate are continuing to let the field to such shows as were previously objected to by them when Mr. Bradford was lessee.
>
> One or two members of the syndicate were in the field on Saturday morning [2 July 1904], arranging, I presume, the position, etc., the tents should occupy.
>
> The stables for the horses are placed at the bottom of the field, parallel with the houses in Well-street, and cause great annoyance to the inhabitants in the immediate vicinity. The smell arising from these stables at this time of year is intolerable, and I may add that the sanitary arrangements for the employe[e]s are anything but desirable.

Local residents protested, but the letting of the field for shows was not something the City Council could prevent.

We're just two months away from St Sidwell's United's first practice game as 'Exeter City' at St James' Park. It was on Saturday 3 September 1904. It's hardly surprising that, given the history, when the Trustees agreed a lengthy lease with the club in 1908, they made sure *all* possible causes of 'nuisance or annoyance' were covered in the contract.

3

Clown cricketers

JUST before the midpoint of the nineteenth century, at around the time travelling shows began to pitch up at the Parish Field, it's clear that little, if any, recreational activity was taking place in the St Sidwell's district of Exeter.

Writing to the *Exeter & Plymouth Gazette* in October 1847, a correspondent who went by the name of 'Medicus' was critical of the fact that no land had been set aside for 'recreation and exercise'. In a 'large and opulent' parish like St Sidwell's with a population in excess of 10,000, surrounded by 'spacious fields', it was a disgrace that 'not a single acre, or even rood of ground' had been provided for sports:

> The importance, the necessity, of such a provision, to the health, morals, and happiness of the youthful population, is so obvious and indisputable, that it were an insult to common sense to make any attempt to prove it. It is altogether idle and absurd to suppose that the best interests of the poorer classes of our fellow-citizens are receiving from those who are more fortunate and influential, that consideration which they demand, while a want so natural and urgent as this, and one at the same time so easily and cheaply satisfied, remains neglected.
>
> Who can calculate the amount of good which a few acres thrown open to the public, in a populous neighbourhood, is capable of producing? What a sum of pleasure in all those cheerful sports and games which are hourly going forward, and in which hundreds are daily partaking! What a fountain of health is opened! What a useful resource is provided for the innocent and beneficial occupation of leisure hours, – otherwise too likely to be spent in idleness and vice, in the streets, the alehouses, or around the ring!

A fairground atmosphere at St James' Field, 1890s
Source: © J.S. Hines

The 'ring' was perhaps a reference to the wrestling matches that took place infrequently in a field near Blackboy Road. The popularity of sport and numbers participating elsewhere may have been exaggerated, but the case for access to sport for the 'poorer classes' was well put.

The letter ended with an appeal to the wealthier parishioners of St Sidwell's:

And now, O Magnanimous Grecians, let us hope that you will lay this to heart. Your great ancestors and namesakes thought matters of this kind deserving of the most serious attention; and they took a world of pains, by all sorts of athletic sports and contests, to train their youth to vigour, health, and fortitude. You refuse to yours the power even to play a game at cricket!

This viewpoint signalled a break from sport as being exclusively a pastime of the gentry, with activities such as cricket, horse racing and hunting. 'Medicus' was voicing the view of the emerging middle classes, the result of which were the first attempts to organise and regulate the sports we play today. But it would take more than 20 years for this visionary perspective to be widely embraced in Exeter – let alone in the parish of St Sidwell's and, by extension, St James'. Not until the 1870s was the Parish Field, for example, used for sport.

Cricket, as 'Medicus' alluded to, *was* being played in Exeter, in the south of the city. An Exeter Cricket Club was formed in the mid-1820s. The club used a ground – 'Quicke's Cricket Ground' – between Haven Banks and Alphington Road. In the years up to 1850, there were annual matches against the Isca Cricket Club, which was based at the Hoopern Fields, near Barrack Road. These informal occasions were socially exclusive: players were gentlemen. Occasionally, military officers took part, and so too did barristers and members of the clergy; in 1849, Exeter even hired a professional, Edward Martin, who'd played for Kent. Gradually, as we enter the second half of the nineteenth century, 'working men' were encouraged to join in.

One of the first sporting events at the Parish Field, it appears, was the athletics held there on a Saturday in October 1872 – if indeed it was the venue reported as 'a field near St. James's Church'. It was the finale to the Isca Cricket Club's season. As well as flat races, hurdles and long jump, there was throwing the cricket ball – 72 yards was the winning throw – and a 220-yard race for cadets in uniform. Later, the Belmont Club used the field for athletic sports, as did St Sidwell's School, which held its first annual sports meeting there in 1892.

St James' Park's introduction to cricket came with the formation of a St James' Cricket Club in April 1875. How appropriate that in one of the first matches to be played there, the locals took on a group of clown cricketers; the circus field seemed the obvious venue. The 'Clowns' XI was made up of professional cricketers, acrobats and talking clowns: a fusion of sport and the big top. Here's how the *Western Times* of Wednesday 23 June 1875 recorded the spectacle:

Yesterday the Clown Cricketers resumed their play in the field adjoining St. James' Church, Exeter, and throughout the day there were numerous spectators. The result of the match on Monday against eighteen of St. James' Club was the victory of the Clowns (among whom are several professional cricketers) by forty runs. The scores were – Clowns 85, the Club 40); the best score of the day – 41 – was made by Charlewood, and Pooly scored 17. Dick-a-Dick, the Australian, who bowls at a great pace, took the majority of the Club wickets. Yesterday eleven of the Club played against the Clowns. The latter scored 88 and the Club 43. A good deal of fun was afforded by the Clowns – who indulged in various comicalities whilst they were fielding.

But the event had no lasting impact. After the entertainers had resumed their tour of the country, the 'St James' Club' failed to gather momentum. With limited success, the club ran into debt and was disbanded.

Three years later, two of the club's officials, the Reverends Dumbleton and Ponting, called a meeting of members of the St James' Parochial Institute with the object of forming a new club. Chairing the meeting, Reverend Ponting made it clear that the club would be run differently from the old one: 'the Cricket Club they desired to establish was not intended to pull on the purse of the Institution, for they considered that with systematic management, it could be made self-supporting'.

Motions were passed, a management committee was agreed and a scale of subscriptions drawn up. The new club was called St James' Institute Cricket Club. Finally, a decision was made to 'secure' Mr Bradford's Field and that they would play there three evenings a week. The first practice game was scheduled for Wednesday 8 May 1878.

'Foot-ball' – i.e. rugby – had been played in the Millbrook area (off Topsham Road) since 1872 when an Exeter club was formed; the club also played at Higher Matford field in the Mount Radford area, and the 'St Thomas Cricket-field', later to be the site of the County Ground. It was being played too at the St Luke's Training College ground on Magdalen Road. At St James' Park, the game dates to the early 1880s. As with cricket at St James', in the parish of St Sidwell's the rugby enthusiasts received support from church officials. The rector, Reverend Spencer, agreed to be club president.

Advert to let St James' Park for cricket

Source: © *Exeter & Plymouth Gazette*, 11 March 1881

CRICKET! CRICKET!!—ST. JAMES'S PARK, Exeter, to LET for the present season.—Apply, T. and E. BRADFORD, St. Sidwell's.

In the following report of rugby at St James' Field in November 1882, interestingly preventing a touchdown, or 'saving', is included in the scoreline:

St. Sidwell's v. Isca. – This match was played on Saturday, on the ground of the former, at St. James's Field. Owing to the continuous rain the ground was in a very sodden condition, which made running and kicking difficult.

In the first part of the game Isca played with the hill, the 'kick-off' being followed by a series of tight scrimmages; in fact, the match proved a forwards' game throughout, every inch of ground being hotly contested. St. Sidwell's were compelled to save the ball twice to relieve their goal-line. On ends being changed the ball was followed up well by the St. Sidwell's men, and Isca had to 'save' in self-defence. The ball soon after going in touch, Richards obtained it from the throw-out, and succeeded in carrying the 'leather' across the Isca goal-line, thus obtaining a touchdown for St. Sidwell's. The kick for the goal was entrusted to Pike, but the Isca men, making a good rush, charged the ball down and carried it half-way up the field. Just before 'time' was called Isca had to 'save' the ball again, the match thus ending in a victory for St. Sidwell's by one try and two saves to two saves. It is needless to mention names where all played well.

As regards the lie of the land, the 'hill', or slope, at St James' Park is worth noting. See how St James Road slopes down to Well Street and you've got an idea of the extent of the original incline. Today's pitch, according to Estates Manager Clive Pring, is 'pretty flat'. There's a slight crown in the middle, and the pitch very marginally slopes away in all directions, but no more than 5 degrees.

When the St Sidwell's Rugby Football Club held its annual meeting at the Church Institute, Summerland Street, in September 1883, once again it was decided to 'secure' the field in 'St. James's-road'. A measure of how rapidly Exeter was expanding is the fact that the Clifford Trust

The Exeter rugby XV, mid-1880s

Source: © *Football Express*, 6 January 1934; photograph provided by Mr Frederick E. Pratt of Exeter

land was chosen as it was 'nearer to the city'. It was the reason too why the St John's Junior Rugby Club – an offshoot of St John's Hospital School – rented the ground in 1893. Not until 1896 did St James' parish have a rugby club of its own. And its home, naturally, was the field adjoining the church.

It wasn't only the fact of a club being based nearer the centre of Exeter that might attract members and spectators. In September 1890, Rougemont, a newly formed rugby club, as well as renting St James' Field, 'as far as practicable arranged their matches so as not to clash with those of the city teams'. A good share of patronage, it was hoped, would be ensured.

Cycling, too, was growing in popularity. In December 1880, it was reported that 'a field adjoining St James' Church' had been chosen as the site for a cycling track. The Devon and Exeter Cycling and Athletic Recreation Company, with offices in Sidwell Street, had been looking for a 'centrally situated' field on which to build an athletics ground with stands and dressing rooms. With a capital of £500, this limited liability company would sell shares at £2 each.

St James' church provides the backdrop for this cycling event, 1890s
Source: © J.S. Hines

The reasons behind the scheme were laid out in the prospectus, as well as the full uses to be made of the ground:

> Cycling by means of either the bicycle or tricycle is now a recognised mode of locomotion, and is extending every day, and as it leads young men into the country in this pursuit of healthy enjoyment, it deserves the support of the Public, especially as it is highly recommended by medical men. The immense number of clubs now established proves the popularity of the sport.
>
> The ground will be available for all kinds of Athletic Sports, and especially bicycle and tricycle races and practice, and as many who now learn in our streets and thoroughfares would much prefer the privacy of an enclosure, it is certain that a large profit will be derived from Members' tickets and admission.
>
> The portion of ground within the track will be suitable for lawn tennis, cricket, football [i.e. rugby], and other athletic sports.
>
> Similar grounds in other districts are known to have cleared their outlay, besides being an attraction to the neighbourhood and increasing its prosperity. The field, being so centrally situated, is sure to command the attendance of cyclists and athletes of Exeter and the County.

Advert for St James' Field
Source: © *Exeter Flying Post*, 3 September 1892

HOUSES & PROPERTIES
TO BE LET OR SOLD.
20 Words or Less, 6d

ARE YOU HOUSE-HUNTING ? – The best way to find what you want is to advertise in the " Evening Post."

TO LET, ST. JAMES' FIELD (St. James'-road) for the Football Season, commencing October 1st.—Apply T. and E. BRADFORD, Purveyors, Exeter.

But, for reasons unknown, the projected site in St James Road was replaced by one in Polsloe Road. There *was* cycling at the Parish Field, but on a more informal basis. For example, in the early 1890s, clubs such as Exeter Roving Tourists, Exeter Cadets and Exeter Rovers organised races there. On occasion, they held other events. On Easter Monday 1894, the Exeter Rovers Cycling Club played the London & South Western Railway team at rugby. For this match, it was possible to book seats in advance.

We are now just months away from the first known association-football match to be played at the Parish Field. An Exeter XI would take on Minehead on 6 October 1894. How and why it took the association code longer than other sports to reach the St Sidwell's area and, in particular, the Parish Field is the subject of the next two chapters, which take us from Matford to Mount Pleasant.

4

Steadily gaining favour

UNTIL a more organised form of the game arrived in Devon around the midpoint of the nineteenth century, an ancient or 'folk' form of football was played. At fairs and on religious holidays, there were games of 'foot-ball kicking'. These games were part of a programme of activities, not isolated events.

An example of this type of 'foot-ball' was played in Exeter in 1845. On 1 February, it was announced in the *Western Times* that in the parish of St Sidwell's Easter Monday would be kept as a saint's day. Special arrangements had been made by a committee of leading parishioners:

> The sum of ten pounds will be divided into four prizes for ringing matches, to be competed for on St Sidwell's church bells, by country ringers. Foot-ball play will be carried on in Pratt's fields, and donkey-racing will animate St Sidwell-street, the course being from the London Inns to St Anne's Chapel. A band of music will perambulate the parish during the day, and some other amusements will be provided which have not yet been decided on by the committee. A good subscription has already been made in the parish, and there is no doubt, from the well-known spirit of the Grecians, that it will soon reach a handsome sum. The committee intend to apply to all employers of labour to give the hands a holyday on Easter Monday, so that none may miss any of the sport.

The last point highlights the fact that when a more orderly form of football appeared, it was introduced by those who had the free time to play it. They had played the game in its various forms at private schools, at universities and in the services. This was before the first attempt to codify football in October 1863, when the Football Association (FA) was formed in London.

Unsurprisingly, versions of pre-1863 football were difficult to describe. Participants, sometimes, had been taught different rules. Compilers of newspaper reports, you sense, were at times struggling to convey what game had been played. In Devon, early examples of organised 'football' were played on the Chapel Hill Cricket Ground in Torquay.

In March 1862, there was 'an exciting football match' between Torquay and Highstead, a private school in Torquay:

> After a spirited contest, during which five bases were kicked, Torquay were the winners, gaining three out of five goals. The game is to be renewed to-morrow (Saturday), at three o'clock, when the attendance of all admirers of the game is invited.

But what game? The word 'bases', i.e. goals, is a reference to the game being played at Harrow School. The Highstead XI included Reverend G.T. Warner, a schoolmaster who had previously taught at Harrow. As explained in Percy Young's *A History of British Football*, the Harrow rules would make important contributions to the first codified rules of association football.

In late 1862, there was a series of similar 'public' contests between 'the Gentlemen of the Highstead Club' and 'the eleven of "All Comers" of Torquay'. These matches, organised by a Sir George Prescott, we are told, 'attract much interest amongst members of the gentry and townspeople'; they were even reported in a London publication *The Sporting Life*. In the line-ups, a distinction was made between those names with an initial (including the clergy) and those without; a pointer no doubt to future class divisions in sport. Before the year was out, a 'foot-ball and athletic club' was formed in Torquay, at a 'meeting of gentlemen'.

Soon afterwards, on Saturday 17 January 1863, a game was arranged between Torquay and Exeter. Exeter, the *Exeter & Plymouth Gazette* tells us, won by one goal. There was some discussion over which rules to use. And in this pioneering period, it was not uncommon for teams to be depleted at the start:

> Torquay only shewed up seven of their original eleven, the other four not making their appearance at the right time. The vacancies were filled by some of the spectators. A little difficulty was experienced at first about the rules, some of the players being accustomed to the Rugby, and others to the Eton and Westminster. Considering the hurried way in which the match was got up, we must say that it was a very successful one, and hope it will take place annually.

Such hopes, however, appear to have fallen by the wayside. At that time, the Rugby School rules were no more important than those of other schools. But this would change. Eventually the 'Rugby' handling game – the rival of the dribbling game – became so popular that a governing body, the Rugby Football Union, was set up in 1871. This was the code that would predominate in Devon.

Before long, shortly after its formation, Exeter Rugby Club played a match at Millbrook, near Topsham Road on the outskirts of the city, on Saturday 19 October 1872. St Luke's College were the opponents. The *Western Times* informs us that 'the play lasted two hours, and ended in a draw, neither side kicking a goal'. In that first season, other opponents included sides from the armed forces such as the Volunteer Rifles and the 11th Royal Artillery. When association football in Exeter finally started to catch on in the 1890s, men from the Devonshire Regiment played a key role.

By the 1880s, Exeter was the foremost rugby club in Devon. The strength of the playing squad was flaunted in the opening match of the 1880–81 season. Styled Oxford and Cambridge versus the World, it was played on the club's ground at the back of Topsham Barracks. For the rest of the decade, rugby consolidated its position as the dominant football game in the county. It wasn't until a Devon County FA was formed in Plymouth, on 8 February 1888, that the association code could begin to develop.

The Devon FA founding meeting took place in the pavilion of the Plymouth Cricket Club. A write-up in the *Western Morning News* explained why the time had come for such action:

> For some years now, the Association game has been steadily gaining favour in this part of the country, and every season brings added names to the already far from insignificant list of clubs playing under these rules. As a necessary consequence of this, there has for a long time been a general feeling that the county of Devon should not be behind its neighbours, but should have an Association on the usual lines chiefly for the purpose of putting representative teams in the field to play inter-county matches.

It was true that at this moment in time there was more association football being played in and around Plymouth than anywhere else in Devon, and contact had also been made with Newton Abbott. From then on, association enthusiasts in Exeter not only had rugby to contend with, but also the fact that influence in their sport came from a governing body based in the west of the county.

Even before the Devon FA was formed, a first county match had been pencilled in against an XI from the Somerset FA, an organisation that had been set up two years earlier. There were trials first, then the game at Weston-super-Mare on 3 March 1888. In the Devon line-up, seven of the founder members were represented (all except Plymouth College): Plymouth, Argyle, Plymouth United, Newton, Carlton Oaks, Tavistock Grammar School and Mannamead School. Players from the schools made up half the team. The *Western Times* tells us that 'the Devon men – for a team that has not played together before – acquitted themselves admirably, and only allowed their more experienced opponents to secure a narrow victory by two goals'. A few weeks later, a return fixture took place at Plymouth.

So, did the fact there was no Exeter representation on the Devon FA imply that the association code in Exeter had been abandoned since that game in Torquay 25 years before? In 1888 in the Exeter area, the association code *was* being played, but only, it appears, in educational institutions, so the game was remaining 'in-house'. There were no association clubs as such.

The Junior Students of Exeter Training College, captained by A. Philipson, of Bootle, have inflicted a defeat of six goals to nil upon the Seniors. The goals were obtained by L. E. Oatey (2), A. Philipson (2), Brooks (1), and Goodwill (1). This is the first time the Seniors have been beaten by the Juniors, and it is a very creditable performance.

Report of association football at St Luke's College (Exeter Training College)
Source: © *Cricket & Football Field* (Bolton), 6 March 1886

From press reports, we know that students at St Luke's Training College in Exeter had been playing association-rules games as far back as the 1860s, but only amongst themselves. It was when Park House, a private boys school based in St Leonard's, began organising matches against other schools that the association code in Exeter had, for the first time, some kind of foothold. It was chiefly down to the efforts of the school's headmaster, Henry Tucker.

Born in Totnes in 1850, Henry Judson Tucker was a graduate of University College London. He'd worked as a schoolmaster in Gloucestershire before coming to Exeter to run Southernhay School; an advert for the school stated that its aim was 'to provide a high-class general education for boys'. In January 1887, Southernhay School moved to premises in St Leonard's Road and became Park House School. The new location provided easy access to land suitable for cricket and association football.

From early 1888 and during that year, as well as 'in-house' matches, there were games against Moorside School from Okehampton, Heavitree-based Regent's Park School, who played at Polsloe

(Left) The land where Park House School played their football, off St Leonard's Road, with St Leonard's church spire in the background
Source: © Aidan Hamilton, 2016

(Right) The building used by Park House School in St Leonard's Road
Source: © Aidan Hamilton, 2016

The building in Regent's Park, Exeter, where Regent's Park School was located
Source: © Martin Weiler, 2018

Park, and Crediton Grammar School. Tucker not only organised the games, he also played in them, as did other schoolmasters; and it was he presumably who made sure the press were informed. To understand the development of the association code, we rely on reports of games and the formation of teams by men such as Tucker. Often, it's all we have to go on.

Despite Tucker's efforts, an indication as to how far Exeter was behind in terms of popularising association football was given when the county town was chosen to host a match against Somerset in November 1888. The venue was the Cowick Fields in St Thomas. The *Western Times* correspondent, prefacing details of the play, doesn't hide disappointment at the lack of local support. For many in the crowd, this was their first game of association rules:

> For the first time in its history, the capital of the County of Devon was the scene, on Saturday, of a first-class exhibition of the Association game, but it cannot be said that the citizens displayed that enthusiasm for it which it deserved. The attendance was very small, when compared with that at a Rugby match, and what was wanting in numbers was not compensated for by the presence of any very defined acquaintance with the rules amongst the generality of the spectators. The greatest amusement was certainly manifest when the players headed the ball, but beyond this and cheers whenever Devon did a good piece of work, the lookers-on refrained from showing their bias one way or the other. The strong breeze from the west may have had something to do with it, but both players, and the rules which they adhered to, were strange to the public, and therefore it was scarcely possible to expect either a big 'gate', or much enthusiasm. – [It must be remembered that the fact of the funeral of Earl Devon taking place on Saturday restrained many from being present at the match. – Ed.]

Alexander Stuart
Source: © *Exeter Flying Post*, 28 November 1891

Later in the report, there's a rallying call for supporters of association football in Exeter. Surprise was expressed that nothing had been done 'to raise an Association club in the Ever Faithful'. After praising the refereeing of Alexander Stuart – and alluding to his previous leading role in the Scottish FA – it was suggested that he was the one to advise and assist those who were keen to form a club. Newton Abbott had made a success of it, why not Exeter?

A further argument was that rugby players would benefit from association-rules football. With the introduction of new 'Rugby' laws, it was 'imperative for a player to have some knowledge of the dribbling game if he was to shine in any department'; contemporary reports of rugby matches do refer to instances of 'association play'. There was then a request for Stuart to call a meeting of those interested in forming an Exeter club.

Regardless of whether a meeting took place, by the end of the year, Stuart and Tucker were involved in an 'Exeter' XI that travelled to take on 'Crediton'. They were described as two 'clubs' by the match report. A return match was played at Matford in January 1889: Stuart played; Tucker selected the team. The same formula was used for a match in February at Matford. This time the team was called 'Exeter District' and the opponents were the 'famous' South Staffordshire Regiment. We're told Tucker had difficulty in putting together a side, leading to several Exeter rugby players being chosen.

The result, coming after two close games against Crediton, stopped any progress in its tracks: the soldiers won 13-1, with the unfortunate Stuart in goal.

While the Devon FA continued to arrange county matches, including one against a newly formed Cornwall FA, the next attempt to put out a side representing Exeter would not be for over a year and a half.

5

At St James' Field

INITIALLY, therefore, it was Henry Tucker, Park House School head, who did more than anyone to promote the association code in Exeter. The code, according to the *Western Times* of 27 December 1888, 'doesn't seem to make much headway amongst us. The only ones that stick manfully to it are the lads of Mr Tucker's School, and a very pretty game they play.' If, following the heavy defeat to the South Staffordshire Regiment, there was discussion between Tucker and Alexander Stuart over the possibility of continuing the Exeter Association XI, it came to nothing. As the 1889–90 season beckoned, Stuart contacted the *Evening Post*'s football correspondent to inform him that he and several kindred spirits were getting a team together. It was based at a church in Newtown.

Stuart, a sidesman at St Matthew's, could count on the support of the vicar. The Reverend Ponting had experience of forming sports clubs. He'd been involved in the organisation of St James' Cricket Club in the 1870s and lent his support to the cricket club at St Matthew's. Parishes that provided physical development and health for local youths through sport were seen as being more advanced in a moral sense. No doubt, in his sermons and at the end of Sunday worship, Ponting would have actively encouraged members of his congregation to join the new club.

Stuart, in his letter to the *Post*, made reference to the two football codes. 'I think you will agree with me', he wrote, 'that there is quite enough room in Exeter for the two different games'. That was all well and good, but his loyalties were divided. Despite the fact he'd been a leading administrator of association football in Scotland, on relocating to Devon, Stuart had decided to throw in his lot with the Rugbyites. When the formation of 'St Matthew AFC' was announced in October 1889, he made it clear he'd only be carrying out secretarial duties on a temporary basis.

St Matthew AFC decided to play their matches at Whipton Lane, where the Heavitree Pleasure Ground is today. That was where the church cricket team played. St James' Field wouldn't even have been considered as it remained firmly linked to the rugby code. At that time, the nearest Associationists got to St James' was Belmont Park, where from 1889 pupils of the newly opened Newtown School had kickabouts. The school building remains to this day in its original spot, adjacent to St Matthew's church.

St Matthew's church
Source: © Aidan Hamilton, 2018

For a brief period, then, Stuart used his knowledge of association football and influence in Exeter sporting circles to showcase the code. It was probably he who suggested the game at the County Ground in St Thomas before an important boxing event in late November 1889, St Matthew AFC v Collingwood House School, and he refereed it. Then, on Boxing Day 1889, St Matthew were back there, Devonport the opposition, and Stuart again officiating. And once again, it was a preliminary to a bigger event, this time a county rugby match. From then on, it appears, Stuart's rugby work took precedent.

So, during that 1889–90 season, it was chiefly a case of Exeter's first proper association club, St Matthew, and local schools – Park House, Collingwood House (formerly Regent's Park School) and Exeter Grammar School – playing return fixtures against each other. The association code also continued to be played at St Luke's College. But there was no representative Exeter XI, not until Tucker took the initiative again, in the run-up to the following season.

The first match of the Exeter Association Club was played in the Matford area on Saturday 25 October 1890. This is how it was reported in the *Western Gazette*:

> ### EXETER (ASSOCIATION) v. CREDITON GRAMMAR SCHOOL
> A match was played on Saturday afternoon between these clubs which resulted in a decisive victory for Exeter by 12 goals to one. This was the opening match of the newly constituted Exeter Club, and the members have no reason to be dissatisfied with the start. James, Goodman and Wright were best for Exeter, whilst Lucas, Hockaday and Edwards did good work for the school.

It was an almost identical scoreline to the one in February 1888, only thankfully for Tucker, this time Exeter were not on the receiving end. In putting together the team, he drew on players from St Matthew AFC – James and Goodman, for example – and Park House old boys. Later, there was even an Exeter B Team. Indeed, there were grounds for optimism at the club's first AGM held at Park House School in September 1891.

Tucker, the secretary, was singled out in the report of the meeting. The fact that expenses had been covered by members' subscriptions alone was down to the 'energetic' work of the secretary 'who has done so much to bring the club into prominence'. One of the new committee members was W.J. Tompkins of St Matthew, later to be secretary of the succeeding Exeter clubs. We are also told the location of the ground: 'the field is situated on the right-hand side of the road going towards Topsham, just below Matford Lane', so a short distance away from Park House in St Leonard's Road.

In the first two months of the 1891–92 season, fixtures had been arranged with Crediton Grammar School, Dawlish (home and away) and Exeter Grammar School. Things were looking up. Then, suddenly, progress was interrupted by a tragic event. Sport and the wider society in Exeter was shocked at news of the death of Alexander Stuart. Over-work in his sporting commitments, it was suggested, led to him succumbing to typhoid fever on 23 November. Stuart, in his mid-thirties, left a widow and three small children.

When news of the death was circulated, as the *Exeter Flying Post* put it, 'a deep gloom was cast over a large section of the community, and doubtless it will be received with genuine grief in many districts even remote from Devonshire'. It was, for as well as being secretary of the Devon Rugby Football Union, he'd also been appointed to English rugby's

governing committee. In an obituary, the *Edinburgh Evening News* called Stuart 'an enthusiastic sportsman'. As a mark of respect, a forthcoming county match was postponed.

There was, you sense, an extended period of mourning. In March 1892, a column in the *Devon & Exeter Gazette* referred to 'the lack of interest recently taken in football in Exeter'. If football, i.e. rugby, was struggling, then spare a thought for the association code. In the press, from January 1892, nothing more was heard of the Exeter Association Club.

The absence of an association-football club in the city was confirmed in a letter to the editor of the *Western Times* in July 1892. The correspondent was an E.T. Wood of 74, High Street, Exeter:

FIRST EXETER CITY TEAM

BACK ROW:—A. E. Denning (Hon Secretary), Littlehales (back), Bayles (goalkeeper) and Carey (back).
CENTRE:—S. Gardland (right-half), H. Byrne (centre-half) and Addis (left-half).
FRONT ROW:—R. G. Davey (outside-right), Nelson (inside-right), J. McDermott (centre), Fletcher (inside-left) and H. Smith (outside-left), captain.

Exeter AFC team, 1893–94 season. This is the oldest-known image of an association-football team in Exeter
Source: © *Football Express*, 20 January 1934

As an association player, may I be allowed to suggest the formation of an Association Club in the city? It seems to me a great pity that with so many clubs playing the Rugby game in our midst, and with Association clubs but a short distance away, there should be no combination which lovers of the game may join here. I have heard several express a wish for the formation of such a club and believe that many would willingly assist were this suggestion brought before them. Will all players and all desirous of becoming players of this noble game, kindly communicate with me (preferably by letter), at their earliest convenience?

Twelve months passed before the suggestion was taken up. The first 'City Club' was formed on 17 August 1893 under the title of 'Exeter AFC'. It began a sequence of association-football clubs representing Exeter that were known as the 'City Club'.

From the outset, there was an attempt to insert the club into the heart of city life. After the founding meeting at the Arcade Assembly Room, there was a general meeting at the Guildhall. The Mayor was invited to become president of the club, the Sheriff of Exeter vice-president. At the well-attended Guildhall meeting, a Mr Collins spoke of his interest in the association code:

The Association game was, in his opinion, the most scientific and not attended with so much danger as the Rugby game. [If] they wanted to form a good team they must have working men, and not gentlemen who would ignore working men when they went on the field. (Hear, hear.) With proper management and judgment, the game should certainly prove a success. If the Association game was properly brought before the Exeter public they would certainly prefer it to the slogging Rugby game.

Aside from the swipes at the sister code, crucially there was emphasis on the desire to take the association game out of the confines of the private schools; Park House, by then, had closed. Here was the first attempt to democratise the game in Exeter.

Another feature of the new organisation was the active part taken by members of the Devonshire Regiment. Sergeant Denning of the Higher Barracks was appointed secretary. In the team, among others in the squad from the Devons, were Sergeant Byrne at centre-half and centre-forward Sergeant-Major McDermott. Denning, like Tompkins, would have a lasting role to play in the running of the 'City Club'.

As to the question of a ground, the Devon County Athletic Ground Company, which managed the County Ground, was contacted. An offer was made, but Saturdays could not be guaranteed as arrangements had already been made with Exeter Rugby Club. So, at the Guildhall meeting, a committee was set up, which included Mr Collins, to interview owners of fields. Perhaps Tom and Elizabeth Bradford were approached as to the availability of the Parish Field? The club ended up letting a field in the vicinity, on the north-east fringes of the city.

We are four years on from the efforts of St Matthew AFC to bring the association game in Exeter to a wider public. For its opening fixture at the Horse Show Field in Mount Pleasant, Exeter AFC managed a creditable 3-3 draw with Plymouth United. For the most part, opponents were from outside Exeter, such as Tavistock, St James-the-Less (a church side from Plymouth) and teams from the armed forces. By the end of the 1893–94 season, 23 games had been played of which 9 were won, 3 drawn and 11 lost. Club officials didn't let an adverse balance of £10 deter them; of the costs for the season, annual rent for the Horse Show Field was £25.

It was at this juncture that a move was made to obtain St James' Field, although it's not clear when exactly this happened. No mention was made of a new ground at the club's first AGM in August 1894. At that precise moment, St James' Field had been booked for the Exeter Rovers Cycling Club annual sports. The *Evening Post* gives us an image of a piece of land that was used to being adapted for a variety of purposes:

> Those who visit the sports [of the Exeter Rovers] will be surprised to see what a transformation has been effected at St. James's Park. The steam roller has manufactured an excellent track, and the ground, roped off and adorned, looks charming.

A report of the event referred to the venue as 'St James's Circus Field'. This, after all, was the essence of the land's identity.

So, when Exeter AFC opened its fixtures for the 1894–95 season with a game at St James' Field, it happened discreetly; there was no fanfare. The *Devon & Exeter Gazette*'s report of the game played on Saturday 6 October was framed by rugby results. It merely said: 'A match under Association rules between Exeter and Minehead, played at St. James's Field, Exeter, ended in a win for the home team by three goals to nothing.'

Other reports were more detailed. There are references to playing 'down the hill', and to the grass in parts of the field being 'knee-deep'. According to the *Evening Post*, there were 'few spectators'.

In contrast, two weeks later, there was 'a numerous company' at St James' Field for the visit of Tavistock. Interest from the public was confirmed on Saturday 24 November when 'a large attendance' gathered for the game against Home Park. We're told Exeter AFC had 'secured the presence' of two patrons, the Mayor and Colonel Milne-Home, and each kicked off a half. The launch, it seems, had been delayed. Nevertheless, the Minehead game is the one we celebrate.

6

A scientific game

AFTER that first season of hosting association-football matches, St James' Field reverted to providing a venue for an event that it was popularly known for. In July 1895, Bostock, Wombwell and Bailey's – a circus, hippodrome and menagerie rolled into one – gave exhibitions over two days. There were two daily shows: at 2.30 p.m. and 7 p.m. The set-up was impressive.

Spectators were entertained in a 'spacious waterproof marquee' with seating for 3,500 plus standing room, we're told, for nearly as many more. The entire show was 'expensively illuminated by electric light'. Riders, acrobats, clowns and wire walkers performed under the canvas, with several acts appearing at a time. The owners boasted that they'd give £10,000 to charity if theirs was not the very best circus performance that had travelled Europe.

When it came to sport at St James', it was hard, too, to break with tradition. Although Exeter AFC managed one more season – 1895–96 – there, the club ran into difficulties. In August 1896, it was announced that a newly formed rugby club for St James' parish would be playing its games at the ground. Perhaps the new club's coup in securing St James' Park was down to the fact that it had an association with the tenant. Tom Bradford had connections with the mother church: he was a long-standing member of St Sidwell's Church Choir.

For the next four years, then, after two seasons of association football, rugby was the sport played at St James' Park in the winter months. As for Exeter AFC, on 8 September 1896 a crisis meeting was held at the Guildhall. There was discussion as to whether the club should continue or a new one be formed. Reg Davey, standing in for Tompkins, the treasurer, passed on the figures: a negative balance of 10s 6d and a debt of £5. When it came to the vote, a majority decided in favour of forming a new club: Exeter United AFC. This club was to last for just over six seasons, the last two of which would be played at St James' Park.

Later in September 1896, we learn that Exeter United had succeeded in renting the ground where the St Luke's Training College played: Magdalen Road. The *Devon Evening Express* Football Notes provide an insight into the partisan nature of the football codes in Exeter, and how this could impact on whether or not a rental agreement was drawn up:

> The Club has been lucky enough to secure the best situated ground in the city, that field is Magdalen Road, so long coveted by the Rugby Club, but which, it was understood, would not be let for football. It is to be presumed that only the 'common' rugby game was meant. Played by a good team, there is nothing more interesting to watch than an Association match, and I rather fancy that a good number of Exonians will be attracted to Magdalen Road.

Back in September 1890, as the Exeter Rugby Club was moving from Matford to the County Ground, it was reported that efforts were being made on behalf of the organisation to obtain the Horse Show Field in Mount Pleasant. Nothing came of it, but it's another indication that – for some officials of the rugby club – St Thomas was seen as being too remote.

Exeter United's first season was a successful one, both on and off the pitch. Of 26 matches played, 20 were won, 5 lost and 1 drawn; while in breaking even, the £11 in gate money was almost half the total receipts for the season. From the AGM report, one thing of note was the importance of the club's military contingent. The meeting at the Guildhall was delayed for almost an hour due to the late arrival, 'through some inadvertence', of the Mace-Sergeants. W.J. Tompkins, continuing the link back to St Matthew, was re-elected as treasurer.

For 1897–98, playing results were much the same as the previous season, with the bonus of reaching the final of the Devon Senior Cup. In that match, United narrowly lost to the 15th Company Royal Artillery, 1-2, at the Rectory Ground in Devonport; the crowd of 8,000 was a sign that association football was gaining in appeal and rivalling rugby. A special train had been laid on for supporters. On the financial side, however, increased expenditure meant there was a slight adverse balance.

Looking ahead, members' dissatisfaction at the lack of strong opposition needed addressing. Clearly, there was work to be done to promote the code at grassroots level, not only in and around Exeter, but in the county as a whole. Exeter United was doing its best. In September 1898, the club introduced a limited number of season tickets at a reduced price, and free tickets were distributed to Exeter day schools. Most important of all, it was announced that a Schools' League was to be formed in Exeter.

A Phil Barnes cartoon showing Norman Kendall championing Exeter City's cause on the eve of their first Southern League season

Source: © *Football Express*, 29 August 1908

J. F. : What are your prospects, Kendall? That youngster of your's has been making enough row this last four months.

N. K. : Fancy you noticing that, now. I bought him a drum and a trumpet, and I said to Thomas, "Let him make as much row as he can; I know our Rugby friends won't mind. It's all in the game." Besides, you know, a little "walking up" never hurt anybody yet.

It's at this point that two names, each having a significant future impact on St James' Park, enter the story of how association football developed in Exeter. A. Norman Kendall, an Exeter United committee member, was the chief organiser of the Schools' League and its secretary; while playing for one of the competing schools, St Sidwell's, was Sidney Thomas. He was, for example, in the line-up for a match against the eventual winners of the League, St John's, in January 1899. Both Kendall and Thomas were to play key roles in Exeter City becoming a limited liability company in 1908.

In the late 1880s, as a member of St Mary's Church Choir in Southampton, Norman Kendall had followed closely the beginnings of St Mary's Young Men's Association FC, the club that evolved into Southampton FC. He was employed as a tailor and a musician, before, in 1892, he moved to Exeter to take up a position as Lay Clerk in Exeter Cathedral.

St John's Hospital XI, March 1900

Source: © *Football Express*, 3 September 1938

In the Schools' League, sides competed for the 'Harvey Cup'. Frederick Harvey was an Exeter United player and committee member, and he'd later become the leading administrator of association football in East Devon. The cup and medals were presented to winners St John's and runners-up Wingfield at the Guildhall in May 1899. As well as St Sidwell's, other competing schools included Heavitree and St Thomas'.

The *Devon & Exeter Gazette's* report of the proceedings including Kendall's opening remarks was entitled 'Rugby v. Association Football'. A measure of the challenges still facing Associationists in Exeter was summarised:

Association Football, as far as Exeter was concerned – and he [Kendall] might say Devon – was practically a dead letter. In comparison with Rugby, the Association game was as different as skittles to billiards. The Rugby game was a knock-down game, and the Association was a scientific one. He looked confidently to the improvement and extension of Association Football in Devon, but the boys were the ones who would have to make that change.

Belmont Pleasure Ground, where association football was played in the late 1890s
Source: © Aidan Hamilton, 2018

There's no doubt that the inaugural schools' competition was a success, and in September 1899 the *Devon Evening News*' football correspondent, 'Spec', who admitted he preferred rugby, remarked that 'the Boys' League … has placed a powerful factor in the hands of the Associationists, and is a dangerous foe to Rugby, as I have discovered by watching the boys in the various Pleasure Grounds'.

It was at one of those pleasure grounds, Belmont, that founder members of the club that became Exeter City learnt how to play 'the Socker game'. They went to St Sidwell's School. In the oral-history project 'People Talking', former pupil Harry Snell recalled how there was resistance among the boys to the school's major sport, rugby:

> The headmaster was Teddy Nicholls. He was a rugby player – course it was a rugby school. He tried to force rugby on you. The majority of us wasn't interested in rugby – soccer was our game. Every day at lunch-time some of us would play soccer in the playground. We'd have one fellow on the corner of the railway bridge in Pennsylvania – he could see Mr. Nicholls's house. When Mr. Nicholls came out, then that boy would pass it on to a boy down the corner of York Road; that one would wave his arms to the boy that was posted up outside the school gates. As soon as you had the signal, 'He's coming!' instead of playing soccer you'd be playing rugby. And if you was in Belmont Park playing soccer – if anyone reported to Mr. Nicholls that some of his boys were playing soccer, you used to get the cane the next morning. And this was for playing soccer after school.

During the 1900–01 season, ex-pupils of St Sidwell's were turning out for two new association clubs: Exeter Wesleyan United and Exeter Athletic. Both played their home games on a pitch in Mount Pleasant where Monks Road is today. Kendall had good reason to be pleased with the way in which the game was taking hold.

Soon these clubs would be playing against Exeter United reserves. United had secured St James' Park. But before the new season got underway, there was a novelty at the ground. On Saturday 25 August 1900, a Fire Brigade competition was held there. Open to brigades in Devon and Somerset, among the events were Four Men Manual Fire Engine (dry drill), Fire Escape Drill and Obstacle Race with Scaling Ladders. These contests would be repeated in the future. One of the earliest images of St James' Park was taken at one of these events: a horse-drawn fire engine with St James' church providing the backdrop.

A horse-drawn steam-powered fire engine at St James' Park, *c.*1900

It wasn't long before a rivalry had developed between Exeter Wesleyan United and Exeter United reserves. Tensions were sparked when the Wesleyans paid a visit to St James' Park on 27 April 1901. After a 1-3 loss, a member of the Wesleyan club wrote to the local press:

> The Wesleyan United were annoyed to find on coming on to the field that the 'First' team was waiting, with Steele and Thorpe, of the Battery, helping them. The Wesleyan defence was very fine, Flood (back) and Allin, who closely marked Steele, playing a splendid defensive game. Of the Wesleyan forwards, Morgan, Eveleigh, and Sellick were undoubtedly the pick, Eveleigh having exceedingly hard lines in not scoring, several times kicking the ball over the goal-post. This is the fourth time the Wesleyans have been down to play the Reserves, and on each occasion, with but one exception, there were a good sprinkling of first men and other Exeter teams. Several other junior clubs seem to have the same complaint to make, and it is rather a pity that the Reserves should put in first men just for the sake of winning a match.

Perhaps it was on the back of this protest that a meeting was arranged, which brought together players from a number of junior clubs.

Reminiscing in 1939 on the early days of 'Soccer football' in Exeter, Sid Thomas refers to 'a meeting of selected youngsters in the city who were known to be good exponents of the game':

> In those days, there was a public-house in Sidwell-street, the actual name of which was the Foresters Arms, but which was more popularly known as the Drum and Monkey – peculiar how Soccer football seems to run in conjunction with licensed houses – and the meeting was held there at which it was decided to run a football team. The club's first name was Wesleyan United. Afterwards it was changed to St. Sidwell's United.
>
> Now, I always say, and I do not think that it can be seriously contradicted, that that meeting in the old Drum and Monkey was the origin of the Exeter City Football Club. Unfortunately, the house was eventually closed down on the grounds of redundancy, but some sort of plaque should be placed on its walls as indicating the great part it helped to play in the formation of the City Club.

Thomas then goes on to say: 'we played the first fourteen matches without defeat'. Here, he seems to be referring to the 1901–02 season; there's no record of him having played for the Wesleyans.

It was after the end of the 1900–01 season that a new organisation was formed, one that effectively replaced Exeter Wesleyan United. The first we hear of St Sidwell's United is when two of their members, Sid Thomas and H. Eveleigh, attend the formation meeting of the Exeter Junior league on 3 June 1901. Seven other clubs entered the competition: St Luke's College reserves, St David's, Friernhay, St John's Athletic, Exeter YMCA, St Leonard's and Exeter United reserves. While it's true that St Sidwell's United appears to have been born out of Wesleyan United, contemporary reports refer to St Sidwell's as being a 'new' club, with the red and black of the Wesleyans being replaced by green and white.

The first St Sidwell's United line-up, in September 1901, contained players from a number of other junior clubs – bearing out what Sid Thomas says about 'selected youngsters in the city'. There were Robinson, Campbell and Hawkey from Heavitree; Avery, Morgan and Eveleigh from the Wesleyans; Sellick and Thomas from St Thomas' Past; Flood from St James'; Mann from St John's; and Coles from St David's. Club secretary George West had been the Wesleyans' secretary. If St Sidwell's United was ever known previously as 'St Sidwell's Wesleyan AFC', it was short-lived.

Sidney Thomas
Source: © *Football Express*, 17 November 1906

Given the needle between the Wesleyans and Exeter United, St Sidwell's would have looked forward to their league fixture with Exeter United reserves on 16 November 1901. But it never took place. The weekend before, the reserves had been unable to field a team and consequently the club decided to cancel all its Junior League fixtures. Two months later, another opportunity came for the clubs to meet. This time, St Sidwell's played a friendly against the Exeter United first team.

On Saturday 11 January 1902, we're told the game at St James' Park was watched by 'but few spectators'. Nevertheless, the St Sidwell's ones present showed their passion for the game, and in booing some of the referee's decisions, overstepped the mark for some. The *Exeter Flying Post*'s report was entitled 'Referee Hooted':

> A free given to Exeter United in their own territory met with the disfavour of some of the onlookers, and the referee was hooted … Towards the end of the game … an opposing forward, who was palpably offside, had the goal at his mercy. The referee gave the free, and the St Sidwell's supporters again showed their dissatisfaction by hooting the referee (Mr Sturdy).

Minutes before the end it was 2-2, and when Exeter United scored just before the final whistle, all hell broke loose:

> It was alleged the referee was five or six minutes late in blowing his whistle, and he and the Exeter touch-judge were subjected to a hostile demonstration by spectators and players off the ground and some distance down Sidwell-street. However much the losing team felt they were aggrieved, such unsportsmanlike behaviour should be denounced in the strongest terms.

The *Devon & Exeter Gazette* agreed:

> Mr Sturdy would have been quite justified had he stopped the game. The supporters of St Sidwell's United should endeavour to treat a referee who is trying to do his duty impartially with a little more respect than they did that official on Saturday.

The referee, Donald Sturdy, was an Exeter United committee member. It was perhaps the first time sport at St James' Park had seen anything like it.

7

'Who are the leaders?'

JUST weeks after that stormy encounter with the city's leading junior club, Exeter United suddenly found itself without a home. Presumably it was a condition of the 1901–02 season-long lease that from March 1902 they had to vacate St James' Park. The ground had been chosen to host the exhibition at the Co-operative Society's 34th Annual Congress.

As there was no hall large enough in Exeter, it was decided to put up a wooden building 'in St. James' field'; unlike the sporting County Ground in St Thomas, St James' Field was still very much land for all purposes. The cost was met by Co-operative Societies from all over the UK. A note in the *Western Times* gives an indication as to what the structure entailed:

In size it will run the Salisbury Hall, which was built on the occasion of the visit of the Premier to the City a few years ago, very close, if, indeed, it does not eclipse it. A good idea of its dimensions will be gathered from the fact that it is about three and a half times bigger than the Victoria Hall. It is 177 feet by 122 feet, and the flooring measures 220 superficial feet … The roof is being covered with vulcanite, and the electricity for lighting is to be generated on the grounds.

It took about two months for the building work to be done. The Congress would last for six days, and the hall was supposed to be temporary. But, as we shall see, the fact that it remained in place for much longer spelled trouble for Exeter United.

The 'Exhibition of Co-operative Productions' opened on Saturday 17 May 1902. Between 60 and 70 of the productive societies had displays; 1,000 delegates were expected to attend. Admission was free. It wasn't the first time the event had been housed in a specially erected facility. On this occasion, however, the wooden structure was unable to keep out entirely the heavy rain on day one. As a result, in parts of the hall, there was extensive damage to some of the goods.

In the Co-operative Society's archives in Manchester, an account entitled 'Proceedings in Connection with Congress' depicts what visitors to the exhibition would have seen:

The exterior of the building was anything but inviting, but inside was a scene of gaiety and animation … The huge floor space was covered with elaborate and artistic show-cases, while the walls and ceiling were concealed with draperies, flags, and bunting of every hue. An innovation was made by the Wholesale Society, and one which had a particularly pleasing effect. Round

CO-OPERATIVE PRODUCTION!

THE 34TH ANNUAL CO-OPERATIVE

CONGRESS.

AN

EXHIBITION

OF

CO-OPERATIVE MANUFACTURES

Will be held on
MAY 17th, 19th, 20th, 21st, 22nd, and 23rd, 1902.

IN THE

EXHIBITION BUILDINGS,

ST. JAMES' FIELD, EXETER.

The Exhibition was
OPENED ON SATURDAY, MAY 17th,
at 5 p.m., by the
RIGHT WORSHIPFUL THE MAYOR OF EXETER
(Albert Edward Dunn, Esq., J.P.).
SIR C. T. D. ACLAND, BART.,
Presided at the Opening Ceremony.
The EXHIBITION WILL REMAIN OPEN
on Saturday from the Opening Address
till 10 p.m. ; on Monday, Tuesday,
Wednesday, and Thursday from 10 a.m.
till 10 p.m. ; and on Friday from 10 a.m.
till 6 p.m.
ADMISSION FREE.

A 3270

Advert for the Co-operative Congress
Source: © *Western Times*, 19 May 1902

the walls, at certain intervals, were hung large coloured illustrations of the Silvertown Corn Mill and the new premises at Bristol and Cardiff.

As for the exhibits on display, the Report of Congress provides examples in a general survey:

> The English Wholesale Society was represented by almost everything – from a biscuit from Crumpsall to a suite of furniture from the Broughton works. Bright-faced girls were deftly making cigars and cigarettes; at another stall, shirt-making was in progress, whilst the tea-packing machine, and the printing-press from Longsight, claimed a considerable share of attention. The delegates were keenly interested in the photographs of the two tea estates in Ceylon, the purchase of which marks the most recent enterprise of the two Wholesale Societies. Middleton jams and pickles were there in tempting array, and the display of crockery from Longton must have roused the envy of many a visitor. The Scottish federation was also well represented with boots, furniture, preserves, tobacco, &c.

In terms of local and regional involvement in the exhibition, one society, Plymouth Printers, exhibited, and the Exeter Society provided a refreshment stall. The general secretary of the Co-operative Society expressed the hope that the Congress would lead to the spreading of the co-operative movement locally.

The Congress itself was held at the Theatre Royal from 19 to 21 May. There were fringe events at Barnfield Hall, the Royal Public Rooms and Victoria Hall; while at the Cathedral, sermons alluded to the principles of fellowship and fairness on which the co-operative movement was founded. For the first time, St James' Park had been the venue for an international event.

To return to the rivalry between Exeter United and St Sidwell's United, the two clubs met for a second time in April 1902. There was, we're told, 'considerable interest' in this fixture at Mount Pleasant. Once again, the scoreline was 3-2 in the seniors' favour, and again there was an 'unpleasant incident' near the end. The *Devon & Exeter Gazette*'s correspondent, 'Behind the Ropes', recorded what happened:

> The St Sidwell's goalkeeper [Robinson] made an unwarrantable attack on Tyte [Exeter United's centre-forward], and Flood [St Sidwell's right-back] also mixed himself up in the affair. A general melee was only prevented by the interference of the players. The referee, whose decisions were most partial, showed a lamentable lack of strength in not ordering at least two of the players off the field.

Monks Road, where St Sidwell's United had its ground
Source: © Aidan Hamilton, 2018

The reporter concluded that incidents such as this were not uncommon but perhaps that was a way of playing down tensions between the two clubs.

It seems Exeter United had banked on taking St James' Park for the 1902–03 season. At the club's annual meeting in May, if the ground situation wasn't mentioned explicitly in the report of proceedings, it was certainly inferred in the description of the previous season as being 'rather a trying one'. Two key officials had left the organisation, as well as a good number of players, some of whom – it's not clear why – had been 'debarred' from representing the club, possibly due to some sort of ineligibility.

Reference, also, was made to the cancellation in November of all fixtures of the reserves and the Wednesday team. Only a few seasons back, members had complained of a lack of quality in first-team opponents: now, there'd been just 9 wins in 22 matches. Nevertheless, finances showed a balance in hand and, by the end of the season, there'd been an upturn in membership. Efforts were made to attract new members by reducing the fee, and it was agreed to restart the reserve team. It was taken for granted, therefore, that St James' Park would be available again.

On the eve of a new season, Exeter United weren't the only association club having difficulties in finding a ground. There were reports that Junior Cup winners St Sidwell's and St David's were facing a similar situation. On Monday 15 September, Exeter United members met at the Red Lion Hotel in Sidwell Street to discuss the problem:

> For several years they have had St James' Park at their disposal, but as the building erected there for the Co-operative Society is still standing and in use, the Club are obliged to seek a new ground. It was decided to ask the hon. Secretary and hon. Treasurer to interview Mr. Pople of the New London Hotel with the view to obtaining a field situated in the Pinhoe-road.

It came to nothing, and so did the suggestion of a 'scheme of amalgamation' with a junior club. A ground share with Exeter Rugby Club at the County Ground was 'not considered feasible'. Couldn't they have made another arrangement with St Luke's College to share Magdalen Road? And why were junior clubs seemingly preferred by landowners? It's extraordinary that Exeter's leading association club failed to secure a ground and, while facing the possibility of folding, was left with no choice but to play 'out [i.e. away] matches'.

There's an irony too in that the 'rapid progress' being made by the dribbling code in Exeter was largely down to the efforts of Exeter United officials. They were the ones who had championed the idea of an exhibition between two professional teams, and the result was a game between two Second Division sides, West Bromwich Albion and Woolwich Arsenal, at the County Ground in April 1902. And when it came to challenging the Devon FA over fairer treatment, Frederick Harvey took the case to the FA, a move that led to the formation of an East Devon association. It's as if for some at United, spearheading the development of the code locally was more important than finding somewhere for the club to play.

Despite the ongoing hunt for a ground, Exeter United got into their stride by defeating the Devon Regiment 4-3 at the Higher Barracks. St Sidwell's had two games at the Barracks, losing 3-4 and winning 8-2, and they followed it up by beating Crediton Grammar School 8-0. St Sidwell's took this attacking form into what proved to be the defining match in the history of association football in Exeter. It took place on Saturday 25 October on the ground in Mount Pleasant that St Sidwell's had secured, close to where Blackboy Road and Pinhoe Road meet.

In the third game between the two Uniteds, St Sidwell's beat Exeter 3-0. For the *Devon & Exeter Gazette*, 'the better team undoubtedly won; the surprise was that Exeter should have lost after being only a goal to the bad at the interval, and having to play with the slope in their favour'. The report, while highlighting the superiority of the Saints' forwards, dished out praise for Exeter's 'back division', and recounted the times that Exeter 'had extremely hard lines in not scoring'. You sense there was respect, a preference even, for the senior club.

'Linesman', writing in the *Western Times*, was forthright and to the point. It was the significance of the result that was important. His column was headed 'Who are the leaders?':

Frederick Harvey: the pioneer of the East Devon Football Association

Source: © *Football Express*, 16 November 1907

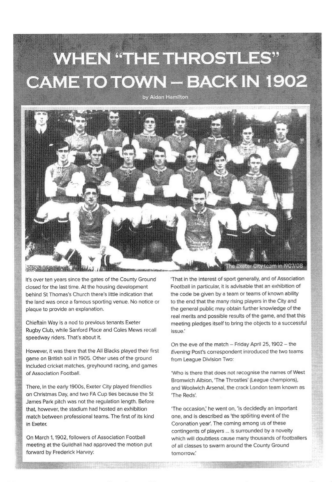

WHEN "THE THROSTLES" CAME TO TOWN – BACK IN 1902
by Aidan Hamilton

The Exeter City team in 1907/08

It's over ten years since the gates of the County Ground closed for the last time. At the housing development behind St Thomas's Church there's little indication that the land was once a famous sporting venue. No notice or plaque to provide an explanation.

Chieftain Way is a nod to previous tenants Exeter Rugby Club, while Sanford Place and Coles Mews recall speedway riders. That's about it.

However, it was there that the All Blacks played their first game on British soil in 1905. Other uses of the ground included cricket matches, greyhound racing, and games of Association Football.

There, in the early 1900s, Exeter City played friendlies on Christmas Day, and two FA Cup ties because the St James Park pitch was not the regulation length. Before that, however, the stadium had hosted an exhibition match between professional teams. The first of its kind in Exeter.

On March 1, 1902, followers of Association Football meeting at the Guildhall had approved the motion put forward by Frederick Harvey:

'That in the interest of sport generally, and of Association Football in particular, it is advisable that an exhibition of the code be given by a team or teams of known ability to the end that the many rising players in the City and the general public may obtain further knowledge of the real merits and possible results of the game, and that this meeting pledges itself to bring the objects to a successful issue.'

On the eve of the match – Friday April 25, 1902 – the Evening Post's correspondent introduced the two teams from League Division Two:

'Who is there that does not recognise the names of West Bromwich Albion, 'The Throstles' (League champions), and Woolwich Arsenal, the crack London team known as 'The Reds'.

'The occasion,' he went on, 'is decidedly an important one, and is described as 'the sporting event of the Coronation year'. The coming among us of these contingents of players ... is surrounded by a novelty which will doubtless cause many thousands of footballers of all classes to swarm around the County Ground tomorrow.'

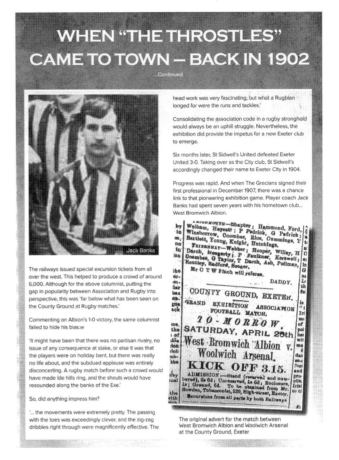

WHEN "THE THROSTLES" CAME TO TOWN – BACK IN 1902
...Continued

Jack Banks

The railways issued special excursion tickets from all over the west. This helped to produce a crowd of around 6,000. Although for the above columnist, putting the gap in popularity between Association and Rugby into perspective, this was 'far below what has been seen on the County Ground at Rugby matches.'

Commenting on Albion's 1-0 victory, the same columnist failed to hide his bias:w

'It might have been that there was no partisan rivalry, no issue of any consequence at stake, or else it was that the players were on holiday bent, but there was really no life about, and the subdued applause was entirely disconcerting. A rugby match before such a crowd would have made Ide hills ring, and the shouts would have resounded along the banks of the Exe.'

So, did anything impress him?

'... the movements were extremely pretty. The passing with the toes was exceedingly clever, and the zig-zag dribbles right through were magnificently effective. The head work was very fascinating, but what a Rugbian longed for were the runs and tackles.'

Consolidating the association code in a rugby stronghold would always be an uphill struggle. Nevertheless, the exhibition did provide the impetus for a new Exeter club to emerge.

Six months later, St Sidwell's United defeated Exeter United 3-0. Taking over as the City club, St Sidwell's accordingly changed their name to Exeter City in 1904.

Progress was rapid. And when The Grecians signed their first professional in December 1907, there was a chance link to that pioneering exhibition game. Player coach Jack Banks had spent seven years with his hometown club... West Bromwich Albion.

The original advert for the match between West Bromwich Albion and Woolwich Arsenal at the County Ground, Exeter

---

The question which will arise in Exeter Association football circles in face of the result of the Exeter United v. St. Sidwell's United match on Saturday, is: Which is the leading Club of the City? Nominally, the distinction belongs to Exeter United. Not only does that organisation bear the City's name, but it had up to last Saturday held undisputed superiority over other Exeter Clubs. Now, however, it has been displaced from its position by that wonderfully promising Club, St. Sidwell's. The latter, to speak of the team in the plural, have now the strongest possible claim, viz. success on the field, to the title. It will not, I think, be questioned by the staunchest supporter of Exeter that the Saints proved themselves a distinctly smarter and more scientific side in the game which ended in their favour by three goals to nil. They are to be heartily congratulated upon an achievement that will rank as not only the most notable, but also as the most pleasing in the history of the Club. The result is one that should have a very beneficial influence on Exeter football. The immediate effect should be two-fold in its character – St. Sidwell's should be greatly encouraged in their laudable effort to raise the standard of the game, and Exeter United should learn by this sharp lesson of experience that disjointed individualism will always be beaten by intelligent combination.

Article by Aidan Hamilton in the matchday programme for Exeter City v West Bromwich Albion (FA Cup), 6 January 2018. The date of the team photo is, in fact, 1908–09
Source: © ECFC/Aidan Hamilton

From that moment, to quote the *Football Express* in 1906, Exeter United 'faded out'.

Initially struggling on, Exeter United played several more friendlies. The fact that the club was on its last legs was evident in a match at Dawlish in December 1902; a 'disorganised team' included three substitutes. What happened to one of their players seemed to sum up their plight:

Soon after the interval one of the Exeter men, who missed his train and cycled to Dawlish, reaching the ground in time to take his place after half-time, was ordered off the field for a reason which was not apparent to the spectators, and which was unknown to the player himself.

By the end of the 1902–03 season, Exeter United had gone. Eventually, as Sid Thomas recalled in 1936, it was a case of the club being 'absorb[ed]' by St Sidwell's United.

In that first half of the 1902–03 season, St Sidwell's United won all 15 of the games they played, including five Junior League matches, scoring 70 goals and conceding 14. And Thomas was on his way to scoring a record 41 goals in a season. Moreover, the club was fielding a second

XI for the first time, and 9 of 13 matches were won. The confidence 'Linesman' had in the organisation was being borne out. Perhaps there were already ambitions to move to Exeter United's former ground, but for that they'd have to wait.

The hall in St James' Field had been acquired by a Mr Walter Little, an art photographer and printer. After the Co-operative Congress had ended, he applied, unsuccessfully, for 'an occasional license for music and dancing'. At the Exeter Police Court on 27 June 1902, we hear that local residents had petitioned the Clifford Trustees, whose solicitors responded by underlining that the tenant must adhere to the conditions of the lease:

> [N]o show was to be allowed to use the field more than once a year, nor for more than six consecutive days, the music to be stopped every night at 10 o'clock, and also on Fridays during Divine service at St. James's Church.

There had been one recent musical event at the St James' Field building: a promenade concert on 2 June to celebrate the end of the Second Anglo-Boer War. In October, the materials used to construct the exhibition hall were put up for auction; however, soon afterwards, Little was organising entertainment there. Apart from roller skating, 'a grand hockey match on skates', and dancing, there were fairground attractions and a steam organ. On 23 December, after complaints from residents, Little was summoned before the Exeter Police Court and fined £5. That same evening, the hall was opened again to the public. Another music licence prosecution followed. Soon, the field reverted to its former use.

In January 1903, there was an appeal to timber merchants and builders for tenders for the wooden structure still standing at St James' Park. By the end of February, it had been taken down and sport was being played there again. But it was rugby, not association football. St James' resumed fixtures on the ground – against Bradninch, and then Tiverton reserves – and on Saturday 11 April, there was a match in aid of the London and South Western Railway Widows' and Orphans' Fund. The Traffic Department defeated the Locomotive Department by '1 goal and 4 tries to nil'. According to one report, there was 'a large number of spectators' present.

It was at this point, in the 1903 close season, that St Sidwell's United finally made its move for St James' Park.

8

Oddities of the pitch

S T Sidwell's United began training at St James' Park in August 1903. The *Devon Evening Express* announced this on Thursday 20 in a column called 'Sport & Pastime': 'Exeter St. Sidwell's United Soccer Team has commenced practising on their new ground, St. James's Park, Old Tiverton-road.' An offer to play home and away matches was made to 'any leading Devon or Somerset Clubs'.

Having twice been champions of the Exeter & District Junior League, now St Sidwell's were one of eight teams making up the newly formed East Devon Senior League; the others were Torquay United, Dawlish, the Exeter Training College, Newton Abbot GWR students, and three Royal Field Artillery Batteries. Fifteen teams, including St Sidwell's reserves, entered the Junior League. Coordinating everything was Frederick Harvey, East Devon FA secretary, from his gymnasium in Sidwell Street.

A Junior League of 15 teams was indeed an indication that interest in association football was gathering pace. As a way of encouraging involvement in the game, St Sidwell's made it known that 'anyone requiring St James' Field for football purposes on any week day' only had to contact Secretary Sid Thomas. There was incentive, too, from the announcement of a trial match in Exeter for the purpose of selecting a team to represent Devon. At last, the east of the county was no longer playing second fiddle to the west over the running of the game.

As Exeter's premier club, St Sidwell's began its League fixtures promisingly. Newton Abbot GWR students were beaten 6-2, and this was followed by an 8-0 thrashing of Dawlish at St James' Park. Then came three losses: 1-6 away to St Luke's College, followed by home defeats to Battery sides. It wasn't just the fact of adjusting to the senior competition; several ex-Exeter United men had to be integrated, notably Ashford, Bailey and Wallage.

There was another example of the difficult situations encountered by referees when St Sidwell's United visited Newton Abbot for a return match in November 1903. On this occasion, the official's decisions had no bearing on the outcome, St Sidwell's winning 5-0. This is how the *Western Times* reported the home side's reaction:

> The home team did not provide goal nets, and a dispute arose over two of the goals. Mr Narracott (Torquay), the referee, allowed the goals, the students contending that the ball had hit the post and glanced outside. On his last decision the home team left the field, despite the fact that only five or ten minutes remained for play.

The failure to provide nets was something that needed addressing. But when it came to the goals, Narracott could only give what he saw, and we don't know how the St Sidwell's side reacted.

Several months later, Frederick Harvey himself was in charge for a friendly between St Sidwell's and Dawlish at St James' Park. An error by him was rectified by a sporting gesture. Seeing the Dawlish keeper take too many steps before releasing the ball, Harvey pointed to the spot. The *Exeter & Plymouth Gazette* recounts what happened next:

> Immediately Mr Harvey gave the decision he became aware he was wrong, but was doubtful whether he could alter the decision once given, and insisted on the penalty kick being taken. The

mistake, however, was so obvious that the St Sidwell's player entrusted with the ball deliberately kicked it outside.

Harvey probably explained his predicament to whoever wrote the report. What it showed was that not even the person who was responsible for examining match officials in East Devon was infallible.

When it came to handling cases of misconduct, a strict precedent was set. At a meeting of the East Devon FA committee in January 1904, suspensions were handed out, including two to St Sidwell's reserve team members. Aplin and Ireland each received a two-week ban for refusing to give their names to a referee when asked to, and Ireland got a further fortnight 'for using improper language'. Sid Thomas recalled in 1939 how, as a lad, he appeared before the governing body 'for some breach of rule and being told by the chairman not to be insolent to that very august body'. It was early days for the East Devon FA, but a clear message was being sent out.

In that first season as tenants of St James' Park, St Sidwell's came third in the Senior League, and were runners-up in the East Devon Cup, losing 1-2 to the 110th RFA Battery at the County Ground. The AGM was held at the Red Lion Hotel in Sidwell Street on 31 May 1904. This was the meeting at which it was decided to adopt the name Exeter City Association Football Club. We also learn that the club had been using a dressing room at the Red Lion during the season. We're still four years away from the club's lease agreement with the Clifford Trustees, which resulted in the radical changes at St James' Park.

Fortunately, we have a personal account of what the Park was like in the years leading up to 1908. Phil Barnes, who went under the cognomen of 'Rover', was the chief association-football correspondent of the *Football Express*, an Exeter Saturday paper. It was launched in September 1906.

Looking back in January 1914, he remembers when the pitch was known as 'Pig's Park', a 'switch-back' type i.e. when it wasn't being used for football, it reverted to a field grazed by pigs. Barnes recalls visiting St James' Park on a Saturday afternoon, pre-season, in 1906:

> It was my first visit to the ground, and I had been told Soccer was making headway in Exeter, and was bound to go ahead. A thin driving rain fell all the afternoon, and not more than fifty people watched this game. Two scratch teams were pitted against one another, and goals were plentiful, the majority being scored by the then young amateur attached to the Dawlish Club, Len Turner [later killed in the First World War]. If I recollect rightly, too, the City's present Secretary [Sid Thomas] was out in his war paint, together with such old hands as Teddy Morgan, S. Andrews, J. Sellick, G. Campbell, Dick Fenwick, H. Eveleigh, and W. and E. Wells.

On the day City played FA Cup holders Aston Villa in the second round in 1914 (see Chapter 14), Phil Barnes chose to highlight, as his column was headed, the 'Contrast with Old Times, When St. James's Was a Mud Patch':

> On the whole, however, it was scrappy football, and the crudeness of much of it, the sparseness of the crowd, its lack of enthusiasm, and the oddities of the pitch – this the principal Soccer pitch in the City – made me wonder whether the statements about Soccer making headway at the Devon Capital were not all foolishly exaggerated. I had been used to the big crowds of first-class football, and all its fascinating environment, and Exeter's fare came, no doubt, as a very cold douche. What writing I did that day was done in an old sentry-box sort of arrangement, which used to serve as pay station, and rigged up near where are now the huge swing doors in St. James's-road.

This was just before City embarked on their second season in the Plymouth & District League. In the club's first season as Exeter City, 1904–05, they'd been East Devon Senior League champions. The step-up to the Plymouth League was largely down to the vision of Club Secretary Sid Thomas. He was also the one who introduced Christmas Day football to Exeter in 1905, despite heavy opposition. These games, which were played at the County Ground, lasted for several years; City also used the ground, occasionally, for other friendlies. This way of showcasing the code was more than justified by the large crowds that turned up.

In Barnes' first season covering the club, 1906–07, City used more first-team players than they've ever done; a total of 42. There were two reasons why. The 'City Club', as we've seen, had always relied on officers and men from the old

Exeter City XI for the 1904–05 season after the name change from St Sidwell's United. Of the players, Thomas is standing second from left; Eveleigh is holding the ball; Russell is seated on the ground (on left)
Source: © ECFC, from the Grecian Archive

and new Batteries at Topsham Barracks, but the removal of the old Battery had left the club's pool of players depleted. Second, young players had been showing 'much aloofness' towards the senior club. A solution to the first problem was for the club to rely on a 'purely civilian side'; as for the attitude of the city's young players, the club would need to work on making the reserve XI a success.

So, the club had a home venue, but if ambitions were to be realised, the rudimentary state of facilities at the Park would have to be dealt with. Soon after 'Rover' arrived, in the late summer of 1906, there was talk of a grandstand being put up. However, the scheme was deemed to be impracticable. Six months later, in April 1907, rumours began to circulate about plans for a new ground in the heart of the city. 'Rover' explained why the 'City Club' should consider moving:

> St. James' is not a model ground, and never will be without the entailment of a big expenditure. If, then, a new ground, more central in regard to site, and with more natural advantages, is available, the City have every reason to seek pastures new.

By September, it was announced that City would be moving to the Barnfield for the 1908–09 season.

East Devon FA Senior League winners' medal, 1905 – front and back
Source: Grecian Archive. Medal belongs to John Tolliday, grandson of George Russell, who appeared for Exeter City in the 1904–05 season

The 'very ambitious' project included the setting up of an Athletic Branch at the ground, which would be equipped for general sports use in the city. The club had the option of a 7-, 14- or 21-year lease, and legal agreements were being arranged. The site was described as follows:

> The enclosure will be adjacent to Denmark-road, Archibald-road, and the Exeter Bowling Club's Green, and a grand stand, it is planned, is to be erected on the Archibald-road side. Natural banks will permit of the building of terraces, and the ground, when finished, will hold 5,000 spectators. The playing area will be 57 by 110 or thereabouts.

The scheme appeared to be at an advanced stage, but unfortunately for the club and its followers there was a hitch in the project. Apparently, it was objections to the enclosure being turned into an athletic and football ground that, in the end, prevailed.

It was not until early 1908 that the Barnfield ground scheme was abandoned. Before that, City had shown their intentions to go down the professional route. 'Rover', in his front-page *Football Express* column of 14 December 1907, one week after the news broke, was particularly enthusiastic:

> At last! The engagement of the professional [Jack] Banks by the Exeter City Club will mark the beginning of a new era for the code in Exeter. It means more than the signing on of one paid coach and player: it means the adoption of the principle of professionalism, and from this unpretentious beginning I look with confidence to a forward march of big developments in the near future. Our Rugby friends, I know, smile at such confident anticipations, but I give them full credit for remembering an old maxim which relates to the slight advantages resting with the 'last laugh'.

Athelstan Road – part of the site of the proposed Barnfield ground in the late 1900s
Source: © Aidan Hamilton, 2018

Jack Banks had played for Oldbury Town, West Bromwich Albion, Manchester United, Plymouth Argyle and Leyton. His best spell was with his home town club West Brom for whom he played in a Cup Final. He was being engaged as a trainer and player. As 'Rover' observed, Banks was 'always popular with his colleagues, and that is a great point to the advantage of a man whose primary duties will be those of a coach'.

For those City supporters who were against the decision to go professional, 'Rover' had a message:

> If such is the fact, I will give these querulous objectors credit for ignorance of what present-day Soccer really means. When they know more of the question, their prejudice will soon fade and vanish, and of this much I am confident: the City Committee will never regret this step they have taken. We shall see what the Code can do in Exeter, now that it has its first real chance.

The remark showed 'Rover' was doing more than endorse the club's position on the issue. He was actively campaigning on the club's behalf. At the end of the report of the club's last AGM, 'Rover' was given a vote of thanks 'for assistance rendered the Club' during the previous season. And in those articles penned by Sid Thomas in the late 1930s, the support of Barnes, aka 'Rover', is acknowledged.

Now to Banks' debut for Exeter City. It was certainly novel. He must have wondered what he'd let himself in for. It was a Plymouth & District League game against Millbrook Rangers. The weather was 'wretched', and the St James' Park pitch 'terribly sloppy and heavy'. City centre-half Bastin arrived late. Early on, Banks was a 'prominent figure directing City's tactics', and then 'the first real shot came from the boot of the pro. Trapping a pass from Sillick, he put in a lunging shot that went at great speed a yard wide.' It was goalless at half-time. Fifteen minutes after the break the visitors went ahead, and five minutes later the match came to farcical end:

"Jack" Banks,

The old West Bromwich Albion, Leyton, and Plymouth Argyle half-back, and first professional engaged by Exeter City. When with West Bromwich, Banks appeared in an English Cup Final. Photo by J. Cann.

> One ball had been burst before the match, and now a second met with a similar fate. The ground officials, however, were utterly unprepared for such a contingency, and no third ball was forthcoming. Players and spectators waited with impatience while officials ran off to headquarters [i.e. The Red Lion], and five, seven, and nine minutes passed, and there was still no ball.
>
> The Rangers' players, elated over their goal lead, began to question the referee as to how long a wait would be made. [Referee] Sergt.-Major Adams waited till the ten minutes had expired, and then, evidently considering this 'a reasonable time,' whistled no side. The Rangers' players immediately left the field, and the spectators, disgusted with the turn of affairs, trooped out of the ground, a new ball having arrived at headquarters meanwhile.

Despite the unexpected ending, Banks had done enough to satisfy his backers, 'proving a fine general – just the man, in fact, that the City wanted'. Now that the era of professional football at St James' Park had begun, consolidation was needed.

9

In the very heart of the city

NOW that the principle of professionalism had been embraced by the club and confirmed with the signing of Jack Banks, the situation regarding St James' Park became all the more pressing. When it was clear that the Barnfield scheme had been abandoned, 'Rover', in a *Football Express* column on 22 February 1908, expressed regret and outlined why a solution to the problem needed to be found before Sid Thomas and co. engaged more professionals:

> They will never get much bigger gates than they get now under prevailing conditions at St. James's Park. The enclosure has one big recommendation, namely, it is central, but beyond this everything is against it. The entrance and pay-box arrangements are against it, and the surface of the enclosure is still more against it. The expenditure of £100 would convert it into a good pitch so far as the playing area is concerned, but in this regard the management has to consider whether the accommodation around the ropes could be rendered such as would recoup the expenditure, and be adequate if events in the near future gave a big fillip to the Club. Suppose, for instance, the City, two seasons hence, have a first-class side in some new Western Sub-Division of a National League, would St. James's Park be big enough to meet requirements? The answer to these questions, I am afraid, is in the negative. Where, then, can the City go? The management are awaiting some reasonable suggestions on that point.

As ever, 'Rover' had his finger on the pulse. You sense at times that he could be ghosting a column for City Secretary Sid Thomas. The club's ambitions are plain to see, and the situation with the ground was indeed a major stumbling block.

Several days after the above comments were published, a historic meeting took place in Queen Street at the home of Norman Kendall; he was the one who'd been behind the formation of the Exeter Schools' League in the late 1890s. Among those present were the City chairman and secretary, and the chairman of the Exeter Junior League. With changes soon to be made to the League structure in England, there was agreement that now was the time to make an application to join one of the two divisions of the Southern League. The best way to go about this, it seemed, was for City to become a limited liability company. The example of Salisbury City of Southern League Division Two proved that it could be done on the smallest of budgets.

The following week, on Wednesday 4 March, another 'private meeting' was held at Kendall's home. It was clear that Division One of the Southern League was the target, with letters of encouragement from two member clubs, Plymouth Argyle and Southampton, being read out. It was decided to organise special canvassing for shares; even without a formal canvass, £250 had been pledged already. There was now only one difficulty to be settled: 'the securing of a suitable ground'.

At this point, Norman Kendall, having observed the growth of the game in Southampton in the 1880s and early 1890s, decided to make use of old contacts. He chose to attend the Southampton–Everton Cup tie on Saturday 7 March. While there, to add to the support of Southampton officials, he obtained promises of support from leading FA Council members and Southern League representatives. On the subject of the ground, Southampton Secretary E. Arnfield, while acknowledging that St James' Park could be adapted, thought that the County

Ground should be considered first, 'because it is ready, and because of the sentiment surrounding it'. It was, after all, the city's leading sporting venue, but if City were to take it, one of the country's traditional rugby clubs would be left without a home.

Within a week, the matter of the ground had been resolved. On Friday 13 March, it was reported that St James' Park had been selected. At a meeting of the Trustees of the Lady Anne Clifford Charity, in Bedford Circus, a lengthy lease of the Park was discussed with officials of the East Devon FA and the 'City Club'. 'Rover' was also there. Sid Thomas was informed by letter that the Trustees were prepared to lease the ground for 21 years, subject, of course, to financial guarantees. The rent would need to be negotiated.

On Saturday 14 March, 'Rover' gave his readers a sneak preview as to what the architect, Frederick Commin, had initially come up with. He also alluded to the future possibility of increasing the size of the Park:

> According to the rough plans already drafted for the laying out of this ground, it will hold 15,000. That, in my opinion, may be put down as the minimum if the banking is judiciously carried out. The grand stands and dressing rooms would be on the side nearest the railway, and, altogether, there would be four entrances. The L. and S.W. Railway Company, I believe, would be willing to lease a small slip of ground on that side at present laid down as allotments, while there is also the possibility of taking in, at some future date, part of the field at the back, and, therefore, extending the accommodation almost ad lib.

Leasing the slip of railway land and extending the ground at the back would both be problematic. On the question of why the County Ground secretary had stuck with the Rugby Club without considering the Associationists' offer, 'Rover' was tight-lipped. There's no doubt that a move to St Thomas would have saved the 'City Club' huge sums, but there were other advantages to weigh up.

Compared to the County Ground, 'Rover' offered three reasons why St James' Park was the preferable site after all – reasons repeated to this day. To begin with, it was the spiritual home of soccer in Exeter:

> It has always been the centre of Association, and such a sentimental point must be borne fully in mind.
>
> Again, the ground there will influence a very considerable amount of money investments, while, lastly, St. James's is certainly more centrally situated than the County Ground. It is, in fact, in the very heart of the city, close to the tram-lines, and right overlooking a Railway Halt, and in such respects can boast material conveniences that scarcely any other ground of a Southern League Club can boast.

'Rover' was getting ahead of himself. There was still a Southern League vote to be won. That week, Norman Kendall and Sid Thomas had travelled to London for a meeting at Southern League headquarters.

A Phil Barnes cartoon featuring Evelyn Lintott, of St Luke's and England, promoting the scheme for a professional soccer team in Exeter

Source: © *Football Express*, 14 March 1908

The club had formed a Special Committee to deal with the professional scheme. The lobbying continued, and there was a visit from Millwall Chairman J.B. Skeggs, an influential figure at Southern League HQ. In advising the City management, Skeggs expressed his satisfaction with the proposed ground, its central position and the thickly populated area in which it was situated. By the end of March, it appeared there would be at least one vacancy in Southern League Division One for the following season.

With regard to the 21-year lease of St James' Park, the Special Committee had sealed the deal without delay; the Clifford Trustees had had an offer from the Exeter Education Committee for leasing the land as a playing field for school children. It was better, then, for now, for the club to accept an inflated price for the lease, and avoid negotiations, rather than risk losing the site. 'Rover' explained what the implications were:

Next year the Park will be rented on the old terms, but after that the new lease opens, and the first twelve months' payment under that new agreement will be £100. That is a huge jump up from what has been paid in the past, but … it is a far, far, cheaper rental than the great majority of Southern League Clubs pay. Many of them have grounds for which they have to furnish a yearly rental of anything from £300 to £500. I know, in fact, of only one Club that is better placed than Exeter is in this particular matter, and that is Watford, who pay but £80 a year as their share of rental for the fine enclosure off Cassio-road. That, however, is quite an exceptional case.

One final hurdle was overcome. That was to persuade the St James' Parish Cricket Club, who were sub-letting the ground during the summer months, to let the football club use the land. With St James' Park secured, and the process for turning the club into a company started, it was imperative that the necessary capital was raised. With this objective in mind, bolstering at the same time the club's Southern League application, a public meeting was held.

On Tuesday 7 April, a gathering of supporters of professional football in Exeter was 'largely attended'. As people arrived at the Royal Public Rooms, the City Band added to the upbeat atmosphere. Despite some enforced absences, which included the Mayor of Exeter, and several leading FA officials, there was no stopping the tide of optimism. The East Devon FA's Frederick Harvey – now Captain Harvey – chaired and gave an address. The 'vast improvement' in the City XI since Banks' signing was proof that the 'tuition of a popular old professional' was beneficial. But it wasn't only the 'City Club' that would benefit from professional football. According to Harvey:

The Bone of Contention.
Will Exeter Walk Off With It?

Phil Barnes' take on the Southern League vote
Source: © *Football Express*, 28 March 1908

A professional club in Exeter would prove a great incentive to the amateurs in the district, and experiences in centres like Plymouth proved that where a first-class organisation was established the amateur clubs went up by leaps and bounds.

He went on to emphasise that Exeter would be able to satisfy the requirements of the Southern League management: 'good ground, a team of class players, and sound financial support'. After naming those Southern League representatives who had made long journeys to be present, such as Skeggs (Millwall), Arnfield (Southampton) and League Secretary Whittaker, Captain Harvey then appealed to as many as possible present to take 'small financial interests' in the new limited liability company, as opposed to a few individuals taking 'big interests'.

Arnfield made the point that local tradespeople, as they'd done in Southampton, should give the company a hand, for they were the ones who'd benefit most from huge attendances. For Skeggs, if facts and figures of the 'City Club' were compared to, say, Swindon, then 'Exeter could easily make a Southern League Club pay'. Moreover, with the Sports Traffic Manager of the Great Western Railway in attendance, Skeggs and Whittaker said how important it was for Exeter to have this company on board.

By the end of the meeting, those present must have felt that Exeter's future Southern League status was all but assured. Norman Kendall proposed '[t]hat this representative meeting of the

A St. James's Park Memory

How many present-day followers of Exeter City can remember St. James's Park as it was thirty years ago? Cattle and sheep used to graze on the field, and there were no stands or terracing to interfere with the rural appearance of the place.

Here is a reproduction of a picture taken in the spring of 1905, when an army of workmen were engaged to design and lay out the football pitch at St. James's. The present generation can now appreciate the transformation that was wrought.

These labourers, members of the local firm of Messrs. Westcott, Austin and White, cheerfully undertook the work of preparing the trenches. Their subsequent experience of trenches ended on a sad note. To a man, almost, they responded to their country's call during the Great War . . . and hardly one of them returned.

St James' Park being made ready for the 1908–09 season. The date in the caption is incorrect
Source: © *Football Express*, 1 September 1934

(Right) Arthur Chadwick, wearing one of his England caps. He was Exeter City's first manager in the professional era
Source: © *Football Express*, 10 October 1908

Bob Watson – City's first captain in the professional era
Source: © *Football Express*, 29 August 1908

citizens of Exeter pledges its support to the Exeter City Athletic and Football Club Company, Ltd., in its endeavour to enter the Southern League'. As the motion was carried, there was 'enthusiastic cheering'. 'Up City!' was the *Western Times* headline the following day.

The club could not have done more to prepare their case for Southern League membership. Sure enough, at the League's AGM in London on 29 May, when the result of the poll was announced, Exeter had come top. With six clubs applying for five vacancies, City secured a record number of votes. The other clubs elected were Leyton, New Brompton, Southend and Coventry. Croydon Common missed out.

One month later, work began on preparing St James' Park for the forthcoming season. First measuring and surveying, and then the spade work. The laying-out of the pitch and the banking would take five weeks to complete. The indenture document of 26 August 1908 between the Clifford Trustees and the club gave a retrospective timescale:

> That the Tenants shall and will within three calendar months from the date of this Lease at their own expense in all respects level the land and premises here demised and embank certain portions thereof and erect and complete Stands and other erections thereon and other accommodation for Spectators so as to fit the same for a Football and Athletic Ground in accordance with Plans submitted by the Tenants to the Lessors.

Advertising outside the ground was forbidden:

> That the tenants shall not nor will erect any advertisement hoarding in or facing Saint James Road nor exhibit any advertisements or placards on the boundary wall of the demised premises facing Saint James Road or on any part thereof.

With a new season in sight, recruitment of players was well underway. Adverts appeared in the Manchester-based *Athletic News* for experienced pros who were told to apply to the secretary, St James' Park, Exeter. Overseeing the process was ex-England international Arthur Chadwick, whose signature alone was a coup for the club; Bob Watson was made club captain. The countdown to the first ball to be kicked at the new-look St James' Park had begun.

10

'Up Grecians!'

RIGHT up until the end of August 1908, finishing touches were being put to St James' Park. While the builders were completing their work, Arthur Chadwick took his players to St Thomas for practice matches at the County Ground. These Probables v Possibles games were a chance to test the professional attack on one side against the professional defence on the other. It was a chance too, since Banks' arrival, for the club's amateurs to have a first taste of playing with a group of professionals. Chadwick's official title was 'coach and adviser to the directors', and he also played centre-half.

On Saturday 29 August, a pros versus amateurs game was scheduled at the Park. It was down to be played in private, due to uncertainty about whether spectating areas would be ready. Then, on the Saturday morning, a decision was taken to allow the public in. Most of the banking had been finished. In the *Football Express*, this is how 'Rover' described the scene:

> In spite of the lateness of the announcement, there was a crowd of 2,000 present when the time for the kick-off arrived, namely four o'clock. The public were allowed only on the Schools' side of the enclosure, and from the grand stand opposite an excellent idea was obtainable of what the ground will look like when (as the Directors hope) it is crowded for next Saturday's first Southern League encounter.
>
> The recent rains had done a splendid service to the turf, which appeared in grand condition, considering the very short time it has been down.

City's first League fixture was away to Millwall (2-2) on Wednesday 2 September. The party left Exeter on the same day at 10.15 a.m. and had lunch on the train. In the starting XI, every single player was making his City debut.

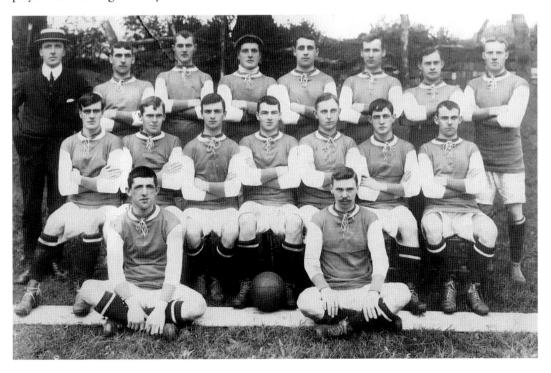

The 1908–09 Exeter City squad. Standing: Chadwick (manager), Amber, Bulcock, Fletcher, Crelley, Banks, Copestake, Wake. Middle row: Drain, Craig, Johnson, Watson (capt.), McGuigan, Bell, White. Front row: Tierney, Parnell

Source: © ECFC, from the Grecian Archive

A Phil Barnes
cartoon of the first-
ever professional
game at St James'
Park: City 3, Bristol
Rovers 3

Source: © *Football Express*, 12
September 1908

BRISTOL ROVER: What a sauce the kid's got; and I thought I had it well in hand, too !

On the following Saturday, 5 September, St James' Park hosted its first Southern League game. Bristol Rovers were the visitors. Special trains ran from Bristol and Plymouth and intermediate stations. The earlier 3.15 p.m. kick off was, although inconvenient, agreed to by City in order to allow spectators to get to the County Ground after the game for the finals of the Cycling Club sports. At such an early stage in the club's life as a professional organisation, it was good PR. Not only that, but cycling, as we've seen, had a history at the Park.

The gate for the Rovers game was almost 8,000. The banking alongside the school building was packed from end to end, and, opposite, the grandstand was 'well-filled'. With City trailing 1-3 at the interval, the home support feared the worst. But they went home happy: 'excitement became intense, and the game progressed to the accompaniment of an almost continuous roar of cheering'. At 3-2 there were shouts of 'Make it a draw, Exeter.' When, finally, the equaliser went in, 'what a scene followed. The enthusiasm of the crowd knew no bounds.'

Just how far the association game in Exeter had come had been emphasised by 'Linesman' in his *Devon & Exeter Gazette* column during pre-season. Suddenly, rugby had a serious rival:

Time was – and that but a few years since – when 'Soccer' was looked down upon in Exeter with something akin to contempt. Less than ten years ago the old Exeter United Club used to entertain 'crowds' which might have been numbered on the fingers of one's hands, and followers of the handling code were wont to sneeringly remark that Association could not possibly 'take on' in the city. The experience of the past few years, however, has divulged a very different state of affairs, for Exeter City have, by dint of hard work and good play, gradually, but surely, obtained hold on the sporting public. And this is not all, for, whereas in the old days there were a dozen junior Rugby organisations to one sailing under Association colours in the city, at the present time the latter outnumber those of the sister code by nearly ten to one.

More than anything, it was the work behind the scenes by administrators such as Frederick Harvey, Norman Kendall and Sid Thomas that had created the conditions for the game to flourish.

After the first-ever professional game at the Park, one month later there was another first. On 3 October, English (FA) Cup football arrived in Exeter with Weymouth as City's opponents. It was the cue for nostalgia on the part of one of the city's association old stagers. Reg Davey, chair of the East Devon FA Council, had played for Exeter AFC in 1893–94. In a game at Weymouth, they'd been beaten 10-0. On the eve of the Cup tie, 'Rover' referred to a letter he'd received from Davey, a postal worker at Brixham:

THE "COOP."

EXETER CITY, to Weymouth: Now then, stop that blubbering. I'm not going to kill you. Besides, many youngsters your size would like to take a hiding at the same price.

[In the English Cup-tie at St. James' next Saturday, Weymouth, a small Western League Club, will be entitled to the usual share of the gate.]

The 'Coop'. A Phil Barnes cartoon

Source: © *Football Express*, 26 September 1908

> True, it is many years ago, but Mr. Davey tells me he took part in that game, and probably the dimensions of the score impressed it upon his mind. At any rate, he concluded his letter by remarking 'Those ten goals MUST be wiped out.' He was not bold enough to add 'on Saturday next,' but I suppose no one will have more welcomed a win of the City this afternoon (if they have won, for these notes were penned at a late hour last evening) than the East Devon Chairman. I suppose, too, he would regard such a happening as avenging the humiliation his side met with at Weymouth fifteen years ago.

Imagine Davey's delight when the result reached him. City's 14-0 triumph is to this day the club's record scoreline. Remarkably, in the next preliminary round, there were double figures again as Longfleet were defeated 10-1 in a replay at St James' Park.

Of course, against Western League Division Two opponents Weymouth, City were expected to win. The 'Club Management' fielded their strongest XI, which included Chadwick in midfield;

Supporters at Exeter City's first-ever Cup tie, against Weymouth, 3 October 1908. The wooden structures to the side of the grandstand were for the press

Source: Dave Fisher collection, Westcountry Studies Library, Devon Heritage Centre

in these early days of professionalism, the directors were involved in picking the team. 'Rover' began his match report by noting the conditions and commenting on the gate:

> The turf was in a splendid condition, though somewhat on the hard side, perhaps, while the weather was bright and summer-like – too hot altogether for the usual robustness of Cup-tie football. An excursion to London to-day, and the Territorial Field Day, undoubtedly affected the gate, and a large crowd was not in consequence expected, for in addition to the counter attractions, supporters of the City were inclined to take Weymouth with little seriousness. At three o'clock there were barely 2,000 present, but subsequently the Flower Pot stand filled up very rapidly, and at the time of the kick-off [3.30] the gate numbered 6,000.

The reception for the City players, we're told, was 'magnificent', with a special cheer for Chadwick who came out last. Even before a ball was kicked, the visitors were at a disadvantage: after winning the toss, City skipper Bob Watson 'set Weymouth to play with the sun in their eyes'.

As soon as City had opened the scoring, 'it was simply a question of target practice for the Green and Whites [City's previous colours]'. Then, three goals were scored in quick succession: 'Weymouth were absolutely helpless against the cleverness, the inter-passing, and the deft side-stepping of the Exeter attack.' The goals kept coming and at 8-0 there were still 15 minutes to go before the interval. At one point, the crowd was amused by Chadwick's back pass to City keeper Fletcher, 'just to keep himself warm'. It was 10-0 at half-time.

When Weymouth came out for the second half, there was an encouraging cheer, 'and most of the side laughed back in good-humoured fashion'. Soon, it was 11-0, and then 'Exeter gave Weymouth much more latitude, and quite an agreeable change came over the game, as their forwards rushed the ball to the vicinity of goal'. There were two more City goals, including a sixth for Bell, before Copestake rounded off the scoring with one of the best goals of the game: 'he received wide out, and taking the defence, who expected him to centre, completely by surprise, put in a brilliant shot which A.R.A. Bell jumped at, but could not stop'.

Hard on the heels of the Weymouth game, 'Rover' proposed holding an informal ballot among supporters to decide on a nickname for the club: 'What of a name for Exeter City?' After St Sidwell's United changed its name to Exeter City in 1904, use of the name 'the Grecians' appears to have faded. So, with City's change of status, now was the time to either choose a new name or resuscitate the old one.

A fortnight later, 'Rover' announced the result of the poll. It was down to suitability, rather than quantity of votes. So, he and his colleagues chose the most suitable name in keeping with the club's origins:

> 'The Grecians' it must be. Of all the 200 or more suggestions sent in for nick-names for Exeter City I think that has most to recommend it. It has been suggested by two or three correspondents, and I know that it is one of the most favoured sobriquets by some of the Club's management, who have taken an interest in this search for a nick-name. There is no reason to refer to the fact that the old St. Sidwell's United, the first Club to take Soccer seriously in hand in the City, were known as 'The Grecians,' and that for some reason or other (is it not connected to Sidwella?) Exonians living in St. Sidwell's have always been called 'Grecians.' The name has even been adopted as a trade sign in that neighbourhood. 'The Grecians,' therefore, would have its appropriateness in more senses than one, and 'The Grecians' it shall be.

So, what of the other suggestions? Some names had an Exeter theme, others paid homage to personalities at the club:

> The players wore their new Club badges for the first time on Wednesday, and it came as no surprise to find several correspondents suggesting 'The Castles,' 'Castlemen,' or 'Castle-ites,' while others went all for 'Rougemonts.' Good these are, but not so suitable as the one chosen. If the selections had gone by a majority 'The Normans' would have been an easy first. A large number of correspondents

suggested this out of compliment to the Father of the Club, Mr. Norman Kendall, but I feel sure he will agree with what I pointed out last week, namely, that clubs have never adopted a sobriquet culled from a player's or founder's name, and that the precedent is, all things considered, a good one. For this reason 'The Chads,' 'The Chaddies,' 'The Daisies,' and 'The Watties' were ruled out. One of the correspondents suggesting 'The Normans,' by the way, wrote from Birmingham, being an official of the Birmingham Post Office Rugby Club.

Apart from the reference to Chadwick, two other players were nominated, James 'Daisy' Bell and Bob Watson. City Director Norman Kendall's popularity is noteworthy: one day there would be a Norman Kendall Gate at St James' Park.

The nickname was a popular choice, and the London press were soon using it. Several weeks later, 'Rover' heard a group of youths in Queen Street celebrating a win at Brighton (2-1) with shouts of 'Up Grecians!' 'When youngsters pick up a football war-cry,' he wrote, 'it dies hard.'

As we approach the end of 1908, there were the first Devon derbies. First, there was a City success (2-1) in the Southern League before 8,000 at St James' Park on 11 November, and then on Boxing Day City won a friendly 1-0 at Home Park. The highlight of the season, however, was the Second Round English Cup tie at Home Park on Saturday 6 February 1909.

'Rover' called it 'the greatest Soccer event ever known in Devon … the Devon Derby of Derbies'. He described the scenes shortly before kick off when the crowd had 'swollen to close on 20,000'. Exonians raced to get to the ground, 'with long waving rosettes, and a hurly-burly of "Up Grecians!"'. Inside there was pandemonium:

'Up the Grecians!' A Phil Barnes cartoon featuring former England internationals Arthur Chadwick and Jack Robinson

Source: © *Football Express*, 21 November 1908

> So great was the crush that at the west end, just before the far goal posts, the railings gave way before the swaying crowd, but the police, rushing to the spot, held the crowd back in very creditable fashion. No fewer than sixty police were on the ground, including the Chief Constable of Devonport, and emergency barriers were soon fixed against the broken fence.

For 'Rover', it was a 'fine open game'. The Exeter forwards, he felt, 'kept the ball too close at times. They would have done better to have imitated the Pilgrims' forward game, and swung the ball about more.' Argyle made the most of 'snap efforts' to win 2-0.

In a fourth 1908–09 meeting between the clubs, the return League game at Home Park on 10 March, the Dandies, as Plymouth were also known, won 4-0. Finally, in what was looked on as the decider for the rubber, 10,000 saw City go down 0-1 in a friendly at St James' Park on 12 April. Still, given the 'comparatively unlooked-for' first two results, 'Exeter City,' wrote 'Rover', 'had worked up the County rivalry to such fever pitch that any meeting between the two teams was looked forward to as a Devon Derby.'

Despite the interest generated by the Argyle games, it's worth noting that City's biggest home gate of the 1908–09 season was on Christmas Day. A *Western Times* report described the ground at the Southern League match against Millwall, won by City 2-1: 'Pretty much every part of the enclosure was packed, and there were at least 11,000 present. Probably the number was much nearer 12,000.' In the pre-First World War period, few other games at St James' Park attracted a larger attendance.

Uncle Tom Cobley

WHAT SAUCE!
SMALL BOY to player leaving Exeter City ground
last Saturday: I say, guv'nor, is it right there is some
good fishing in St. James's Park?

I N the haste to make St James' Park ready for the 1908–09 season, one aspect of the work was given less attention than was needed: the pitch. So, when there were continuous rains in December 1908, problems with the drainage were exposed. The part of the ground to be affected most was the lower end, in front of where the Big Bank is today. 'Rover' commented that, along with the defect in the drainage, 'the fact that the soil is very clayey, has resulted in the water settling on the surface in large patches'. The Southern League game against New Brompton on 19 December survived, but only just.

Of particular concern for the City management was the fact that the state of the pitch – 'sodden, heavy, and hacked about' – nullified any advantage of playing at home. It could lead to the players' form being affected, as it did in the 1-3 loss to New Brompton. Another worry was the effect of a bad pitch on a busy Christmas period, when there was extra money to be made. For 'Rover', 'good layers of sand' would be the best remedy: 'sand would be trodden in instead of churned up on the surface and would subsequently serve to soak up the rain'.

& MAY'S
VESTAS

Thankfully, two narrow home victories addressed the club's concerns: the 2-1 defeat of Millwall on Christmas Day with a bumper crowd, and then of Watford 1-0 on 9 January. We're told after the Watford game that 'the turf showed much improvement, the main drains having been got to work this week. The ground, in fact, although sticky, was better than it has been for weeks.' Later in the season, Arthur Chadwick commented to 'Rover' that his team might have been pushing for Southern League honours if they'd only had a decent surface to play on.

During the club's first Southern League season, the St James' Park pitch was used too by the reserves playing in the Plymouth & District League, and local schools played there. There was also a charity match in March 1909, which recalled the ground's former use as a circus venue. Celebrated comedian Fred Karno, stage name of Exeter-born Frederick John Wescott, had brought his company to town. They were performing 'The Football Match' at the New Hippodrome, a 'Cup struggle' between the 'Midnight Wanderers' and the 'Middleton Pie-cans'. It was the show that gave Charlie Chaplin his big break in 1908.

So, a match was arranged between the City reserves and a Karno XI, drawn from the cast, which included former professional footballers; Chaplin may well have been with the company at that time, but he's not in the line-up. It was played at a wet St James' Park on Wednesday 31 March. One verdict? 'If it had not provided tip-top football, the game had been a source of no little merriment, and, in this respect, anticipations were realised.' But with the bad weather a deterrent, just a few hundred spectators were there; for the record, City won 5-2.

Fred Karno's XI
Source: © *Devon & Exeter Gazette*, 31 March 1909

In June 1909, work began on improving the drainage at St James' Park. Repairs to the drains six months earlier had been but a temporary remedy. Director Tom Oliver, licensee of the Red Lion Inn, got together a group of helpers, made up of his regulars most probably, and on the eve of a new season 'Rover' reported that there was a 'vast improvement' to the playing surface. 'No one suggests that it is yet perfect,' he wrote, 'but much good work has been done, and the City's ground is now well up to the standard of Southern enclosures.'

Now that the club had the ground to itself, use was found for it in the close season, filling the vacuum left by the St James' Cricket Club, whose last summer at the ground was in 1907. On 12 July, Exeter City applied for a music and dance licence, two weeks after a temporary one had been granted. The application at the Exeter Police Court was made by City director and local barrister Michael McGahey on behalf of club Secretary Sid Thomas; he was up against a Mr Tarbet representing owners of property in St James Road. McGahey, later to become City chairman, laid out the case for the licence. He referred to recent entertainment at St James' Park:

> I defy any witness to point out anything objectionable in this performance. On the first night a resident, named Miss Stone, complained of lads climbing on to the railings in front of her house, but the Company engaged a policeman to be on duty outside every night, and the children were then under control. A policeman was also on duty inside the grounds. Residents in Well-street sat at their top windows and watched the performances, which they evidently enjoyed, and they had signed a petition in favour of the license. Indeed, there were residents in St James'-road who had signed the petition.

McGahey was backed by comments from a police constable, City Director Fred Parkhouse and a Mr Dempsey whose company had been providing the entertainment.

Opposing the application, Tarbet outlined why the evening performances were 'a great nuisance'. It was the St James residents' battle against the travelling shows all over again:

> It took place between 8 and 10 p.m., when most of the residents liked to spend a quiet time in their homes. The entertainments were attended by from 150 to 200 people, who frequently joined

in the 'catchy' songs which were being rendered on the platform. Children assembled outside the grounds in such large numbers that one policeman could not control them. He asked the Bench to read the police reports. Eighteen months ago, when an attempt was made to have entertainments in the Barnfield – a less populous district – the residents very properly objected, and the Justices declined to grant the license.

After deliberation, a majority of the Justices decided that the license should not be granted 'under any circumstances'. It was the rowdiness outside the ground that was the deciding factor, not so much what went on inside it. It seemed harsh, as all that was needed was an increased police presence.

The first annual meeting of Exeter City Athletic and Football Company took place at the Red Lion Hotel on Wednesday 22 September 1909. The balance sheet showed a profit of £165, or 28 per cent, on the subscribed capital. Concerning St James' Park, McGahey, in the chair for the absent Captain Harvey, pointed out that when the club had managed to pay off the whole of the cost of the ground, the shareholders would be owners of a valuable property. For the coming season, despite the fact that the rent would be going up from £40 to £100, an increase in advertisements 'would go a long way towards meeting this'. It had been a 'most successful' year, business-wise as well as sporting-wise.

There was also an assessment of the benefits of the club becoming a professional organisation:

'Final Harmony'. Phil Barnes' take on the end of City's first season as a professional organisation
Source: © *Football Express*, 1 May 1909

The advent of the Club had given many in the city the advantage of seeing Association football as it should be played, while it also increased trade, consequent upon the visitors brought into the city. He was pleased to say junior Clubs were increasing, and the directors hoped that the time was not far distant when they would be able to include in their team amateurs who would prove as good footballers as some of the professionals.

FINAL HARMONY.

It was important to give encouragement to local amateur players, especially given the fact that the team that finished sixth in the club's first Southern League season was made up entirely of pros from the north of England. Two years later, Arthur Chadwick would discover Dick Pym playing for St Margaret's in Topsham. And in the 1920s, local schoolboy Cliff Bastin began his path to fame (more on Bastin in Chapter 19).

When a new season arrived, Rover's first home match report made reference to two established features of matchdays at the Park: the programme and the brass band under a Mr George Newman. For the game against Bristol Rovers on 11 September 1909, we're told the band were 'in the full glory of a uniform'. When Bob Watson led his men out, they struck up the now-familiar 'Uncle Tom Cobley'. Newman's band was still operating after the First World War, but sadly without one of its members. Drummer W.R. Wilkey of Summerland Street was killed in action at Wulverghem, Belgium on Christmas Eve 1914. He was with the 1st Battalion Devonshire Regiment.

Since the start of the club's second season as a professional organisation, it was regularly getting gates of over 5,000. And that was the case for the friendly against Bristol City on Wednesday 3 November. It was the first time the 1909 Cup finalists had been to Exeter, and a 'strong side' included the internationals Wedlock and Cottle. In a game won by City 4-1, for the *Western Times* reporter, 'exchanges were of an excellent sporting character, and, for a friendly, keen and fast'.

For atmosphere at the Park that season, nothing could beat the Devon derby on Monday 27 December. In the *Western Times* report, there's particular reference to both ends of the ground, including a problem containing the crowd:

The ground presented a very animated scene before the start, and for the first time, a large number crowded on to the banking behind the lower goal. Long before the start, every corner was crowded, and streams of would-be spectators were still crowding in. Exeter were first out in all white, and Argyle, in green and black, met with quite as uproarious a reception. Palpably the Dandies had a very large following. Bells and hooters kept up an uproarious din, and coloured umbrellas were everywhere. Both goalkeepers before the start were presented by enthusiastic supporters with their Club colours. There was an ominous breaking over the fencing at the St James's end just before the start, and Directors hastened over and stopped an ugly rush. Police, too, had to be requisitioned. At this time people had clambered on to the top of the advertisement hoarding overlooking the railway, and the crowd must have numbered from 12,000 to 14,000.

It was reported that many spectators had been turned away. As for the result, City lost 2-4. It was the first home loss of the season and followed a 0-1 defeat at Home Park on Christmas Day. The fact that the club had recently been knocked out of the English Cup prompted an alarmed 'Linesman' of the *Devon & Exeter Gazette* to remark that this latest loss to Argyle 'brings the City management face to face with a serious situation'. It wasn't their only worry.

In 1910, St James' Park was inspected by a Southern League official. Millwall's visit to the Park on 29 January allowed their chairman, Mr Skeggs, one of City's backers in their 1908 election campaign, to make 'a thorough inspection of the enclosure'. The fact was that Portsmouth had reported the ground to the Southern League. Writing in the club's defence, 'Rover' was his usual partisan self:

"HALF TIME!"

THE GRECIAN (whose in and out form has been much criticised of late): Here, half-time! some of you chaps.

'Half Time'. A Phil Barnes cartoon showing the Grecian under fire after a poor run of results. Note the reference to NK: musician Norman Kendall

Source: © *Football Express*, 20 November 1909

Admittedly, the touch-line on the left-hand side is somewhat close to the grand stand railings, but in how many grounds, where Clubs have been particularly fortunate in regard to acreage, do we see any space to spare? Numerous enclosures could be mentioned quite as confined as that at St James's, and when it is remembered, on the other hand, that the City's dressing and bath room accommodation is the equal of any in the League and vastly superior to the greater number, the Council would surely hesitate before they singled it out for condemnation. Pompey are the only visiting Club from whom a word of complaint has been heard, and while admittedly their men have experienced the only two accidents of anything like a serious nature which have happened there, one of these accidents occurred in the middle of the pitch, and by no stretch of imagination could be attributed to the state of the ground, while Buick's mishap was the result of an unusually (for him) reckless charge – or an attempt at charging.

For 'Rover', there was nothing wrong with the state of the pitch: 'so well has the drainage been improved that at the finish of the game against Millwall it was in as good a condition as last year it would have been after, say, a couple of heavy showers'. This was the ground about which a complaint had been made to the Southern League management.

A few weeks later, 'Rover' followed this up by rubbishing a rumour that the City management still had their eye on the County Ground. A remedy could be found to the one difficulty at St James' Park – the under-length playing area for English Cup matches – and the capacity of the ground could also be increased. In short, too much had been invested in the venue:

Sporting memories: recalling warning notices at St James' Park following a League game against Crystal Palace (3-4) on 14 September 1910

Source: © *Football Express*, 17 September 1938

To hear some people talk it might be imagined that scarcely any money had been put into St James's Park, instead of which a big sum was expended there, and some of the ground's equipments, in consequence, are as good as anything of their kind in the Southern League. After this expenditure, is it likely that in five minutes fresh pastures are going to be sought? There are a hundred and one reasons, in fact, why a change should not be made.

But until a way could be found to purchase the adjoining property at the lower end of the ground, there'd always be speculation about a possible move to another site.

Sporting Memories

No 4 : Warning Notices at Park !

READING an old "Football Express" file for the year 1910, I came across a report which referred to the posting of warning notices at St. James' Park. This instruction followed on an incident after the City v. Crystal Palace match, and the City directors were asked by the Management Committee of the Southern League to post notices warning followers of the club against disorder on the ground.

*　　*　　*

THE incident in question did not occur inside the ground, but outside, mud being thrown at the Palace officials and players while on their way to the station by a group of rowdy youths. The League Management Committee accepted the City directors' explanation of the affair.

*　　*　　*

Tailpiece. . . In the self same season Exeter City and Crystal Palace agreed to pool their gates.

12

Strangely different

IN little over two years, from the summer of 1908 to November 1910, the basic ingredients that make up what the 'City Club' is today were established. Once the professional route had been taken and a place in the Southern League assured, first, the ground at St James' was laid out with banking and a grandstand. Second, there was confirmation that Exeter would be known as 'Grecians'. Third, starting in 1909, close-season activities took place at the Park. Finally, to top it off, new club colours were chosen.

In 1910, close-season entertainment at the Park was varied. On Friday 1 July, there were two performances by the band of HM Irish Guards – under the auspices of the football club. While in August, having recently added 'Athletic' to its name, Exeter City ran a sports day. Events included various flat races, a one-mile open cycle handicap and a local footballers' relay race; the two handicaps for professional footballers 'excited the keenest interest'. At the end, there was a full practice match involving City pros, 'Greens' v 'Whites'.

Around the beginning of the 1910–11 season a number of Southern League clubs – including Coventry, Norwich and Portsmouth – changed their colours. So, it was as part of this superstitious trend that the City players approached the directors to request replacing the old St Sidwell's United green and white. The choice of red and white vertical stripes was unanimous. 'Rover', as ever, had his ear to the ground:

> I was aware that the players had got tired of the green and white, and that several of them, including the old hands, had got it into their heads that luck would never change while green was a predominate part of the Club's colours. I am giving away no secret, now, when I mention, also, that the wives of the married members of the City's team were even more insistent upon the matter than the players themselves.

These women had probably had enough of dealing with downcast husbands, struggling to find a reason for inconsistent results. Once it was taken, the decision to change colours was kept under wraps. The new jerseys were due to be collected at Paddington Station to coincide with the team arriving for a game against Queen's Park Rangers (QPR) at Park Royal. Had the jerseys been there, they'd have been worn the same day, and City's travelling support would have been left scratching their heads. In fact, they were worn for the first time a week later, on Saturday 12 November at St James' Park.

For the Southern League game against West Ham – Grecians v Hammers, the report by 'Rover' was headed – new colours weren't the only change on show. Bandmaster Newman's musicians, 'in a brand-new rig-out', had a new

THE SUPERSTITIOUS GRECIAN.

" There I go again! I no sooner change my colours than I walk slap-bang under a ladder. I wonder if I ought to go back and have another change ? "

Exeter City have changed their colours, the players, in a superstitious mood characteristic of footballers, having concluded that their recent bad luck was due to the old Green and White jerseys.

A Phil Barnes cartoon: 'The Superstitious Grecian'

Source: © *Football Express*, 12 November 1910

name: The Exeter City Professional Band. As for their repertoire, there was a promise – superstition again – that there'd be no more renditions of 'Uncle Tom Cobley'; in its place was a favourite march of the Devonshire Regiment, 'We've lived and loved together'. The band warmed up by playing on their way to the Park. 'Rover' gives us a flavour of the scene before kick-off:

> The ground appeared in fair trim, but each goal area had a liberal sprinkling of sand …
>
> In strict accordance with the Management's usual luck, the rain, which had held off all the morning, started in a drizzling shower at 2.30, or half an hour before the start, when the crowd had just begun to assemble in force.
>
> Prior to the start, Bob Watson received a telegram from White, captain of the Reserve team, which was at St. Austell, wishing the Firsts good luck.
>
> West Ham were out five minutes before the start, and were quickly followed by Bob Watson at the head of Exeter City. No sooner had the teams taken the field, than the little daughter of Trainer Jack Banks was led on the ground and presented the home skipper with a horse shoe, decorated with the Club's new colours, the mascot being deposited at the back of the net.

Here's an early equivalent of the present-day ritual of tying a scarf to the back of the goal net. It also provides a context for a photograph that was discovered during the dismantling of the Old Grandstand in 2017: a horse shoe being presented to City officials, possibly during the 1930–31 Cup run. More about horse shoes and mascots later. What of City's first game in new colours? 6,000 saw it end 0-0.

Later that month, with the prospect of a home FA Cup tie on the horizon, once again the under-length pitch was discussed. In December 1909, City had been forced to play their Cup replay against Stoke at the County Ground, due to St James' Park being under the FA's minimum length of 110 yards. In November 1910, having drawn away at Reading in the fourth qualifying round, it was 1-1 in the replay at the County Ground when fog forced an early finish. City won the rearranged tie 1-0. It turned out to be the last time the club used the rugby ground for a home game; no other ground has been used for home games since.

Cup games should have been a financial asset. Instead, on top of paying expenses to the visiting side, City had to pay for use of the County Ground. And what if a tie clashed with an Exeter

The popular bank crowd with St James' church in the background, exact date unknown

Source: Dave Fisher collection, Westcountry Studies Library, Devon Heritage Centre

CITY V ARGYLE Nº 1.

Rugby Club fixture? The cricket ground at Gras Lawn was a possibility, but the club would have made a loss if they'd played there. After the 1910–11 Cup run had ended with City losing what should have been a home tie at Burnley (0-2) – 'the FA refused to comply with the City's request to recognise the County Ground' – 'Rover' estimated that in the region of £2,000 had already been lost by not having the use of St James' Park for Cup ties.

The County Ground before the land was developed for housing. Exeter City played Cup ties here in 1909 and 1910 as the pitch at St James' Park was under length

Source: Photograph © Martin Weiler, 2006

At the club's AGM in January 1911, there was a résumé of the ground difficulty and a hint that perhaps a solution had been found:

> The Chairman [Michael McGahey] said the directors deplored the fact that the ground at St. James's Park was not of regulation size for Cup-tie matches. Two years ago, they tried every possible device to see if, by any manner of means, it could be done, but the best architectural schemes proved of no avail. However, there was a likelihood of other negotiations taking place, and he trusted that those negotiations would be successful.

The owner of the land at the lower end had previously stated that either all or no part would be sold. Another possible solution was a ground share with Exeter Rugby Club. This was one of the topics for discussion at a public meeting on Monday 1 May at the Queen's Hall. The other issue was summer wages. It had got out that some on the board were considering not re-engaging players and saving summer wages until August; 'Rover' described the proposals as 'cheeseparing' and, as a result, an aggrieved Arthur Chadwick delayed re-signing.

EXETER CITY FOOTBALL CLUB.

St. James's Park.

SATURDAY NEXT,
AT 2.30.

GRAND SIX-A-SIDE

FOOTBALL TOURNAMENT.

Sixteen entries, including all the leading Amateur sides of the district.
Admission: Reserved prices.
S. H. THOMAS, Secretary.

Advert for a six-a-side tournament at St James' Park

Source: © *Devon & Exeter Daily Gazette*, 20 April 1911

The summer wages situation was eased with contributions from supporters. At the public meeting, just over £100 was guaranteed; and as for the ground, those present 'affirmed the desirability of remaining at St. James's Park, and requested the Directors to acquire sufficient of the adjoining land to enlarge the pitch'. What finally brought an end to the ground question was the intervention of local MP Mr H.E. Duke. Having had a letter of support read out at the 1 May meeting, he purchased the whole property at the lower end of the ground for a price in excess of £3,000. This timely action, wrote 'Rover', 'immensely improved the outlook of the Club, and relieved the Directorate of an anxiety which had long, like a cloud, overhung them'. The club stood 'at the threshold of what should prove a new era in its affairs'.

By the start of the 1911–12 season, work on the pitch extension had begun. For the visit of New Brompton (8-1) on 9 September, we're told 'huge alterations' had already been made at the lower end: 'the trees have gone, and excavations have been carried out half-way across'. When Luton visited a week later, further changes were noted:

> The 'Football Express' score board had been transferred to its new position at the back of the flower pot stand, the excavations for the extension of the playing pitch having now been practically carried right across the breadth of the ground at the back of the far goal, and the terracing already extended on the cheap side.

In late September, with QPR the visitors, the flower-pot side had extended 'twenty yards or so', and there was new fencing behind the goal at the St James Road end.

During the excavations, the discovery of a horse shoe led to more talk of superstition. 'Rover' explained what he'd heard:

According to rumour … this shoe has been preserved not in the usual way by tacking it on to a door for all and sundry to see. Oh, no! It was buried (I wasn't at the ceremony, so I can't vouch for the truth of it) as near the spot as could be picked out from where Bob Watson scored the first goal of the season. If that is so, then there is either something radically wrong with this particular horse shoe, or else the talk about horse shoes bringing luck is a miserable fraud, for it was near that very same spot last Saturday that Bob Watson had the hard luck in the first five minutes to just fail by inches to get at a fast pass when a touch would have meant a certain goal.

But the horse shoe symbol *was* common; a miniature one in red and white had been sent to Arthur Chadwick by a former Southampton teammate, Clawley, before the trip to Burnley the previous season. Meanwhile, the club had a new mascot: a sheep dog called 'Laddie' owned by City goalkeeper Walt Whittaker. Later, there'd be a kennel put up under the *Football Express* telephone box.

The Grecian to his new mascot, Walt Whittaker's sheep-dog : My only fear is, "Laddie," that what with all this talk about you, and the enlarged ground, and the bigger grand stand, people will be expecting miracles from me this season.

This Phil Barnes cartoon features City's sheep-dog mascot 'Laddie'

Source: © *Football Express*, 2 September 1911

The first game on the new pitch was on Saturday 14 October. Just as it was for the new colours a year earlier, West Ham were the Southern League opponents. For the opening of the extended pitch, a new feature of the ground was in place, a flagpole on which the Grecians' and their opponents' colours were displayed. It was Norman Kendall's idea. Mr Duke was unable to be present due to ill health, so his daughter performed the opening ceremony. This is how 'Rover' described it:

Across the lower part of the ground exactly where formerly stood the goal posts had been strung red and white ribbons. The new fencing behind was in its permanent position, with cinder banking behind … and the whole ground looked strangely different to last season. Archdeacon Sanders was an early arrival, and was shortly followed by several members of the City Council and well-known citizens and their wives, the party who accompanied Miss Duke to the tape drawn across the enclosure numbering about fifty. The breaking of the cord was followed by cheering, and the playing by the band, under Mr. Geo. Newman, of the National Anthem.

Afterwards Mr. Archibald Lucas, as architect, presented Miss Duke with a solid silver inkstand as a memento of the occasion, while Mr. J.H. Stile, the contractor, presented Miss Duke with an inscribed silver penholder. The inscription on the inkstand ran: 'Presented to Miss Duke, October 14th 1911, by the Architect, Mr. J. Archibald Lucas.' A handsome bouquet of red geraniums and white carnations was presented to Miss Duke by little Miss Norman Kendall, daughter of Mr. Norman Kendall, and subsequently the Club's flag was unfurled amid cheering.

The game that followed was watched by an estimated 7,000. Three times City were behind, before eventually drawing 3-3. City keeper Walt Whittaker played the whole of the second half with a broken middle finger, and two of his teammates played on after picking up injuries. 'With their three crocks they were hopelessly handicapped,' wrote 'Rover'.

In the official programme for this game, there was mention of the new holding capacity of St James' Park. The extending of the terracing behind the goal, it was said, increased the total capacity by another 7,000 or 8,000 spectators. Perhaps this was the architect's estimate based on what the old ground proportionately held, but for 'Rover' the figure was too high. Since professional football started at St James' Park, estimates of attendances had 'varied to a strange degree'. Agreement between newspaper reports was rare. Given the correct holding, no one calculating a crowd of up to 6,000 should be a thousand out, but that was often the case at the Park.

The reason, explained 'Rover', was that in 1908 the given holding capacity was far too high. From 18,000, it dropped to 15,000. This figure stood until the Argyle game on 27 December 1909. Capacity, as we saw in Chapter 11, was reached on that day and the gates were closed:

On that occasion, in the pressure of a congested crowd, 300 or 400 passed in without payment, or, in other words, the gates were rushed to that extent. Anyone who was present doesn't need to be told that the ground was absolutely filled, and that it would have been impossible with safety to have packed any more in. Now, allowing for the gates being rushed, the takings on that occasion showed the crowd to have been 12,000, and this figure, therefore, may be accepted as the holding capacity of the old ground. Probably not more than 5,000, or, at the most, 6,000 could be got into the extended portion while the steps on the flower pot side remain as wide apart as they are now, and, therefore, we get the present holding capacity of St. James' Park as 18,000.

In the past, without a reliable guide to go on, it wasn't the fault of 'Rover' and his colleagues that inflated figures had been given. At least now the public would have a more realistic idea as to the club's takings.

13

Unparalleled happenings

GIVEN the numbers attending games at St James' Park, it was only a matter of time before a Supporters' Club was formed. At the start of City's fourth season as a professional club, 1911–12, the idea was suggested by 'Rover'. He'd managed to get his hands on a rules card of the Watford Supporters' Club, along with a badge worn by members. He outlined how subscriptions were used, and what the rates were. Anyone interested in starting a similar club in Exeter – an 'enterprising supporter of the Grecians' – would at least have something to go on.

Two months later, a Grecian Supporters' Club was proposed. A former director of QPR, Mr H.A. Devenish of 'Mont-le-Grand', Thornton Hill, Pennsylvania, Exeter, asked those wanting to join to contact him. 'Rover' again alluded to Watford, pointing out that its Supporters' Club often funded away travel for members. And addressing those who intended answering Devenish's call, he referred to the difficulties City were currently experiencing: 'there is never a time when one can show real loyalty to a club and a genuine desire to see it prosper like that when things are "rocky"', a situation encountered by City fans many times down the years.

A NASTY BLOW FOR THE SAINT.

After the problem over summer wages and the way it was dealt with, the City board continued to be divided over how the club's finances should be managed. Certain directors were 'pulling one way', while a minority were 'pulling the other'. Worse, details of the split were being discussed outside of the board room; the players themselves knew what was going on. The paying public, insisted 'Rover', 'have a right to demand that this meaningless bickering should end. The shareholders have a better right still.' His column on 9 December was headed 'Recent Troubles of Exeter's Management.'

One week later, City Secretary Sid Thomas had a letter published in the *Football Express*. In an attempt at transparency, speaking on behalf of the directors, he explained to supporters why it was necessary to increase gate receipts for two games on public holidays, with funds for the ground being one reason:

> The Directors of the Exeter City Football Club have decided to raise prices for our home Southern League match with Plymouth Argyle on Boxing Day, and also the match with Reading on Easter Monday next, and they think it only fair both to themselves and the public that an explanation be given as to the reasons which have prompted their action. During the next few months heavy calls will be made upon the Club in connection with the ground, and the early exit from the English Cup Competition has rendered it essential that the extra charges be made for the objects named. My Directors feel sure that having had the reasons explained to the supporters there is no one but will agree with the course taken. The matter has had the most careful consideration of the Directors, and they think that the local public will show their sporting loyalty and interest in the Club and do all they can to make its future safe; and, for the small matter of an extra sixpence to

For 'Rover', City's 2-2 draw against Southampton in December 1911 was one of their best performances ever. Earlier in the year, City had beaten Saints 3-1 away

Source: © *Football Express*, 11 February 1911

themselves, be the means of very considerably aiding the Company in fulfilling its many obligations. Our supporters may rest assured that were it not for absolute necessity, no such extra call would be made upon them.

It is thought right to mention that the alteration to our ground has increased the accommodation by four or five thousand, and there will be no recurrence of the disappointment experienced by the many hundreds of visitors on the occasion of Argyle's visit on Boxing-day two years ago.

This was different to previous interaction with supporters on the cost of tickets. In January 1911, there'd been a meeting between City officials and supporters to discuss ticketing at the forthcoming Argyle game. The suggestion to double prices was put to a vote. The crowd of two thousand or so, who'd just watched a reserves' game, elected to keep usual prices if bought in advance, otherwise it would be double prices on the day. The formation of a Supporters' Club would formalise links between management and fans, and it would soon become clear that the club's survival depended on fund-raising efforts.

These may have been difficult times for City *off* the playing field, but *on* it, two days before Christmas 1911, there was a reminder of why the game has such appeal. Southampton were the visitors to St James' Park. With four players out injured, Chadwick picked a former St Luke's College amateur, T.R. Kent, who happened to be in Exeter for the festive period, to play inside-forward. Another surprise were the colours worn. With Southampton – the senior side – playing in red and white, the Grecians came out wearing green and white. As usual, the band was in tune to the occasion: 'Auld Lang Syne' was played in recognition of Chadwick's and Kendall's links to the Saints.

The story of the match turned on events half an hour after the start. First, City's keeper, Chapman, was carried off injured. Shortly afterwards, Saints were given a penalty for hands. City skipper Bob Watson, who'd taken over in goal, saved the first effort and the ball was cleared. Here's how 'Rover' described what happened next:

The referee [Mr C.J. Ross from Aldershot], though, ordered the shot to be taken again for a technical infringement, amid great booing. Bob saved Eastham's second shot, but the Saints' skipper followed up and scored. The booing now came from all parts of the crowd. Still more exciting scenes were to follow. Fort fouled a forward near the penalty area and following the free kick Brown scored [2-1 to Southampton]. Feeling had naturally crept into the play now, and in midfield Cornan was deliberately kicked by Brown. The referee at once ordered the latter off, and would listen to no protests. In the excitement which followed even a spectator jumped on to the enclosure from the popular stand and entered into the counselling of the referee. He was pushed away by the Southampton players, but Brown had to go. He went off as Cornan was being helped to the dressing room by Chadwick.

These, of course, were unparalleled happenings for Exeter's ground, and one team now had nine players including a cripple, while the other had but ten. Was ever luck like Exeter's? With three forwards they struggled on, but it was a hopeless fight.

To add to Chapman and Cornan leaving the field, Coates also picked up an injury. Cornan did come out after the interval, but in his 'Notes', 'Rover' commented:

There was, of course, ill-feeling among the players following the injuries to Coates and Chapman, but, thank goodness, the crowd's better judgment prevailed, and what looked like developing into a very ugly scene when the penalty was ordered to be retaken, was happily averted.

Since professional football began to be played at St James' Park, it was the first time a player had been ordered off. 'The 5,000 spectators,' 'Rover' summarised, 'will never see a more remarkable game, and they will certainly never again see a team handicapped as Exeter were.' Given City's heroic second-half display, which included an equaliser to make it 2-2, 'Rover', who'd been watching City since 1906, was convinced this was 'among the very best performances ever credited to Exeter'.

What of the state of the pitch? At the start of the Exeter–Southampton game there were 'ugly patches' within the penalty areas and sawdust had been spread on the goal lines. One month later, before the visit of Brentford, we're told the pitch 'was in a shocking state, and the mud near the penalty line at the lower goal was ankle deep'. To counter this, 'the goal posts were brought in, making the length of the pitch only two yards longer than it used to be before the extension'. In February 1912, when Millwall visited, the pitch was 'still "pudding-like" in places, and likely to cut up badly, especially in midfield'. The lower end goal posts remained in the 'short distance' position.

As regards the atmosphere at St James' Park, there was much in common with today. Match officials, as we saw in the Exeter–Southampton game, would come in for barracking. Players, too, might be singled out, even by their own supporters. But in early 1910, it was felt that some of the barracking at the Park had overstepped the mark. A friendly bit of banter was one thing; what was objected to was, as 'Rover' put it, 'the levelling at one or two or three different players a running fire of the most caustic criticism, calculated to put the best good-tempered players off their game'. So, there was debate even back then as to what constituted fair criticism.

On another occasion, in November 1911, 'Rover' was asked by the City management to remind one or two 'ebullient spirits' in the flower-pot stand to moderate their choice of language. He appealed to this handful of supporters

> to remember when they are giving voice to very emphatic opinions about men and play that sometimes ladies are near at hand, and that there are quite a number of ways in which one can express one's feelings about an indifferent game. Try a new way.

At St James' Park, women were by no means peripheral. In March 1912, 'Rover' referred to the club's loyal 'lady supporters', and to the fact that 'they have always been to the fore, too, when a little extra assistance has been required'. Once again, the spirit of the reminder about bad language echoes in modern-day campaigns such as the EFL's Enjoy the Match launched in April 2017. At the Park, there are also matchday PA announcements voiced by young fans to encourage supporters to see 'football as a family sport', to 'respect one another, the players and the match officials' and to not use 'abusive language or aggressive behaviour'.

Now that the Supporters' Club was up and running, bucket collections were a feature of matchdays, just as they are still a feature today. One of the most significant ones was in aid of the 'Titanic Fund'. Several days after the disaster, City had a home League game against Crystal Palace on Saturday 20 April. 'Rover' describes how the Park had special reason to commemorate and to support the fund:

> Harry [Henry] Dyer, whose tragic death, in the 'Titanic' disaster, all Exeter athletes and football followers deeply grieve, was in his time one of the stalwarts of the old City Amateur Club, and a back of more than average skill … It was not unfitting, surely, that the hymn which is to become a classic now and which was played by the 'Titanic's' band as the great ship went down, should have been rendered last Saturday on the ground where one of the leviathan's victims, then in the prime of his youth, often held the breach. His fine young form was in the memory of many of his old friends as the music, touched to a note of tragic sadness, was begun under the baton of Mr. Geo. Newman.

Over £10 was raised, with the band foregoing their usual collection. And in keeping with all football grounds, the flag at the Park was flown at half-mast.

During the 1912 close season, the results of an FA inquiry into Exeter City's finances were made public: for not keeping its books in order,

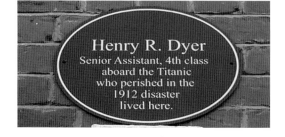

The Titanic
Engineers' Memorial
in Southampton.
Henry Dyer, former
City player, lost his
life in the disaster

Source: © Aidan Hamilton,
2018

the club was fined £20, several directors were censured, and one was suspended. Meanwhile, further improvements were made to St James' Park. New terracing had been put up on the 'reserved sides' (possibly a reference to either side of and in front of the grandstand) and as a result there was an increase in the holding capacity of about 1,500. When Watford visited on 7 September, the ground was looking 'smarter than it has ever appeared'. It was announced, also, that the board room had been 'rather lavishly furnished', one of the directors having paid for the work.

The Watford game, City's first at home in the 1912–13 season, provided a first for St James' Park in terms of the official attendance figure. One of the City director's, Mr J.I. Pengelly, had criticised the local press for the way gates were estimated. When 'Rover' made the point that the club had never provided any information on one single gate, it wasn't long before he was supplied with a figure. The crowd at the Watford match numbered 4,879. All ticket holders were included, the only ones not counted being 'the Directors themselves and the players and visiting officials, who did not pass the turnstiles'. It was proof that estimates of previous crowds had indeed been over the mark. When City had been struggling, some crowds had in fact been fewer than 3,500.

For 'Rover', it was calculation of the numbers on the flower-pot side that had led to mistakes in the overall attendance. He explained what the problem was:

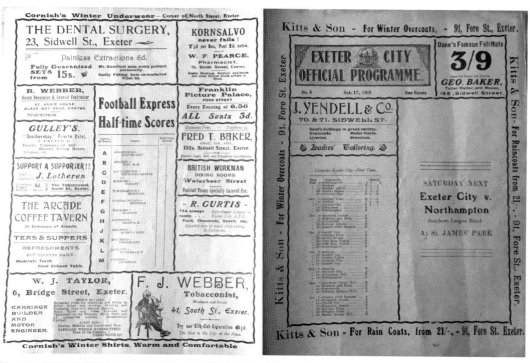

It has often appeared full when it has been nothing like it, and allowance has not been made for the fact that it was badly designed, in a way, in fact, that renders inevitable a lot of sheer waste of room. The terracing is too wide altogether. For some reason or other it was built with the idea that spectators would stand two, or even three, deep on each terrace, and, of course, they do nothing of the kind. Each terrace – save under exceptional circumstances – has its one row of spectators, and the rest of the accommodation is wasted. A taking up of the whole of that banking and relaying it would increase the holding of the enclosure very considerably.

What the club needed was a big Cup draw at Exeter, one that would fund the improvement to the flower-pot side of the ground. Two seasons later, in January 1914, the plum Cup draw duly arrived.

14

Record day

N O sooner had celebrations died down – following City's magnificent 4-0 win at Fratton Park in the English Cup first round – than there was more excitement. When the draw for the second round was made on Monday 12 January 1914, City were paired with Cup-holders Aston Villa no less; the tie to be played at St James' Park. Delighted at the City's luck, this is how manager Arthur Chadwick assessed their chances:

> I saw Aston Villa play Burnley this season, and on that form we shall beat them. In fact, they'll have to play a lot better than they did that day to put Exeter out of the Cup. Our defence, so far as backs and halves go, is a lot better than theirs. Will it be played at Exeter? So far as I know, certainly. I sincerely hope it will, at any rate.

The last comment reflects doubt as to whether or not the club would receive an offer to move the tie to Villa Park. By the following Saturday, when Crystal Palace visited for a Southern League game, offer or no offer the City directors had decided to keep it at St James' Park. And it was reported that 'banking is now proceeding at the lower goal end, and it is hoped to accommodate at least 5,000 there at a shilling charge'. The price for the flower-pot side, the popular terrace, would be two shillings.

In Doleful Memory
OF POOR OLD
PORTSMOUTH,
Who were defeated at Fratton Park by Exeter City
in the First Round of the English Cup,
ON SATURDAY, JANUARY 10TH, 1914.
4—0.

When the football match was over, / Everywhere was desolation,
And they came to count their cost, / Silenced then was every one,
Then we heard poor POMPEY wailing, / Poor old POMPEY they were beaten,
For the match that they had lost. / By the GRECIANS it was done.
It was a glorious victory, proclaimed the whole way round,
How the GRECIANS beat POMPEY on that famous football ground.

Image from a scrapbook kept by Edgar Uzzell recording Exeter City's 4-0 Cup win away to Portsmouth, 10 January 1914
Source: Uzzell family, from the Grecian Archive

What follows is part of the *Football Express* report that appeared shortly after the Cup tie on Saturday 31 January 1914. Who better than Phil Barnes, alias 'Rover', to describe the biggest day in City's history to date, and what the tie meant to Exeter and beyond?

> ***ENGLISH CUP***
> ***Exeter City and Aston Villa at St. James's***
> ***RECORD CROWD***
> ***Incidents in the Grecians' Great Test***
> ***CITY UNLUCKY LOSERS***
>
> It used to be a common thing for writers in opening a description of any particular English Cup Final at the Crystal Palace to say that all roads led to the slopes of Sydenham. It would certainly be said in a local sense that all Exeter City's roads to-day led to St. James's Park. From noon, when the gates were opened, a stream of spectators, apparently ever increasing in numbers, converged upon Exeter City's ground.
>
> It was a record day for the Club – a record in pretty well every sense of the word. Ever since the last draw was made, and it was known that the Grecians' opponents in the Second Round of the English Cup were to be none other than the holders of the trophy, and probably the most famous of all famous Clubs, namely, Aston Villa, little else had been talked about in the City and for miles around. The Cup fever, as it is called, gripped the Ever Faithful at last, and everywhere the City's

colours have been flown, while scarcely a tradesman's window but had some decoration; quite a number of shops, in fact, devoted one whole window to a Cup-tie display. Not only had Exeter in this manner caught the fever, but it had spread to towns and villages for many miles around, and one could not go to the smallest hamlet but some question would be asked about the City's chances, and more often than not by an individual who from appearances one would have least suspected of taking any interest in it. No football event in Exeter, in fact, has ever aroused over so wide an area the excitement this tie between the City and the Villa had aroused. It is safe to say, too, that Exonians in many of the Colonies were eagerly awaiting the result this afternoon. From as far away as Montreal and Toronto, former citizens have written to this office stating that they and their friends would be desperately anxious to learn the news this evening.

Exeter City, of course, earned the right to oppose Aston Villa to-day by their brilliant victory at Portsmouth in the First Round three weeks ago. It was the finest performance they had ever placed to their credit, and their form that day made one hopeful that they would even hold in check the Villains. So many questions are still being asked about the City's past Cup records, and so many mistakes have been made in the Press on one particular point, namely, as to whether the Grecians had previously got as far as the Second Round, that we make no apology for again printing a full list of the results. These are as follows:

1908–09.

Exeter, 14; Weymouth, 0.
Longfleet St. Mary, 1; Exeter, 1.
Exeter, 10; Longfleet, 1.
Exeter, 4; Whiteheads, 0.
Kingswood, 0; Exeter, 2.
Barnet Alston, 0; Exeter, 3.

COMPETITION PROPER
Wrexham, 1; Exeter, 1.
Exeter, 2; Wrexham, 1.
After extra time.
Plymouth Argyle, 2; Exeter, 0.

1909–10.

Exeter, 7; Nunhead, 1.
Stoke, 0; Exeter, 0.
Exeter, 1; Stoke, 1.
First Cup-tie decided at County Ground.
Stoke, 2; Exeter, 1.
Played at Fulham.

1910–11.

Reading, 1; Exeter, 1.
Exeter, 1; Reading, 1.
Abandoned through fog. Played at County Ground.
Exeter, 1; Reading, 0; at County Ground.
Nelson, 3; Exeter, 4.
Choice of ground forfeited.

COMPETITION PROPER
Burnley, 2; Exeter, 0.
Choice of ground forfeited.

1911–12.

Exeter, 1; Merthyr, 1.
First Cup-tie at St. James's extended pitch.
Merthyr, 0; Exeter, 0.
Merthyr, 2; Exeter, 0.
Played at Bristol.

Exeter City official programme for the League game a fortnight before the Aston Villa Cup tie, 17 January 1914

Source: © ECFC, from the Grecian Archive, Norman Shiel collection

1912–13.
Cardiff, 5; Exeter, 1.

1913–14.
COMPETITION PROPER
Portsmouth, 0; Exeter, 4.

'Rover' goes on to comment on how similar are the records of Exeter City and Aston Villa, albeit in different leagues. He also noted the two teams were evenly matched in terms of weights and heights before bringing readers down to earth with a bump when comparing the footballing pedigree and trophy cabinets of the two clubs.

Cup fever had descended on the city of Exeter. Here 'Rover' describes the arrival of Aston Villa:

The Villa team were welcomed at St. David's at 8.12 last night by about 200 enthusiasts, who cheered them to the echo. Outside the Rougemont Hotel another small crowd waited for them, and one of the players jokingly remarked, as he walked into the Hotel, 'Every promise of a big crowd tomorrow.'

One reserve was brought, this being Whittaker. The party numbered about thirty, and included Messrs. F.W. Rinder (chairman), J.E. Jones (vice-chairman), P.W.M. Bate, Howard Spencer, the old International (Directors), C.S. Johnstone and F.W. Cooper (vice-presidents), and Geo. Ramsey (secretary).

They travelled by the G.W.R route, through Yate, Standish, and Cheltenham, and left home at 3.55. About nine o'clock last night all the players visited the Exeter Hippodrome, and the City team were also there. A packed house applauded the Manager, Mr. Fitchett, himself an old inter-League player, when he came forward and briefly thanked the teams for their attendance.

Street Scenes

All this morning drizzling showers fell, but nothing could damp local enthusiasm. At an early hour, wearers of the claret and blue were to be seen parading the city streets, and these had evidently left nothing to the chance of a late excursion arrival, preferring, instead, to pay the extra fare of the ordinary trains. The City colours were flying everywhere, and two ebullient spirits spent the whole morning riding on the top of a tram-car waving a red and white umbrella. The mascot goat, which had been bought for presentation to Skipper Rigby by City taxi-drivers, was marched through the main streets about eleven o'clock, decked in the Grecians' favours. What is its fate, now?

The Villa players walked from the Rougemont Hotel to the ground early this morning and spent some time on the pitch, subsequently going back to their headquarters for a light lunch, served at 11.45. About that time, the cinema operators began their work in the City's streets, and, despite the miserable weather conditions, it was early apparent that this was to be, as prophesised, a day of days in the annals of Exeter sport.

The Crowd on the Ground

As early as 11.15 small batches began to gather outside the ground, and as soon as the doors were opened at noon there was the first rush. From that time a continual stream made their way to St. James's, and every tram-car from 12.30 onward carried its full freight of enthusiasts. At 1.30 there were already 8,000 on the ground. The new bank was filling, and all parts of the enclosure were speedily being occupied. Ticket holders were also early arrivals, fearing, no doubt, a closing of the gates.

As time went on, it seemed that the arrangements made by the local management were excellent. The barriers and division bars were answering their purposes admirably, and the Villa 'checkers' were all agreeably surprised.

A few youngsters climbed on to the top of the 'Football Express' score board, but were promptly ordered down in case of accidents. Red and white umbrellas were being waved from the shilling bank, and intermittently the City's 'war songs' rang out. It was a lively, good-humoured crowd, and inside the Directors' office everything was reported to be running smoothly. The Villa secretary, Mr. Ramsey, was outside the big Well-street swing doors, and his Directors were early on the scene, among them the old international Howard Spencer, looking as fit as ever.

The first fight took place on the shilling bank at 1.55. The two combatants had a lively two rounds before the police got to them. The police strength was about fifty, and, in addition, there was a large contingent of St. John Ambulance men, under Supt. Bowden and Head-Sergt. Rivers. Two mounted constables were outside the ground.

At 2 p.m. the crowd was at least 11,000. Photographers and cinema men were on the pitch hard at work, and the band was struggling with its enlivening airs.

The pitch was in a good state considering the rains, and had been well rolled. It was, of course, on the soft side, however, and liable to be cut up quickly.

The Villa players arrived on the ground exactly at two o'clock, being conveyed from their hotel in six of the Exeter Blue Elite Taxis. The City players were already present. Holt had a badly swollen face, and had been in bed with a cold all day yesterday. He was, however, as anxious as anybody for the fray.

Message from 'Father' Skeggs

Shortly after two o'clock a telegram arrived from Mr. Skeggs, of the Southern League Association and Millwall Club, which read:

'Millwall did; so can Millwall's child.'

Mr. Skeggs, of course, regards himself as the father of the Grecians, having played a big part in getting the Club admitted to the Southern League.

A drizzling rain was still falling when 'Artful' Thomas led on to the pitch the City mascot goat, and posed with it for the cinema operator.

There was still room for more at 2.30, and the lower end of the 'Flower Pot' stand was not nearly filled up. The crowd had massed at the higher end. It was probable, in fact, that the prediction about the possible closing of the gates as early as 2 o'clock had kept a good many away. At 2.30, however, the shilling bank was absolutely packed. Several Plymouth Argyle Directors occupied seats in the Stand.

'Artful' Thomas
Source: Exeter Memories

City team group
published on the
day of the Villa Cup
tie. Standing: Lagan,
Fort, Pym, Strettle,
Smith, Chadwick
(manager). Middle
row: Holt, Lovett,
Whittaker, McCann,
Marshall. Front row:
Brooksbank, Rigby
(capt.), Goodwin

Source: © Chandler and Co./
Football Express, 31 January
1914

A couple of enthusiasts took their stand on the roof of one of the villas in St. James'-road.

At 2.45 there was still room and to spare on the ground, and the crowd certainly did not reach expectations.

The Teams

Six minutes before the kick-off the teams filed out on the ground as follows:

EXETER.

Pym;

Fort, Strettle;

Rigby, Lagan, Smith;

Holt, Lovett, Whittaker, McCann, Marshall.

●

Edgley, Bache, Hampton, Stephenson, Wallace;

Leach, Harrop, Barber;

Weston, Lyons;

Hardy.

ASTON VILLA.

Referee: Mr. E.W. Child, London.

Linesmen: Mr. J. Down and Mr. J. Haxell.

In the *Football Express*, there is a detailed match report by 'Rover' – 'The Game' – of Exeter City 1 (McCann), Aston Villa 2 (Hampton 2). After the report, there are the following 'Notes by "Rover"':

It was a case of experience being too much for slog and unbounded enthusiasm.

Yet one is inclined to say that from Exeter's point of view it was a game thrown away.

They had chances enough to have won it, and they failed to round off efforts which were magnificent in their pluck and thrust.

Why, too, was not McCann given that penalty?

St James' Park on the day of the Aston Villa Cup tie
Source: © *Devon & Exeter Gazette*, 2 February 1914

Times out of mention I have implored that he should be reserved for penalty kicks.

I don't blame Fort. I blame the policy of standing aside the one man who in temperament and shooting powers should essentially be the City's penalty taker.

I shall always look back on this game with the keenest disappointment.

A good thrashing would have left no room for cavilling. We could have accepted that and made the best of it.

But here was a case where a game was lost by the narrowest margins when it should have been won. Had that penalty been scored, I thoroughly believe Exeter City would have beaten the Villa, and even had they but drawn I should still have been confident of their surviving in the replay in Birmingham.

Why? do you ask. Simply because after a hesitating start they played the Cup-holders in the best of cup fashion, and for long stages undoubtedly had the best of it.

People thought that the Villa's class was going to make the Grecians look small fry, but nothing of the sort happened.

The City had their full share of a hard, gruelling game, and the Villa players welcomed the final whistle with expressions of relief.

Up to a point the homesters played splendidly, and they have the satisfaction of knowing that though they lost, they gave the Holders a fright, and came near, so very near, to springing a huge surprise on the football world.

The Villa have the opportunism of Hampton to thank for their victory. It was he who pulled them through, and those two goals of his were the sort of efforts which have made him famous.

Apart from his scoring, however, he shone but little, for Lagan had him shadowed, and gave him no rope.

The Villa, on to-day's showing, were not too stiff a proposition for Exeter, and English League's best football was not better than the Southern League's best.

It was just that lack of finish which kept Exeter from beating Hardy on several occasions.

I blame no man for the defeat. Indeed, the team acquitted themselves with great credit, and no doubt they are as disappointed to-night as the most disappointed supporter.

Had they got through to-day we should all have had great hopes of their making history in the competition.

Let none of those who crowed about the Villa and the next-door-to-certainty of their piling up a big score, crow to-night. They have nothing to shout about, and they are lucky not to be trying to explain away a Villa defeat rather than celebrating a Villa victory.

Ah, well, it is over. The Grecians may still hold their heads high. Their day is to come. The last I heard of the goat it was bleating very pitiably somewhere near the stand. Probably the odds are slightly against its having survived till now. Several were after the blood of this unfortunate new mascot.

The gate realised £910 2s 8d. These are the official figures. The number of the crowd had not been exactly ascertained up to 5.30, the whole of the tickets not having been checked. Approximately, however, the figures are given out as 9,600.

Mr. Stuart Palmer, with ticket No. 16, won the City Supporters' Club's goat.

15

A flourishing example

I F the Villa Cup tie was the biggest pre-First World War *sporting* event at St James' Park, the biggest non-matchday equivalent by far was the fete organised by the City Supporters' Club. Since this club's inception in early 1912, fund-raising activities had gone from strength to strength: from whist drives and dances to firework displays, and from concerts to sports days. Local businesses were roped in too. In March 1913, for a week's entertainment programme at the Exeter Hippodrome, the theatre management wrote the Supporters' Club a cheque for 25 per cent of the value of tickets sold; it amounted to £22, over £2,400 in today's money.

The 'Grand Fete' held in July 1913 ran for three days and featured 'any number of side-shows and entertainments'. The idea was based on the Bristol Rovers annual carnival. Before the gates of the Park opened at 3.30 p.m. on Thursday 10 July, the *Western Times* correspondent had a sneak preview of the ground:

> The football pitch, save on its extreme edges, has not been touched, so that the whole of the middle space of the Park will be open to the public.
>
> It is around the back of the goals and touch-line spaces that the entertainments and side-shows have been erected.
>
> Bordering on the St James's-road wall a huge marquee, big enough to accommodate 400 or 500 people, has been put up, and it is here that the concerts by Mr. W.H. James's party and others will be given, while the Jollity Boys' entertainments and the evening boxing contests open to local amateurs, will also take place in this tent.

It will also be the scene of the biggest attraction of the whole fete, namely the Exeter Flitch trials on Saturday afternoon and evening, when the selected claimants for the two flitches [i.e. two sides of bacon] will be tried before judge, jury and counsel in full court paraphernalia, on the lines of the famous Dunmow flitch trials.

Teas and refreshments will be served before the grandstand, and here, too, will perform each afternoon and evening the Band of the 3rd Devon Regiment, under Bandmaster A.W. Lowther.

Advert for the Grand Fete at St James' Park

Source: © *Devon & Exeter Daily Gazette*, 10 July 1913

Side-shows included the greasy-pole competition, bowling for ducks and fowls, and penalty kicking, with City pro Charlie Pratt helping out. Use was even made of the board room where there was palm reading by a well-known local chirognomist. How close, you wonder, did she come to predicting City's future Cup form or fortune?

We're told the various events received 'gratifying patronage' over the three days. The flitch trials were indeed a particular success. Dating to the Middle Ages, this custom of rewarding marital harmony was revived in the nineteenth century, and continues to this day in Great

Dunmow. A *Devon & Exeter Gazette* article entitled 'Football Fete' describes how the trials were run:

> [T]he two flitches, which were to be awarded to two couples whom the Court decided had not quarrelled for a year and a day, were hung at the entrance to the tent. Accommodation was provided on the platform for judge, jury, counsel, and witnesses. The judge, jury, and counsel – one of the latter for the applicants, and one for the flitch – were all well-known personages in Exeter, and the jury was composed of six ladies and a like number of gentlemen.

Festivities ended with 'a confetti fete and dancing', and prizes were presented. When the receipts of the fete were added up, the total was in excess of £200. Allowing for expenditure, this left a balance of £71. At one of the Supporters' Club's weekly meetings at the Park, it was decided to hand over a cheque for £50 to the football club. It is a sobering thought that in little over a year's time the carefree innocence of the Edwardian era would be brought to a sudden halt.

Occasionally, the regular collecting at League games was suspended. As with the contribution to the 'Titanic Fund', a similar one was made following the Senghenydd Colliery disaster on 14 October 1913 in which 439 miners were killed, the result of an explosion and subsequent release of poisonous gas. There was a collection in the ground before the Northampton game on 25 October. On this occasion, those City pros who were not playing, assisting Supporters' Club members, 'went in and out among the people with boxes'. From the crowd of more than 5,000, £17 was collected for the *Devon & Exeter Gazette*'s Relief Fund.

In 1913, there was debate among supporters about the level of their involvement in decision-making at the football club. One suggestion was that 'the moneys of the Supporters' Club be invested in the Exeter City Football Club, so that the supporters might have a voice in the conduct of its affairs', but in a letter to the *Daily Gazette*, someone calling themselves 'Shareholder' 'deeply resented' the idea. In April, it had been rumoured that supporters were unhappy about the figure at which Ben Ives was sold to QPR; not only that but also the Supporters' Club had not been informed before the transfer was made public. 'Rover' took the directors' side on this one:

> There are a good many members of the Supporters' Club who have been responsible for a lot of hard spade work in the Grecians' interests, and have helped the Club to achieve in some degree the best aims of a Supporters' organisation. It would be a pity, therefore, at this stage, if an attempt were made to go beyond the confines of a Supporters' Club legitimate range of activity. The Directors, I have no doubt, would welcome useful criticism, but until one is in possession of all the facts relative to Ives' transfer and the amount paid by the Rangers, to say nothing of the nature of the negotiations which are pending for further transfers, it is impossible to offer such useful criticism. Plain, too, it must be to everyone, from the point of view of good business, that the Directors cannot divulge the negotiations, step by step, which they have entered upon. No Club ever does it; it would be showing one's 'hand' to every other player at the table.

After a 12-month existence, the Supporters' Club, with already a membership of over 700, was making its presence felt, and not just in Devon. In a *Portsmouth Evening News* item on the growth of supporters' clubs, the one in Exeter was cited as a 'flourishing example'.

When City were drawn at home against Villa in the Cup in January 1914, the directors, it seems, were keen for the match to be played in Exeter. Chairman McGahey told one reporter, that 'if £500 were offered, the match would not be taken away from Exeter'. McGahey also added that for supporters to get their wish they must accept an increase in ticket prices. Once the decision was taken to play the tie in Exeter, it was the Supporters' Club who heard it first through director Norman Kendall.

Following the work done to the Park – the banking and stepping at the lower end – in the run-up to the Villa game, the subject of ground development returned in April 1914. Chairman McGahey attended the Supporters' Club meeting and responded to a proposal to cover the popular side of the ground. Despite the improvement in the club's finances – record takings

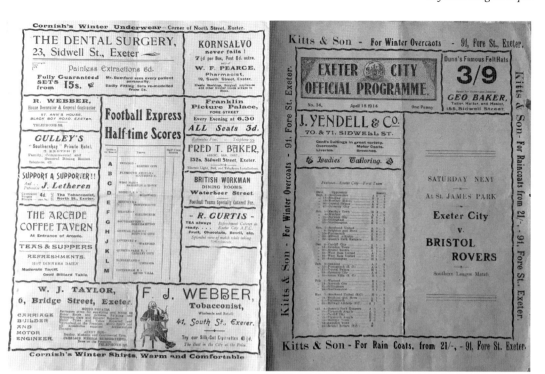

Exeter City official programme for a reserves' game, 18 April 1914

Source: © ECFC, from the Grecian Archive, Norman Shiel collection

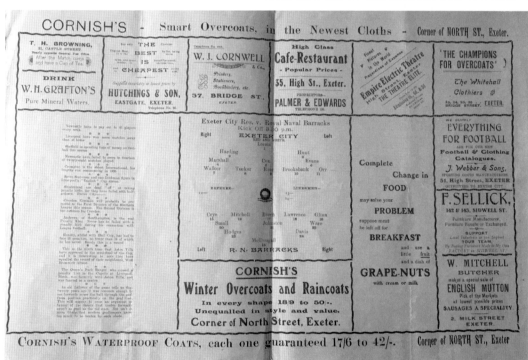

overall for League and reserve-team games, and the performances in the Cup – he felt the idea for the covered stand was 'a little premature':

> The overdraft had been very considerably reduced, and he believed he was accurate in saying that it did not now exceed £600, whereas, previously, there was £600 owing at one bank, and about £900 at another [total debt of around £170,000 in today's prices]. The financial difficulties had been very much relieved, but at the same time they had not been completely overcome. The Club was still in debt, and the Directors, of course, were responsible for such debts. It was also a fact that the Club still owed a couple of transfer fees on two of this season's players, and that, further, they would, this summer, have to pay a lot more in transfer fees than they had ever had to pay before.

The club would need to keep the present team intact, given the upcoming tour to the Argentine. Allowing for new players to be brought in, summer wages would be higher than they'd ever been. Even with the Supporters' Club's offer to contribute £110, McGahey made it clear that the club

City and Argyle drew
0-0 at St James'
Park before a crowd
of 11,000, 13 April
1914
Source: © *Devon & Exeter
Gazette*, 14 April 1914

EXETER CITY v. PLYMOUTH ARGYLE.

was in no position to pay the rest of the bill for a 'covered-in stand' that would cost upwards of £500.

What members of the Supporters' Club wanted was for 'some specific work' to be done, serving as 'a sort of memorial'. Something tangible, such as a covered stand, to represent the significant contribution supporters had made to the survival of the football club – something to benefit supporters. One week later, a meeting of the Supporters' Club decided to allow a further £100 to be handed to the football club for 'management expenses' but it would be the last such payment. In future, Supporters' Club funds, it was agreed, should be devoted towards 'the covering in of the ground'.

Five years would pass before the next discussions between supporters and City directors over the erecting of a new stand on the popular side. One week after Britain entered the Great War on 4 August, it was announced that a sports meeting arranged by the Supporters' Club had been postponed. The same applied to a banquet for the team, recently back from their South American tour. In May, a repeat of the fete had been deemed 'impossible' to arrange; penny tickets were issued instead. When whist drives began again, 25 per cent of the proceeds was given to the Devon Patriotic Fund to support wives and families of those serving in the armed forces and the sick and wounded. Later, donations were made by the Supporters' Club to other war charities.

Meanwhile at the Park, in late August 1914, attention turned albeit tentatively towards the next Southern League season. Two practice matches – stripes v colours – raised money for the Prince of Wales' National Relief Fund. However, it wasn't long before there were calls for professional football to stop. In the press, the *Devon & Exeter Gazette*, for example, began a campaign against Exeter City. This is an extract from an article entitled 'To the Colours! Not to football':

We do not, for a moment, question the deep-seated patriotism of those responsible for the conduct of the affairs of the Exeter City Club. We know – and it is well that the general public should appreciate this fact – that their action has been dictated by the Football Association. What we do say, however, is that the majority of Britishers would sooner resign office than actively participate in furthering the game at this critical moment. They may say – and with a certain amount of justice – that if a team fails to fulfil its engagements it will lose its place in this or that particular League.

Can the future of any Football Club be referred to in the same breath as that of the nation? Will a victory at St. James's Park do anything to minimise the sorrow, and, perhaps, hardship of the dependants and relatives of those killed or maimed by German bullets? By all means let men keep fit, but let it be through the medium of training of use to their country, and not simply to amuse those who would cheer the scoring of a goal within the hearing of the widow who may, perhaps, at that very moment have had placed in her hand a telegram announcing that he whom she loved dearest in all the world has sacrificed his life for his country's honour.

Flyer for a practice match at St James' Park, August 1913

Source: © ECFC, from the Grecian Archive, Norman Shiel collection

It was emotive stuff. The decision by the FA to continue League football was described as 'a disgrace to the country which gave us birth'. So, on the eve of the club's first competitive fixture – a home League game against West Ham on Saturday 5 September 1914 – Club Secretary Sid Thomas, responding to the critics, laid out the position of his directors in a letter to the press. The FA, after consulting the War Office, had decided 'that it is not in the national interest that football should cease'. Exeter City, with reluctance, had no alternative but to carry on 'at great financial loss owing to decreased gates':

The Exeter Club, whatever may be its own wishes, is only one of many under the control of the Football Association, and is bound by its rules to act on the decision of the Association in conjunction with the Leagues. As indicative of the position of the local Club, I may mention that, instead of over £200 being received in season tickets, we have not yet taken £20.

Despite the financial difficulties, the club would do all it could to support the war effort. We learn that portions of the gates from the practice matches had raised over £43 for local charities and the Relief Fund, and that such donations would continue throughout the season. St James' Park was already being used by the local military authorities, with troops being drilled there on a daily basis, but how far would this go to appeasing the anti-football brigade?

16

A deserted scene

IN Sid Thomas' letter to the *Daily Gazette*, published on Friday 4 September 1914, there was mention of forthcoming matchdays at the Park. Southern League games would be an opportunity for recruitment, with advertisements and a recruiting sergeant on hand. There'd also be a public meeting after each 'large match', encouraging young men present to enlist; presumably this was a reference to all Southern League fixtures. The reserves would also use the ground during the 1914–15 season.

On Monday 7 September, far from commenting on how City got on against West Ham, the *Devon & Exeter Gazette* took to shaming those on the terraces at St James' Park who weren't in khaki. Occupying practically half a page was a photograph of a section of the popular stand; a City goal was being celebrated. For the newspaper, the image showed

> that with some people there is little thought for those who are giving their lives for King and country when a lad imported from the North of England scores a goal for the 'Ever Faithful!' Some of the young fellows who found themselves next to gentlemen in khaki must have felt heartily ashamed of themselves – provided, of course, they retain any self-respect. Our advice to the latter is to cut out the above photograph, preserve it, and hand it down to those who are to come after them in remembrance of 'what they did when Britain was at war with Germany in 1914.'

'More Men Are Needed'. The popular bank at St James' Park

Source: © *Devon & Exeter Gazette*, 7 September 1914

THE DISTINCTION.

PATRIOTISM.	PROFIT.
At a meeting of the Exeter Avenues A.F.C. held under the chairmanship of Mr. Lea Turner, it was reported by the Hon. Sec. (Mr. M. R. Kingwell) that no fewer than fourteen members of the club had enlisted in the Army, and that many others intended to follow their example. In view of this and the present crisis, the Committee unanimously decided to suspend the whole business of the club sine die.	The Management Committee of the Football League has unanimously adopted the following resolution: "In view of the request from certain people to stop football, the Management Committee have taken counsel with their Clubs. The Committee are even more decidedly of the opinion that in the interests of this country football ought to be continued."

Exeter City Club deal in the latter.

Anti-association football advert

Source: © *Devon & Exeter Gazette*, 9 September 1914

Above the image were the words of a War Office communiqué: 'MORE MEN ARE NEEDED'. Sarcastically, the *Gazette* did concede that 'in fairness to Exeter', the majority of first-team players were 'importations', pointing to the tensions between amateurs and professionals, locals and non-locals.

Elsewhere on the same page, there was more criticism directed at the club. Retired academic and politician Sir Roper Lethbridge responded aggressively to the points in Sid Thomas' letter. If the Devon Battalions were to suffer the losses others were experiencing, 'would Mr. Thomas celebrate the event by the shouts and screams of a huge white feather brigade looking on at the exploits of a white feather team on the Exeter ground?'

White feathers were given to those thought to be 'shirkers'. Lethbridge branded the matches 'unseemly and sordid shows'. If they continued, he wrote, 'there must soon come a time when no self-respecting Englishman will consent to be seen on the ground, or to contribute another penny to the funds of the Company'. Up and down the country, wherever professional football was being played, similar outrage was shown.

Exeter City carried on as best they could. Gates were down, and the contracted players accepted reduced wages. From now until the end of the war, press news on the club was mostly sporadic; the detail and focus depended on the newspaper. In November 1914, the *Gazette*'s anti-football protest was still going strong, centred on the column 'Football and the War'. The rhetoric was reinforced by quotes from the national press and national figures such as Poet Laureate Robert Bridges. Bridges concluded: 'It is high time that our footballers let the world see what they are really made of, and that they do not deserve the execration that is falling upon them.'

Meanwhile, on Monday 23 November, the *Western Times* included a short item on the previous Saturday's League game against Millwall:

> There were several wounded soldiers at Exeter City football match at St. James' Park Saturday. These included Sergt. Hyde, of the Devon Regiment, who will be remembered as a former Soccer player in Exeter City's amateur days. He is also well-known as a cricketer. Sergt. Hyde was wounded with a bullet in the back of the neck, and had a very narrow escape.

Hyde's story was an illustration of the realities of warfare, and the fine margins between death and survival. Around this time, news reached St James' Park that George White, the captain of the City reserves, had been killed in action in France. White, an amateur, was the first of 13 known City players to die as a result of the conflict.

'Your King and Country Need You': QPR official programme for the game v Exeter City, 14 November 1914

Source: © QPR FC, from the Grecian Archive, Norman Shiel collection

Given the unrelenting venomous criticism of the professional game, and the fact that former players were sacrificing their lives, it does seem remarkable that the Leagues weren't wound up. At a national level, despite the lobbying, at the end of November 1914 the British government stopped short of suppressing professional football matches. What Prime Minister Asquith hoped was that discussions with the football authorities 'would meet with good results in the matter of recruiting' but such results had already proved to be pie in the sky.

On Saturday 19 December, during the interval of City's home League match against Southampton, an officer of the Sportsmen's Battalion, Lieut. A.E. Dunn, made an appeal to the crowd, described here:

> [I]n uniform, [he] crossed the ground from the stand side to the popular part, and delivered a stirring recruitment speech to a crowd of about 1,500. He referred to the enemy's recent raid on the Yorkshire coast and to the dastardly murder of women and children, remarking that their having brought the horrors of Kultur's [Germany's] methods of war close to the Englishman's home, would undoubtedly arouse the young men of the nation who had not already done so, to take up arms against a foe who threatened modern civilisation. Lieut. Dunn expressed pleasure at seeing so many young men present that afternoon in uniform (quite 30 per cent of the crowd on the popular side were clad in khaki), and urged the claims of the Sportsmen's Battalion upon the followers of football. He remarked that he did not tell them to go, but asked them to come, he himself having joined the Battalion as a private. At the close of the speech Lieut. Dunn was heartily cheered.

We don't know how many were persuaded to enlist but reports from other grounds suggest that such methods remained miserable failures. As for the current City organisation, besides a number of amateurs – and two board members and the trainer – several professional footballers responded to the call: Stan Cowie, Arthur Evans (Sportsmen's Battalion), Fred Goodwin (Footballers' Battalion) and Alf Green (4th Devon Territorials). Following a meeting of the Southern League, clubs had been requested 'to urge their players to join some branch of the Regular Army'.

In early 1915, as well as Southern League and reserve-team games, St James' Park hosted charity matches such as the one in February between Eastman's Ltd and Exeter Tramways Staff in aid of the Mayoress of Exeter's Clothing and Emergency Fund. At long last, in April, days before City's final League fixture away to Southampton, FA Secretary Wall announced the cancellation of Cup ties and League matches for the following season.

Soon afterwards, the City directors decided to 'cease all operations' until the resumption of the Southern League competition. St James' Park was loaned to the Athletes' Volunteer Force for use as a drill ground, the rooms under the grandstand serving as headquarters for the regiment. As a result, the rent of the ground had been reduced to a nominal amount by the Clifford Charity

GREAT XMAS ATTRACTION AT ST. JAMES' PARK, EXETER.

FOOTBALL MATCH,
EXETER CITY v.
COMBINED BATTERIES,

To-Day (BOXING-DAY)
KICK-OFF, 2.30 P.M. SHARP.

Admission, 3d. 6d. and 1s. Proceeds for Mayoress of Exeter's Hospitality Fund and Equipment Fund of the City Volunteer Force.

The Exeter Battalion V.T.C. Band will kindly attend, by permission of the Commandant.

Trustees. In May, over the non-payment of rates for the ground, City were summoned to appear before the Exeter Police Court. The case ended with the local Council accepting part payment of the amount, given the club's insolvency and inability to meet liabilities.

Around the time a new season would have been due to start, we hear from 'Rover', on Wednesday 1 September 1915. His *Express & Echo* piece is entitled 'City Footballers'. The Park was a lonely place:

> In normal times September 1st is a great day with the Soccer football public, both players and followers. Another campaign is started with all its hopes and brightly-painted prospects. Probably St. James's Park would have been the venue of a Southern League fixture this afternoon, and the Grecians' followers in hundreds would have trooped to the ground to see the team of 1915–16 at serious work. September 1915 has seen the great majority of old City players, however, engaged, instead, in more serious duties with the Colours or in munition work, and St. James's Park this afternoon was a deserted scene.

Then, with real feeling, he refers to the fallen:

> Looking over the enclosure one recalled some of the players who have gained popularity there and who now are far distant from the City's old ground. There are two who will never don the Grecians' jerseys again, who have died in the service of their King. Poor 'Cadie' [George] White, a sergeant of the Devons, was killed 'somewhere in France' quite early in the war, and a rough wooden cross marks the resting place of the former City Reserves' captain. One of his former team-mates, Chapman of the R.F.A., has seen the grave, having made, when near the spot where White fell, a successful search for it. Poor 'Cadie' was one of the most genial souls that ever kicked a ball for the City Club, bubbling over always with good spirits and enjoying the hardest game and the hardest knocks. He was an amateur of the best type, and for that reason made an almost ideal captain. It seems difficult to believe that we will never again see him racing on to the ground at the last moment (he had a knack of cutting things fine), and bursting into the players' room with some joke and his infectious laugh.
>
> The other player who lies buried in France is John Webb, an Exeter lad (his parents live in St. Leonard's), who learned his football with Friernhay. A robust centre half, he was tried in the Plymouth League team under White's captaincy in the latter part of the season 1913–14, and created such a fine impression, for he was strong, bustling, and in the very pink of condition. He was regarded, in fact, as one of the 'finds' of the season.

'Rover' goes on to mention Grecian Ashley Pim of the Royal Engineers receiving a DCM for bravery. Other players with the Colours he cites include Club Captain Jimmy Rigby (Army Service Corps), Sammy Strettle (Engineers) and amateurs Fred Bailey (Royal Army Medical Corps) and Fred Hunt (Wessex Territorials in India).

For the rest of the war, alongside the Volunteer Training Corps activities, there was the occasional charity match at the Park. The first such event, on Saturday 16 October, was watched by a crowd of between 1,500 and 2,000:

> Many wounded soldiers from the Exeter hospitals attended by invitation. The game was organised by Q.M.S. Stokes, of the V.T.C., in aid of the Mayoress of Exeter's Hospitality Fund and the V.T.C. Equipment Fund. The teams were City of Exeter and Combined Batteries. The former included Pym, Pratt, and Fenwick (Exeter City F.C.), and the latter Sergt. Voisey (Millwall). Mr. George Campbell was the referee.
>
> The result was a draw of three goals each. Bombr. Benford, Sergt. Voisey, and Bombr. Jones scoring for the Batteries, and Selley, Barker, and Bombr. Evans for City of Exeter.

A similar match was played at St James' Park on Boxing Day 1915. Despite bad weather, over 1,000 turned up. With the 'Exeter City' XI was the former amateur centre-forward Fred Bailey, home on leave. In one of the tragic stories of the war, six months later, 22-year-old Bailey lost his life on the first day of the Battle of the Somme.

Later, charity matches would often feature two military sides. Local army officers approved of them as they were 'a valuable means for promoting physical fitness and esprit de corps'. In November 1916, for example, the 16th Battery Royal Field Artillery took on the London Rifle Brigade – in front of 'a fairly large crowd, in which khaki predominated'. Sometimes these games included well-known former professional footballers who were serving with the forces. In November 1917, almost £20 – about £1,300 today – was raised for the Prisoner-of-war Fund. The *Western Times* reported:

> This helpful amount represents the proceeds of the recent Cadet's match, England v Scotland, at St. James's Park. It is the largest amount yet taken for war funds at St. James's and the match was such a splendid success that those interested in soccer at Topsham barracks will no doubt repeat the experiment.

When the Cadets beat Bristol City 2-1, one month later, we're told 'the game will rank as the very best since the League days at St. James's'. Former City professional Charlie Pratt, who'd been doing munitions work, refereed.

In August 1917, it was announced that the FA would permit matches to be played in one year's time, 'provided the gross receipts are paid to war funds or charity funds'. Perhaps that was what prompted City Chairman Michael McGahey's comment at the club's AGM in December 1917. He mentioned that 'during the past few months the St. James's Park ground had been, after a lot of work, put in thorough playing order again, so that it was quite ready when League football was resumed'. However, followers of the association game in Exeter would have over a year and a half to wait before that happened.

17

Serious losses

IN early 1918, St James' Park continued to be used on a regular basis by troops stationed at Topsham Barracks. Games between the Royal Field Artillery Cadets and the Permanent Staff were a particular attraction, and military charities benefited.

On Wednesday 24 April, a match at the Park between the Royal Navy and the Cadets 'produced a fine, rousing game before a good gate'. It was in aid of the Devon Regiment Prisoners-of-War Week. 'The grand stand,' we're told, 'was well filled, and the Fund should benefit materially.' It did – to the tune of £54, equivalent to around £3,000 today. City Secretary Sid Thomas, liaising with officers at the Cadet School, 'carried out the local arrangements'.

By the end of August 1918, with the war starting to be won, there was optimism in the air. On Saturday 31, the Exeter and District Band of Hope Union held their 'summer treat' at the Park; the Union was a children's temperance society. Members assembled at Bedford Circus, and marched in procession to the Park, headed by the Exeter City Military Band. About 500 children participated. The sports featured races for senior and junior boys and girls, and there were throwing the cricket ball and tug-of-war events.

Several months into the war, wounded soldiers had been invited to attend Southern League games. In September 1918, patients from the local military hospitals were entertained at 'St. James' Football Field' by the Exeter Cycling Club. Around 200 accepted the invitation. Some of the guests even took part:

> Amongst other events there were musical chairs, a hat trimming competition, a boxing contest, the combatants being blind-folded with jingling bells round their necks to give some indication of the position of one to the other, a tug of war between five ladies and four wounded Tommies, the latter using one hand only, which the ladies won, kicking the football, etc.

But the highlight of the afternoon was the clowning around of a local character in top hat and tails. Many of those present would have recalled seeing him at the Aston Villa Cup tie in 1914, leading the City mascot goat onto the pitch. Here, he was in his element:

> 'Artful' Thomas, as the dude [dandy], created much amusement by his antics. He very good-humouredly allowed himself to become the butt for all and sundry to shy at in the little show he provided described as 'Topping the Topper.' He was quite an acquisition, and the soldiers appeared to thoroughly enjoy this item of the programme.

For the rest, there was a band conducted by City Director Norman Kendall, cigarettes were distributed and tea was provided 'on the grand stand'. Sid Thomas was one of the stewards.

When the Armistice was signed on Monday 11 November, reaction in Exeter, a snapshot of the national rejoicing, was captured by a *Western Times* reporter:

> Long before one o'clock the great majority of business establishments closed down for the day, and all classes of people gave themselves over to the sweeping wave of sheer joy that had surged through the city. Impromptu processions still filed up and down High-street, St. Sidwell's and Fore-street, and it was wonderful how many thousands of flags had suddenly come to light. The whole city

was ablaze with them – simply ablaze, and by this time the posters had already announced the afternoon Cathedral service, and services at many other places of worship in the city. As one read these announcements, one gave a thought – a deep thought – to the dead, the great dead, who have made the Supreme Sacrifice for this Supreme Victory of Right, the Immortal Dead. In an hour like this, their memory is a thousand-fold precious, a thousand-fold revered.

One week later, there was an Armistice celebration for local children: 'Children's Night at Exeter'. The 'St James's Football Ground' was the venue for the main event. First there was a fancy-dress competition, followed by an hour-long firework display. Finally, the children lined up for a torchlight procession through the main streets led by the Exeter Cadets' Band. The event was arranged by the High Street drapers' Colson & Co.:

From all parts of the city the children rolled up in crowds, and were marshalled into long queues in front of St. James's by members of the regular and special city constabulary. On entering the ground each guest was given a large slice of plum cake, a by no means small item in these days.

Between five and six thousand children took part. The procession ended back at the Park, where there were brief speeches and the singing of the National Anthem.

Four years after suspending operations, Exeter City Football Club began to prepare for the resumption of League football. At a meeting of the Southern League, it had been decided to restart the old competition in September 1919. Soon there would be discussions with the English Football League on the question of amalgamating the Leagues – with the formation of a Third Division. We learn that the Supporters' Club would start meeting again and that directors were in touch with Arthur Chadwick over the vacant manager's position.

In February 1919, Chadwick's reappointment was confirmed. In an interview with 'Rover', he made it clear that attracting young players from the North would be difficult. Most of the ones in the Forces had already signed on for English League clubs, and the ones in the coalmines, shipyards or munition-making would be reluctant to give up good wages, unless alternative employment could be found in addition to football. His job, he said, would be to develop local talent in Devon:

Exeter, you know, have fared badly with its players in the war. Poor Arthur Evans and Gus Harding, to mention only the first eleven, have been killed; Smith has lost a leg, and Marshall, I gather from a letter of his which I have seen, has finished with football. Those are serious losses. Still, I hope for the best, and shall certainly do all I can. I should like to see some test matches played at St. James's this season – matches where local talent would be on show. When we are getting our house in order, it is necessary to give an eye to the young players who have been coming along in Exeter and the district.

Harding, in fact, had not been killed, but it would be months before that was known. Chadwick himself, doing munition work, had survived an explosion, we're told, in Morecambe – perhaps the one at the White Lund factory in October 1917.

In addition to Arthur Evans, three *former* City pros had lost their lives: Spencer Bassett, Joe Bulcock and William Kirby; along with eight City amateurs: Fred Bailey, Edwin Clark, Fred Hunt, Evelyn Lintott, Len Turner, John Webb, George White and Percy Worner. And around the time of Rover's interview with Chadwick, news came in that one more City amateur, Billy Stoneman, on his way back to England, had died from influenza at a hospital in France. Reviving the business of professional football seemed incidental but it was underway nonetheless.

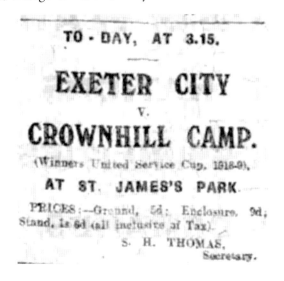

At St James' Park, in keeping with Chadwick's suggestion, a series of friendlies was used to 'test' local youngsters. The matches began on Saturday 1 March, Crownhill Camp, United Services' League champions, winning 6-0 at the Park. After a second game, on 15 March, 'Rover' saw encouraging signs:

Exeter City are reaping their reward of their trial of local talent in practice games. There were 2,500 present to see the match against Aglabs, Capt. Priest's [Agricultural] Labour Corps side from the Higher Barracks, and the queues lined up in St. James's-road before the start were remindful of Southern League days. There can be no doubt, in fact, that the Soccer revival at Exeter is going to be a big thing in the near future. The enthusiasm displayed on Saturday proved that, if proof were again needed.

One of the players to stand out was 18-year-old Charles Lincoln from Heavitree, an apprentice at a local printing works. He'd been recommended by Supporters' Club Secretary George Campbell. On Easter Monday, 21 April, 7,000 saw City beat Argyle 2-1 at the Park. A final trial against Devonport Dockyard resulted in a 2-1 win, Lincoln providing the cross for the second goal.

At the first post-war Supporters' Club meetings, the main topic of discussion was direct supporter representation on the board of directors. But the proposal for a covered stand on the popular bank side hadn't been forgotten. More than that, in May 1919 the

Express & Echo revealed that plans approved by the board to erect 'a big new stand' had been drawn up by the club's architect. Given the capacity of the existing stand – 750, we're told – the project being considered was 'both ambitious and comprehensive'. The *Express & Echo* outlined what it entailed:

[W]here the playing pitch touches the popular bank a sinkage of six feet below the present surface level will be made, thus enabling a new terraced slope to be cut out. This slope will be covered in, and will constitute a first-class enclosure running the whole length of the ground, and capable of holding fully 2,500 spectators. The new stand, which will be erected at the top of the slope, will have seating accommodation for about 2,200 people.

So, similar to the main grandstand, there would be a standing area in front of raised seating. And that wasn't all: 'A new "popular" bank will be built at the far end of the ground capable of holding up to 6,000 persons. Under the scheme, the total accommodation of the grounds would be increased from 12,000 to 15,000.'

The New Stand
Project
Source: © *Football Express*, 14
February 1920

As for funding, a 'stand shares' scheme was proposed by the board: '£10 shares bearing five per cent interest, the dividend and sinking fund being the first charge upon the increase in the receipts effected by the improvements'. Club Chairman McGahey explained the funding idea to supporters in September. But before tackling the £5,000 cost, the board wanted first to 'get the Club's "mouth above water"'. One week later, the Supporters' Club resolved to let the question of board representation stand over; the priority was to assist in the reconstruction of the club – and that meant raising money and increasing the club's membership. Soon, fund-raising began, all proceeds going towards a supporter-controlled New Stand Fund.

Meanwhile, the club's first Southern League games since the end of the war had brought two draws – 1-1 away to Southampton, and then 2-2 at home to Reading on 3 September. The Reading game was watched by 'about 3,000', the weather being 'unfavourable to a large gate'. In October, when Millwall visited, 6,000 were at the Park. The *Football Express* reported that

the playing field was in perfect condition, and the crowd streamed in fast – many sporting the effective red and white rosettes which had been prepared by lady supporters of the Grecians, the proceeds to be devoted to the fund for the new covered stand.

The Exeter City Military Band greeted the teams with 'Auld Lang Syne', the old acquaintance being Millwall full-back Jack Fort.

Back in August 1919, in the first edition of the Football Express since 1914, one whole page was devoted to detailed biographical sketches of the players, old and new, and service during the war. There was an item on 'Players now off the roll'. Cyril Payne, aka 'The Chiel', a replacement for 'Rover' who'd taken up the post of sports editor of the *Bristol Evening News*, referred to a letter from Billy Smith to Arthur Chadwick:

With regard to Smith, than whom none of the men in the last team was more admired, and who Chadwick himself speaks of as 'the makings of one of the best half-backs in England,' the City Manager had a letter from him the other day, addressed from Hyde, in Cheshire. He has now been discharged from hospital and 'living in a state of retirement.' Speaking of his artificial limb, he says: 'I must not complain, as I am able to get about very nicely, and hope to umpire as time goes on. The only complaint I have is that it won't play football. So I shall have to be satisfied with a place amongst the spectators. I am anxious for the opening of the season, so that I can follow accounts of your team, and I trust you will have every success.' Mr. Chadwick has written, in reply, inviting him to come down to Exeter for a few weeks, feeling sure the Exeter people would be glad to see him again.

Having secured a move to Everton, Smith had been wounded just weeks before the Armistice.

On Thursday 4 December, Billy Smith attended a packed Supporters' Club meeting at St James' Park. He was presented with a cheque for £40, the amount raised following a collection at the Northampton game on 22 November; City players and officials had contributed to this fund. Amid the fund-raising for the new stand – the fortnightly whist drives and a 'Watch Scheme' (minute cards were sold at 3d a second, two gold watches to be won) – there'd been a pause to rally round in support of a popular player. It was a reminder of the toll the war had taken on the Grecian family, both on and off the field.

Billy Smith at St James' Park in December 1919, with from left to right Charlie Pratt, John Dockray, Arthur Chadwick and Dick Pym

Source: The Grecian Archive, from the collection of the descendants of Billy Smith, photographer unknown

18

Turnstiles clicked

ONE year after the announcement of the 'big new stand' for the 'popular bank', there was a setback. On 8 May 1920, it was reported in the *Devon & Exeter Gazette* that the City Council's Streets Committee had rejected the plans 'as not being in accordance with the bye-laws'. That was all the short news item stated. As a result, the focus of development at the Park switched to ways of modifying the existing stand, as well as improving other areas of the ground.

When work on the improvements began, there was a fresh incentive. For the next season, 1920–21, the club would be competing in the Football League Division Three. The decision to expand the Football League competition was taken at the body's AGM on 31 May 1920. This followed an application from the Southern League. Their members were eligible to join en bloc – northern non-League clubs would have to wait.

For Southern League clubs, promotion was a possibility at last; the two bottom clubs would seek re-election. Sid Thomas called it 'the biggest and most revolutionary step we have had in football for very many years'. Arthur Chadwick reacted by saying: 'It's the finest thing that could possibly have happened.' But things could have been very different.

What Chadwick feared was the formation of a Third Division made up of 'two-thirds only of the Southern League clubs' and 'the pick of the Northerners'. Had that happened, Exeter would have been 'left out in the cold'. Eventually, for the 1921–22 season, there would be two Division Threes, a southern section and a northern one. At City, in the summer of 1920, just like in 1908, there was an air of expectancy at the prospect of a new venture.

In early July, 'The Chiel' reported on the 'extensive alterations' and improvements to the ground. Once completed, Exeter City would be able to boast 'one of the prettiest and most convenient first-class grounds in the country':

> The stepping of the popular bank is now well on the way, and will ensure increased comfort and a good view to every spectator who takes up a position there, whilst at the same time it will give room for another two thousand people. The extension to the enclosure at the St. James's-road end, and right along past the stand, will prove another big improvement. The new iron railings fronting the enclosure have yet to be fixed.

The cost of the railings had been met by a Supporters' Club donation. There were plans for banking not only on the popular side, but also behind both goals. Chairman McGahey told a Supporters' Club meeting in June that the work on the ground would cost 'close upon £1,000' (over £40,000 in today's money). A first practice match in mid-August was watched by about 3,500 – various charities benefiting from the gate – and the turf was in 'splendid condition'.

In the run-up to the new season, it was announced that the admission charge for first-team games would be raised, from 1s to 1s 3d. Extra commitments needed to be covered. As well as the cost of improving St James' Park, there was a bigger wage bill, football equipment had gone up in proportion to the increase in gate charges, and win and draw bonuses would be paid. Also, away trips for the reserves, now in the Western League, would involve going as far as Swansea and Swindon. For 'The Chiel', arguing in favour of the increase, 'the shilling will go to the club, and the 3d to the Government in the shape of Entertainment Tax'.

City's first Football League game was at home to Brentford on Saturday 28 August. A crowd of 6,000 to 7,000 saw Exeter win 3-0, with new signings Wright, Vowles and Feebury the scorers. Beforehand, a young supporter presented skipper Dick Pym with a horseshoe tied with red and white ribbons. Pym duly won the toss, 'much to the delight of the spectators, who regarded it as a good omen', and elected to defend the St James Road end. A programme advert for Thurston's Sweeteries refers to Pym: 'Save like "Pincher" by getting in "Touch" with our Home Made Sweets & Chocolates.'

Season ticket for the 1920–21 season – City's first in the Football League

Source: From Exeter City Football Club Museum donated by the holder's youngest daughter, Dorothy Simmonds

Programmes at 2d, printed at the *Express & Echo* offices, were a single double-sided sheet with two folds. There were brief editorial notes; adverts for everything from fish and chips to furniture, char-a-banc hire to wedding cakes; a space for half-time scores; and a list of the teams and match officials. A note under the line-ups reads: 'Should any alterations be made in the Officials or Teams at the last moment, a board will be sent round the Ground notifying the corrected names opposite the numbers corresponding with those on the programme.' The invention of the public-address system (Tannoy) was a few years away.

Since City turned professional, the club had had attendances of 12,000 to 13,000 for games against Plymouth Argyle. 'Derby days' would often happen over the Christmas period; back-to-back home and away matches. But on Boxing Day 1920, St James' Park couldn't cope with the crowds. The Chiel's report transports us to what he calls the 'exciting scenes' in and around the ground:

Even at that early hour [noon] there were people waiting for admission at the grand stand entrance – mostly enthusiasts from a distance who carried their mid-day meal in their pockets, and desired to get on terms with it in the quiet comfort of the stand. Round the corner and up St. James's-road the queue had already formed, and the crowd in waiting must have run into several hundreds. Then a heavy rainstorm came on and several bethought themselves of something they had forgotten, and returned home to see about it. Others stayed on, and they got the choice positions when the gates were opened.

The crowds grew and grew; the turnstiles clicked as they have never clicked before. As the hour for the kick-off drew nigh, and as the ground became more and more thickly populated it became apparent that nothing short of a miracle, or an accident, could enable all who wished for a view to get inside in time for the start of the contest. The accident came. At the popular entrance one of the gates burst open, and nearly a thousand people swarmed through the breach. At the other approach in Well-street a couple of thousand people were surging and swaying to and fro whilst a single turnstile tried to achieve the impossible, and pass them all through. Lots of young fellows, and some old ones, also, became impatient and with a smartly-executed flank attack shinned over the palings by the railway embankment. And presently a policeman got busy with a notebook and pencil. He must have collected a pocketful of names and addresses.

Many people fainted in the crush, and eventually it was found necessary to open one of the big double doors, and admit the seething mass in quicker if less business-like fashion than the turnstile permitted. At the corner of the ground where the enclosure joins the popular bank, the crush was so great that at 2.15 o'clock about twenty yards of the fencing were broken down, and two people were assisted to the stand by the St. John Ambulance men. Happily, none sustained serious hurt.

It certainly seems lucky that there were not more serious casualties.

Before the start of the match, there was the now familiar ritual of Pym being presented with a lucky charm (or mascot, as they were then referred to):

Whilst the players were kicking in, one of the members of the Exeter City Military Band led the youngster who rejoices in the name of 'Busty' Goldsworthy – and who wore the City shirt and white knicks – across to Dick Pym, and the little fellow solemnly handed the City goalkeeper and captain a horse-shoe decked in the Grecians' colours. Pym stooped down and gave the kiddie – he is about three years old – a kiss, and as solemnly deposited the mascot in the back of the City net when he had won the toss.

Reflecting on the scenes outside the ground, 'The Chiel', in his *Football Express* column, emphasised the fact that it *had* been 'a record crush'; arrangements for admitting spectators had been 'ample' in the past, and recent improvements to the ground had been made. Putting the attendance at 18,000, he reckoned St James' Park could have held a further 2,000 people, 'if the popular bank had been properly packed'; 'Rover' had said as much ten years before. Of course, being tenants, there were limits to what club directors could do to increase the Park's capacity, and make structural changes to make access easier. But that was about to change.

It's around this time – pre-Christmas 1920 – that the football club successfully concluded negotiations to buy the ground, not only the part on the old 'St. James's Field' owned by the Clifford

'Members of Exeter City team in training'. The grandstand, built in 1908, can be seen behind
Source: © *Western Morning News*, 1 December 1921

Trust, but the land at the lower end, which the club had been renting from Sir Henry Duke. The news was released by Norman Kendall at a Supporters' Club meeting on 22 December, albeit prematurely as contracts had not been signed, and the Charity Commissioners had yet to agree on the valuation.

When the purchase, at a cost of £5,000, was finally completed in June 1921, Michael McGahey explained why it had been a wise move on the part of the directors:

[U]nless they bought, by the terms of their lease they were subject, when the lease came to an end, to grave increases of rent, and if they gave up occupation every penny they had spent upon the ground and on structural improvements would have been thrown away, as one of the conditions of the lease was that if the club gave up possession, the ground must be restored in its original state.

Economically, it was the ideal time to buy. On the back of the club's most successful ever financial year, there was income from transfers, beginning with the sale of William Goodwin to Manchester United in June 1920. It is often said that the sale of Dick Pym paid for the purchase of the ground but Pym's transfer to Bolton Wanderers took place in June 1921, by which time the deal had already been announced many months prior. However, it did enable City to recoup their outlay.

As for the development of St James' Park, improvements in the short term were minor; plans for a new stand remained postponed. In December 1921, in the run-up to the derby game, 'The Chiel' reported on work done to improve access to the ground:

[I]n order that the unpleasant crushing and delay experienced by sections of the crowd outside the entrances last season may be avoided on this occasion, and in future years, a special additional entrance has been constructed in Well-street, adjoining the railway bridge, connecting up by a wide pathway with the big bank at the far end of the ground over by the 'Football Express' score board.

Three new turnstiles will be in operation at this new entrance, whilst a big sliding door has been constructed so that a wide and clear exit may be available at the close of each match. This Well-street corridor is a very valuable addition to the amenities of the ground. The old yarn about the first-man-out who took a stroll round Stoke Canon and passing through St. James's-road again on the homeward journey found people still trying to get out of the ground will now be right out of date.

This, it seems, is a first reference to what is now known as the Jungle Path – transformed almost a century later with artistic 'Walk of Fame' boards, running adjacent to the railway line, featuring Exeter City strikers old and new.

Later, during the 1922 close season, the bank at the 'Duke's end' (also known as the 'Score Board Bank', today's Big Bank) was 'made larger', and at the foot of it new railings, provided by the Supporters' Club, were put up. The railings were formally presented to the directors at a ceremony in the board room. In thanking the Supporters' Club, Michael McGahey mischievously revived the idea for a grandstand on the popular terrace – and then settled on provision of cover for this area:

'Netted'. Cartoon by R.C. Letts following a 2-0 home win on 3 April 1922

Source: © *Football Express*, 8 April 1922

Adverts for games at St James' Park

Source: © *Football Express*, 6 May 1922

> The railings were of much assistance to the Club and indicative of the great help the Supporters' Club gave. He [McGahey] looked forward to the time when the Supporters' Club's gift would be a grand stand on the popular side, this being the crying need of the ground. Then spectators could always watch the games in comfort. Times were not prosperous at present, prices were high, and it was difficult to carry out the scheme. He hoped that, in future, with the aid of the Supporters' Club, the Directors would be able to cover in the side, if not the ends as well. The Supporters' Club had been the greatest possible assistance to the City, and was not too critical, as many such Clubs were.

Covering the ends of the ground? That would take decades to achieve. A roof for the popular side? That remained a realistic objective.

Walk of Fame at St James' Park

Source: © Aidan Hamilton, 2018

19

Burning to ashes

I N the early 1920s, while City Supporters' Club officials and directors of the football club did their best to make ground improvements a priority, *on* the field the club was struggling. In the first three Football League Division Three seasons, Exeter finished a lowly fourth, second and third from bottom. After the 1921–22 season, the club successfully applied for re-election; and in December 1922, long-serving manager Arthur Chadwick moved on. The problem then – as it is now – was achieving stability on the playing side, while relying on income from selling players to keep the club afloat.

Away from League matters, the 'City Club' were doing more than they had ever done to assist in the development of amateur football locally. Various competitions were staged at St James' Park. These included the Wednesday League, the Victory League and the Schoolboys' League; and the club promoted and hosted the Exeter & District Gold Medals Competition, which featured leading amateur clubs, an initiative coming from Sid Thomas. In May 1921, one of the Gold Medals matches attracted over 3,000 to St James' Park: 'the enthusiasm was positively infectious, for the play reached a high standard', wrote 'The Chiel'. Unearthing promising talent was clearly as important as it is today.

In other uses of the ground, in August the Supporters' Club continued to organise a programme of sports. The fixture was strictly run according to the laws of the Amateur Athletic Association and the National Cyclists' Union rules. It attracted competitors from across the south of England, such as sprinter Cecil Griffiths and steeplechaser Percy Hodge, both Olympic champions. Prizes consisted of medals and an assortment of dinner-service items. For holders of lucky numbers on programmes and admission tickets, there were City season tickets to be won. Music was provided by the Exeter City Military Band and, to cap it all, the City pros would have a practice game.

Dick Pym returned with Bolton Wanderers for a friendly (0-2) in September 1922, the first of many visits. Some 5,000 attended. Almost twice that number were at the Park in May 1923 for the joint benefit organised by the Supporters' Club on behalf of Jimmy Rigby and John Dockray, the oldest players on City's books. A present Grecian XI drew 1-1 with a past one. For 'Observer' of the *Devon & Exeter Gazette*, 'Pym showed the spectators a few of the saves by which he helped Bolton to carry off the blue riband of the football world [the FA Cup, in Wembley's first-ever final]. One of his saves, from a terrific shot by Crockford, was extraordinarily clever.' The match set a precedent for player tributes at the club.

As for atmosphere on matchdays, there was much of what exists today – and more. 'The Chiel' gives us a flavour of this as he depicts the

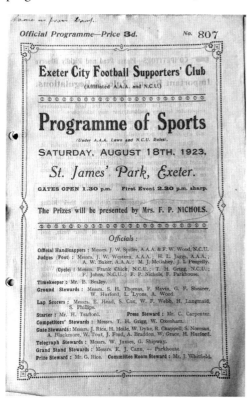

Programme of Sports at St James' Park, 18 August 1923

Source: © ECFC, from the Grecian Archive, Norman Shiel collection

build-up to a League game with Bristol City at the Park in February 1923:

> The 'gates' were opened earlier than usual, and the stand filled quickly, and as also did the covered part of the enclosure. By three o'clock the attendance numbered 6,000, and the crowd was then streaming in fast. Many spectators had brought monster rattles and bells, while in the intervals between the selections by the Exeter City Military Band popular choruses rolled out from the packed mass in the middle of the big bank. Just after the hour a terrific rainstorm swept over the ground, and a mass of umbrellas sprang into prominence in all parts of the terracing. With a rich vein of humour the spectators on the popular bank, with one eye on the cosy stand occupants, burst out with a chorus about the 'difference that money makes you.' A lull in the storm was greeted with 'Sally – You brought the Sunshine to our Alley.'

'Community singing' was common. Sometimes 'Artful' Thomas would make an appearance. Before a Cup tie against Watford in 1924, he was 'in rare fettle on the playing field', advertising with his hobby horse a forthcoming rugby attraction at the County Ground. And still the collectors' boxes for the new building fund did the rounds of the terraces and grandstand. Roofing in a section of the popular bank had been priced at a cost of £300. In November 1924, 'The Chiel' tells us, the sum of £240 had already been raised.

By the following season, 1925–26, work had begun on the galvanised iron roofing on a section of the popular bank. Supporters' Club Chairman George Rice, writing to the local press in August 1925, thanked all those whose donations had made it possible, and then announced the continuation of the building project:

> Sir, – I am instructed by the Committee of the Exeter City Supporters' Club to thank the innumerable subscribers to our funds for assisting in rendering possible the very fine weather protection erection in course of construction at St. James's Park. We shall not be content until the whole of St. James's Park spectators space is under cover, and, so far as our limited powers will permit, we shall leave no stone unturned to bring about this desired result.
>
> It is intended in future that all monies coming to the Supporters' Club shall be used for the above object. Therefore, we ask that all supporters of the City Club, not only in Exeter, but the whole of East Devon, will attend St. James's Park to-morrow (Saturday) in their thousands for our annual sports.

This sports event was the most successful of its kind to date, about 5,000 turning up; a promising start towards funds for covering the whole ground. But just as it seemed the club had turned a corner, both on and off the pitch (in the previous League season City had finished seventh), disaster struck.

On Tuesday 17 November 1925, ten days before a First Round FA Cup tie at home to Swansea, the grandstand at St James' Park was completely destroyed by fire. The players had trained in the morning and later, before everyone left for lunch, playing gear was hung around a slow-combustion stove to dry. 'The Chiel' described what happened:

> Picture the state of mind of the vice-chairman of the club, Mr. J.I. Pengelly, who lives just across the road from the ground, and was early on the scene. Think of the feelings of the Secretary, Mr. S.H. Thomas, as he surveyed the wreck of the stand and offices, in which were most of the club's records, burning to ashes.
>
> Imagine the emotions of the Manager, Mr. Fred Mavin, who at considerable personal risk had salved some of the club's books and a few chairs from the office, and was now watching the greedy flames licking up the stand like a voracious living monster, devouring, amongst other things, the players' gear.
>
> A crowd of people swarmed in at the top entrance in Well-street, and from the 'flower-pot' terracing watched the big blaze across the width of the field, on which were grouped the players themselves. At the back of the stand, in Well-street, were the firemen, working strenuously, but

almost futilely. Yet they did manage to save the refreshment booth nearby, and other minor effects.

Here, too, behind the stand, could be seen the immense volumes of dense black smoke which, sweeping away over the railway cutting and to the Pennsylvania district, carried for miles quick and insistent tidings of the club's trouble.

… With so many others I watched the flames eat their way rapidly along the stand and devour it. Then in a flash the 'Football Express' box was involved, and as the voracious flames reduced the structure to nothingness, I thanked my stars I was not inside. Jove! How it burned.

Later that day, 'The Chiel' saw some of the players in the High Street; they'd just bought new boots. Half-back Ellis Crompton told him he'd dreamt on Monday that 'he was having a desperate time sweeping back a big fire with a broom'. Seven years earlier, the grandstand at the County Ground had suffered a similar fate.

Despite offers to play it elsewhere, the Swansea Cup game (1-3) went ahead at the Park on 28 November. There was 'ample seating accommodation', but none under cover. The gate was just under 10,000. Tents were placed on the site of the old stand for use of players and officials. As improvised dressing rooms, Swansea used decorators Messrs Neal's in St James Road; City changed at the Red Lion in Sidwell Street.

Work on a new stand began at the end of the 1925–26 season. Up until then a tarpaulin was used to cover seats, and a large army hut put up for the players inside the shell of the old stand. As the amount from the insurers wouldn't be sufficient for a new structure, public funding would be needed. The appeal was a success. In August 1926, 'The Chiel' reported on progress with the new grandstand, a 'vast improvement' on the old structure:

When finished, the building will be as smart as anything of the kind in the South. Accommodating over 2,000 spectators, the stand will be well equipped with all the necessary offices and dressing and training rooms. Kiosks for the sale of refreshments, cigarettes, etc., will be installed at the distributing gallery within the stand, and in the arrangement of the building the comfort of the patrons has been the prime consideration.

And the state of the playing surface?

St. James's Park is in wonderful trim, considering the amount of work done on the stand, and the extensive returfing scheme carried out in mid-field and before the goals. Hundreds of tons of poor soil have been removed and good earth substituted for it, and it is hoped that by this means the very heavy mud patches which were so conspicuous last season will have been done away with entirely.

The coming season, 1926–27, proved to be the club's most successful at home since the war. In

The grandstand following the fire in November 1925

Source: The Grecian Archive, photographer unknown

the 21 games, 46 goals were scored, 18 conceded – including a record League victory, 8-1 against Coventry City.

It was at the end of 1927 that 15-year-old Cliff Bastin first appeared in a City shirt. He made his debut for the reserves on Christmas Eve, scoring twice in a 6-1 Southern League win against Bath City. As *Exeter City: A Complete Record* notes: 'Nothing seemed to panic this young man and even when Arsenal came for his signature in 1929, he had to be talked into joining one of the world's most famous clubs before he went out for a game of tennis!'

Bastin made his full Exeter City debut in April 1928, aged 16 years and 1 month. This record, as the youngest ever City player, stood until August 2016 when Ethan Ampadu, aged 15 years and 10 months, was selected for an EFL Cup game.

To return to 1926, having raised all of £1,800 since 1912, in November the Supporters' Club announced that it was disbanding. It had been forced on them, the result of the FA placing an embargo on certain money-raising schemes. This meant the club's bread and butter – the various draws that took place at St James' Park – had to stop; the most recent ones were the gold-watch scheme and a competition estimating the number of local tram passengers on a certain day. But two activities would continue: the running of the annual sports meeting and the organisation of the Exeter Schools' Cup. These would be overseen by the Supporters' Executive Committee. The Supporters' Club would reform in 1935.

Derby days at the Park continued to attract large attendances, and in December 1926 the 20,000 mark was reached. Packing on the flower-pot terraces was still a problem, and there was a plea from 'The Chiel' for a prototype of the 'family enclosure':

> The official figures, on a recount being made, prove to be 19,500, and it is estimated officially that quite 500 others secured free entry to the ground by divers routes which do not appear on the club's ground plans. In short, this latest Exeter-Argyle derby was attended by 20,000 people.
>
> With efficient packing at least 1,000 more spectators could have found accommodation on the terraced bank, but there were some people present in other parts who could not get a perfect view. And in this connection I should like to plead the cause of the boys. An enclosed space somewhere on the popular bank would give the youngsters a chance on great occasions like this, and such an arrangement should not be very difficult.

With 'divers routes' being used to enter the ground illegally, inevitably there were casualties. Examples of injuries sustained included: falling while climbing a pillar at the front entrance to the ground; hands cut on barbed wire after a fence collapsed while it was being scaled; and falling from a roof overlooking the popular bank. Surprisingly, just one incident of crushing was reported.

In January 1928, the club would have expected a repeat of the 1926 Argyle gate. Blackburn Rovers were City's opponents in the Fourth Round of the Cup. In an effort to achieve the highest gate possible, special arrangements were made. On the eve of the tie, Club Secretary Sid Thomas wrote to the local press:

Cliff Bastin – one of City's greatest players – on his way to the big time: 'probably the cleverest forward of his years seen in the Exeter district to date'

Source: © *Football Express*, 6 March 1926

> Clifford Bastin, the Ladysmith-road Soccer captain, and skipper of the Exeter boys' team in their English Schools Shield games this season, is probably the cleverest forward of his years seen in the Exeter district to date, and as such is a great credit to the organisers of the local Schools League which has "brought him out." To-day he is playing at inside left in the South team at Brighton—in a trial game against the representatives of the Midlands.
>
> It is interesting to note that besides being nominated by Exeter for this trial Bastin received very warm support from Bristol, where when playing in the Exeter team in a Shield match at Christmastide he "fairly took Bristol by storm." The honour now accorded him is greatly appreciated throughout the county, Bastin being a highly popular favourite everywhere in Devon.

THE CUP!!!

Exeter City
v.
Blackburn
ROVERS,
At St. James' Park, Exeter.
TO-DAY, at 2.45. Gates Open 12.

Stand Ticket Holders are invited to take their seats by 2.15. Entrance, Well-street.

PRICES: GROUND **1/6**. ENCLOSURE ONLY **3/-**. BOYS **6**d.

Advert for the Cup tie v Blackburn Rovers

Source: © *Football Express*, 28 January 1928

Sir. – The Directors of the Exeter City Football Club desire me to inform the public that the holding capacity of the ground is nearly 20,000. The ground can be filled to this capacity if the public who desire to see the match will assist.

Two men with megaphones will be on the playing pitch, and a number of stewards will help to marshal the crowd, so that the utmost use of the ground may be made. If the spectators will follow the instructions given, everyone may be comfortable, and have a good view of the match.

The Directors appeal to spectators to pack themselves as closely as possible, so as to leave room for others. When the ground is comfortably full the gates will be closed, and no one else will be admitted.

Detailed traffic and parking arrangements were made by the Chief Constable of Exeter. Ground admission was increased to 1s 6d.

In the event, 'wretched weather conditions' meant the ground record remained intact, the attendance being given as 17,330, but gate receipts reached a new high of £1,781. Here's how 'The Chiel' described the moments before the 2.45 kick-off:

By 2.15 o'clock it was clear that almost the entire mass of spectators had taken up their position inside the ground; the turnstiles had slackened off greatly. The crowd was a very orderly one, the people being content for the most part to reserve their vocal organs for the match itself, and steam silently in the warm rain during the period of waiting.

It was not found necessary to close the gates, as, although the ground was well filled, there was no crushing. In the few minutes before the teams fielded 'Artful' Thomas, a well-known local character, equipped with a megaphone, led in some very successful community singing.

With the score 1-2 near the end, it finished 2-2: 'How the City fought their way back to equality,' wrote 'The Chiel', 'will long remain an inspiring memory to the great crowd which watched the match.' Blackburn won the replay 3-1 and went on to win the Cup.

When Argyle were promoted to Division Two in 1930, Cup ties such as this became the big draw.

Police v Garages programme, November 1926: St James' Park was often made available for local amateur football

Source: © ECFC, from the Grecian Archive, Norman Shiel collection

SOUVENIR PROGRAMME.

Challenge Association Match.

CITY POLICE
v.
EXETER
UNITED GARAGES

Wednesday, Nov. 24th,
AT   1926
ST. JAMES' PARK
EXETER.
(By kind permission of the Exeter City Directors)

Kick Off 3.0 p.m.

" *Express & Echo*," *Printers, Exeter.*

20

'Dido's Day!'

ARLY in the 1930–31 Cup run, in December 1930, there was consensus among *Football Express* correspondents on City's best ever Cup win. It was the 4-0 triumph away to Portsmouth in January 1914. In the space of a few weeks, in early 1931, this was eclipsed. Having beaten Northfleet United (3-0 away) and fellow Division Three side Coventry (2-1 away, after a 1-1 draw), City for the very first time defeated Division One opposition – not once, but twice. As the official programme editorial for the Derby County game on 10 January 1931 made clear, the fact that two recent First Division visitors to St James' Park – Blackburn in 1928, Leeds in 1929 – had been 'fortunate' to force replays, gave grounds for optimism:

> We have every respect for the talent of the First Division, but a cup tie with all its excitement, tense situations, and hurried football, is a great leveller, and we have some solid grounds for hoping that the time may have come when Exeter City will succeed in getting the better of First Division opponents.

After the win against Derby (3-2) at St James' Park – followed by victory at Second Division Bury (2-1) – City then beat Leeds United 3-1 in a Fifth Round home tie. Said City skipper Charlie Miller following the Leeds tie: 'Now we are ready for the next, and we don't care who they are. We have great hopes of going to Wembley.' Even before the Leeds game, the City board had agreed provisionally to take 7,500 FA Cup Final tickets at a cost price of £1,822 (over £100,000 in today's money).

So, we arrive at the quarter-final tie: away to Sunderland, a club just below mid-table in Division One. On the day of the game, Saturday 28 February, the *Sunderland Echo* introduced

The City team that took on Sunderland on 28 February and in the replay at St James' Park on 4 March. Standing: Clarke, Barber, Davies, Angus, Houghton, Purcell. Seated: Armfield, Baugh, Miller (capt.), Doncaster, Varco
Source: © *Football Express*, 14 February 1931

the visitors from Devon, front-page headlines including the words 'Weird Cup Mascots in Sunderland' and 'Mysterious "Birds"'. It was reference to 'Dido', City's seagull mascot, named after a whippet owned by Exeter groundsman Harry Greenaway. Since the Derby County game, the bird had been getting quite a reputation.

At the end of January 1931, 'The Chiel' reported on a sighting of 'Dido' in the run-up to the Bury tie:

> Mr. W. McDevitt, the Players' Manager, told me at Bury last Saturday that the seagull mascot was doing his bit nobly again on the Friday morning, just before the Grecians set out for the North. 'When I went out on the field,' he said, 'the first man I met was the old gull. The groundsman said to me: "There you are; just look at that." And the bird was strolling about the playing pitch in fine style.'
>
> As an old lady of my acquaintance says: 'It's wonderful, though, what luck the City are getting when the gulls are about.'
>
> Two of Exeter's best-known tradesmen, who were in the grand stand at Gigg-lane, vouch for it that two seagulls flew over the pitch just before the match started. They were almost indignant when I told them that I had not seen the serial visitation, through being busy with pencil and paper at the time.

Advert for Exeter City v Sunderland
Source: © Devon & Exeter Daily Gazette, 3 March 1931

At Roker Park, 'The Chiel' described the 500 or so 'excursionists' from Devon: 'Exeter supporters warmed up to their work wonderfully and seagull feathers in great variety, and relieved with the Grecians' colours, were held aloft. The cheering, too, was deafening.' One of them told the *Sunderland Echo*: 'Dido has never been known to let us down. It flew over the train when we left Exeter last night, so we are sure to win!' And they almost did. It finished 1-1, Percy Varco having a chance to win it moments before the final whistle. The attendance was 51,642.

Imagine the scenes at St David's Station when the train carrying supporters, players and officials pulled up; expected at 8 a.m., it didn't arrive until just before 1 p.m.

F.A. CUP REPLAY.
To-Morrow (Wed.) at 3
At St. James's Park, Exeter.

EXETER CITY
v.
SUNDERLAND.

All Stand Seats have been disposed of, but there are still a few Flowerpot Enclosure Tickets at 3/-.
Prices of admission: Ground 2/-, Enclosure (St. James's-road) 3/-; Boys 6d.

The *Western Morning News* estimated there was a crowd of 10,000 outside the station – 'a Cup-tie crowd in itself':

> By midday a congested mass of many thousands crowded the precincts outside the station. For another hour these were rapidly augmented till the crowd extended some distance back to the Railway Hotel, and further into the higher ground to St. David's-hill.
>
> Exeter City Band was on the spot, and in addition to their selections the crowd relieved the tedium of waiting with cheers, the singing of popular songs, and other diversions.
>
> Favours of the City colours were displayed everywhere. Rattles and other instruments broke out frequently, and the display and waving of flags completed the gala complexion of the assembly. The cheering was intensified when a large covered charabanc wended its way through the press to await the Exeter party. …
>
> As the train at last steamed into the station, the 500 Exeter excursionists on board joined in the general demonstration. Hats, hands, mascots, and colours were waved vigorously from the carriage windows, and the hearty acclaim of the platform was drowned in the great shout that went up from the assembly outside.
>
> People clustered round the team and officials, showering them with congratulations and handshakes, demanding cheers at almost every step. Miller, the gallant skipper of the team, smiling delightedly, carried the horseshoe mascot which the team had used at Sunderland.
>
> Assisted by the police, the party pressed through the crush to their charabanc, where the immediate section of the crowd demonstrated afresh.

When safely aboard, however, the party could not move on for two or three minutes, the vehicle being hemmed in by enthusiasts, one of whom from an elevated position called for cheers for each individual member of the team. These were given in salvoes.

The band struck up a lively march, and then the coach slowly forced its way through the crowd, the party being cheered to the echo until they disappeared on St. David's-hill.

Having passed through the ordeal of the football battle, the happy team also escaped injury from their almost too attentive supporters. They appeared to be perfectly fit, though tired, after all the turmoil. Houghton, the hero of the equaliser, seemed almost overcome by the warmth of the reception.

Three days later, many of those present took up their places at St James' Park for the Cup replay.

What follows are extracts from the *Express & Echo* on the day of the replay, written by Cyril Payne (aka 'The Chiel'):

Vendors of the colours of the rival clubs were about early, and doing good business, too. The dismal weather conditions did not damp the ardour of the football following fraternity, and there were apparent all the elements usually associated with an important Cup tie. Rattles sounded, football was discussed on all hands, and miniature 'Didos' were sported by the locals.

Excursions from all parts of the South West began to pour into the city this morning, and three specials were run from Plymouth alone.

An elderly lady with whom I got into conversation this morning did not know which team she wanted to win. The fact was that she was born at Exeter, but now resides at Sunderland.

Another person, presumably of Scottish descent, was also in a quandary. His difficulty was the colour question. He

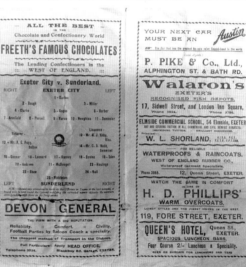

Exeter City official programme for the Sunderland Cup replay, 4 March 1931
Source: Dave Fisher collection, Westcountry Studies Library, Devon Heritage Centre

was an Exeter supporter, and had forgotten that the City this afternoon would be playing in red and blue. Rosettes of these colours were on sale, side by side with red and white favours (Sunderland's usual colours). Here was the puzzle. If he purchased a red and white rosette, it would come in handy when the Grecians wore their normal uniform. Yet on the other hand, he might have been taken today for a Sunderland partisan!

How he overcame a knotty problem I do not know. But, perhaps, in a moment of weakness, he purchased both sets of colours. Had he done so, he would have been replete with red, white and blue, and he would have been all right for Empire Day and other National occasions.

This afternoon all the elementary schools in the city were closed because of the Cup tie. Never before has this happened on account of a football match in the city. Yes, Exeter has caught the Cup-tie fever badly. …

From about nine o'clock yesterday morning onwards, rain fell steadily at Exeter and almost without intermission, all day and all last night, and again all this morning. Optimists believed, somehow, that the conditions would improve in time for the match, but the playing pitch was waterlogged, of course, and the wet weather was a big disappointment for the intending spectators, there being only a very scanty bit of covered accommodation at St. James's Park outside the grand stand.

Excursionists from Sunderland put in an appearance in force this morning just after nine o'clock, the party numbering about 250. For the most part they sported the Red and White colours common to both teams, but a few wore rosettes of white – the Wearsiders' colour for to-day.

Mr. A.F. Fogg, of Bolton, the referee, was among those who paid a visit to St. James's Park this morning. He inspected the playing pitch and took the opportunity of doing a spell of sprinting, to loosen his limbs in readiness for the match.

There was a regular procession of telegraph messenger boys between the General Post Office and St. James's Park, dozens of telegrams of good wishes being received by the City Club from all parts of the country – one, indeed, came from the Devonians aboard a warship at Monte Video.

Colonel Acland Troyte, M.P. for the Tiverton Division, wired best wishes for the team's success from the House of Commons and Mr. Harvey Moore also sent a telegram saying he hoped to see the Grecians at Wembley.

Mr. Clifford Hamilton, of the 'Journey's End' Company, wired to Mr. Percy Dunsford, of the Theatre Royal, Exeter: 'Cheer the City for us, and hope their journey's end will be Wembley.'

Exeter City players and officials had lunch together at Deller's before the match. The Sunderland team and officials were at the Royal Clarence Hotel. Exeter relied on the eleven which drew at Roker, but the visitors were without Morris, their right half back, who is down with the 'flu.' Hastings moved from left half to the right flank, and Andrews, former first team player, stepped into the vacancy on the left. Teams:

EXETER CITY

Davies

Baugh, Miller,

Clarke, Angus, Barber,

Armfield, Purcell, Varco, Houghton, Doncaster

•

Connor, Leonard, Gurney, Devine, Eden,

Andrews, McDougall, Hastings,

Shaw, Hall,

Middleton,

SUNDERLAND

Referee, Mr. A.F. Fogg (Bolton); linesmen, Messrs. R.J. Kidby (Gloucester) and C.A. Webb (Somerset).

Many Exeter business houses closed down especially for the afternoon to allow their employees to see the Cup match; other firms made special arrangements so that as many workers as could be spared could attend at the Park. …

The Exeter City Club, in their official programme for to-day, expressed their appreciation of the sportsmanship shown by the Sunderland Club both on the field and in the Board Room at Roker, last Saturday, and also of the very hearty reception given the City players on their return from Sunderland.

By 2 o'clock there were fully 14,000 people inside St. James's Park, and the turnstiles were then clicking at a great rate.

'Dido's Day!' was the general comment when the spectators saw the watery playing pitch, and pictured the old seagull mascot taking his bath in the puddles.

As in the case of the Leeds United match the juveniles were allowed inside the railings, but this time they stood because of the wet state of the ground. All the time the drizzle descended, and the misty air was more like a November effect than a day in March.

The spectators cheered lustily every now and then as a seagull passed by overhead.

Alderman Charles Warren, the Mayor of Exeter, was among the early arrivals in the grand stand, and there was a big assembly of other Exeter notables.

By 2.45 o'clock the popular banks looked full to overflowing, but still more people squeezed in. The field lines were marked out with sawdust, and there were big patches of sawdust directly in front of the goals. The playing pitch became wetter and wetter – and so did the vast majority of the spectators!

As the teams fielded the Exeter City Military Band, under the conductorship of Mr. George Newman, played 'There's a good time coming' – just as they did at the Leeds United game. Sunderland were first out, and then a mighty cheer and the ringing of handbells signalled the appearance on the field of the Exeter City team.

A record number of Press photographers picked their way through the mud to the centre circle to 'snap' the referee and the captains. McDougall won the toss, but this carried no advantage.

Here are some extracts from The Chiel's review of the game, 'Good-bye to the Cup':

If anyone locally had stated seriously last November that Exeter City would go into the 'hat' for the Cup semi-final, well, what would his friends have said? Yet this was achieved by the Grecians.

Team spirit, grit, and good football have been the secrets of their success. They have gone further than any Third Division side in history, and their record is likely to stand unbeaten for a very long time.

Yesterday was positively the last time they could have appeared at home on the competition, and the whole of the West Country rose to the occasion in great style. The traffic into the Devonshire capital by road and by rail was exceedingly heavy, and in spite of the rain which had been falling steadily for thirty hours, and which continued on into the evening, there was a 'gate' of record proportions, both in the number of spectators and the receipts. The figures were 21,015 and £2,564 [a new and double record for St James' Park].

Just now I referred to the rain and the 'gate'. How about the rain and the match? I believe Mr. M.J. McGahey, the chairman of the Exeter City Club, hit the nail truly and neatly on the head when he stated after the match that the Grecians' chance of success would have been better on a dry ground. To think that at Chelsea and at Wolverhampton the weather was beautiful! The same conditions here, and the City might still have been in the Cup.

People who saw the two games with Sunderland will agree that the First League side was much more solid and decidedly stronger on the wet Exeter playing pitch, and that their marksmanship with the heavy ball was much more impressive. Shot after shot sailed over the Exeter crossbar at Roker. Here, the shots kept low.

Andrews, brought into the Sunderland team at wing half-back in place of Morris, improved the line, I thought, and right through the visiting eleven there was strength and exceptional ability.

Exeter's lighter forwards were not so much at home in the slosh as they would have been on a heavy ground which did not splash, or, on a dry surface, and this applies particularly to the home left-wing pair, who have done so much damage to other teams' Cup prospects this season.

Mr. McGahey also said that the ball did not run favourably for Exeter in yesterday's match. This was noticeable, often, especially in the case of an exciting scrimmage in front of the Sunderland goal at the time when the visitors were leading by three goals to two. At the height of the struggle the ball ran actually along the Sunderland goal line with as many as seven or eight players close at hand staring at it with round eyes, and straining to reach it to turn it in or out, as the case might be. With what gentleness and care Hall, the Sunderland left back, met that ball near the post! How gingerly he diverted it into the field! How tantalising the position for Exeter! An equaliser then, and anything might have happened.

Perhaps that was where Dido failed.

Still, one must keep faith with the mascot and with the game. And it is but right to say that well and gallantly as Exeter played the visitors deserved their victory. They started off at a great rate and maintained a cracking pace until they had got a two goals lead. Then Exeter did some meritorious attacking. And, as you know, when Exeter scored – and they scored twice – Sunderland buckled to and replied. Those two early goals did the damage. Until they encountered Sunderland

Exeter City did not concede a first-half goal to any opponents in the Cup-ties.

And, by the same token, until they met Sunderland Exeter City had been opposed always by teams dressed in blue and white, or white and blue – which is much the same thing, but not quite. Sunderland intimated that they would wear white shirts and blue knickers, but, apparently they had heard a thing or two, and their knickers were black.

Of course, by the time the game ended yesterday both teams were a dirty brown colour – but that by the way.

Sunderland's forwards were masterpieces. They showed wonderful craft whenever they gained possession. And as their half-backs were adepts at intercepting the Exeter passes

Sunderland's front-line men had quite a lot of the ball. There was little or nothing to choose between the teams in the matter of defence. Baugh and Miller and Davies put in some grand work again. But at half-back, and in the forward line, Sunderland showed up famously.

The goals:
Connor in 15 minutes.
Gurney in 22 minutes.
Varco in 37 minutes.
Connor in 60 minutes.
Purcell in 70 minutes.
Eden in 78 minutes.

[T]he City's great Cup performances have brought much trade into the city, and have brought great delight to the sporting public of the South West. With the defeat of Exeter City and Chelsea yesterday the South had lost touch with the Cup competition, but now that we have got so near a Wembley appearance we shall all feel we have a direct interest in the final stages which rest now between the Midland and the North-East.

The results of the semi-finals were Birmingham City 2, Sunderland 0; West Bromwich Albion 1, Everton 0. The final was West Bromwich Albion 2, Birmingham City 1.

One week after the Cup replay, the City directors, meeting at St James' Park, looked to build on the success in the competition. It was agreed to extend manager Billy McDevitt's contract for a term of two years. And, after a letter from Tottenham showing interest in Harry Houghton had been read out, it was 'resolved not to transfer any players that the Club desired to retain'.

21

Under cover

SUCCESS in the 1930–31 FA Cup competition *did* lead to improved League form. Twelve months on, with a top-ten finish in Division Three South in sight, club chairman Michael McGahey outlined fund-raising plans with two aims: to retain players by being able to pay summer wages; and to cover 'the greater portion' of the popular enclosure, the part of the ground later known affectionately as the Cowshed.

The Bond Scheme introduced in April 1932 was almost identical to the one that had raised £3,000 towards the cost of re-building the grandstand. McGahey hoped the scheme would be 'warmly welcomed by all those sports who love a flutter'. Each year, ten winning bondholders would receive the face value of the bond and five per cent interest, the first five out of the hat, in addition, receiving bonuses. A fixed proportion of gate money would fund interest and repayment. If, by extending the covered accommodation at the Park, the 'bob' supporters could be encouraged to attend on the wettest afternoons, the increased takings would help to ensure successful and sustained team building.

In the early 1930s at St James' Park, a Grounds Committee would prepare specifications for summer work. Fencing had been put up along the popular bank and the grandstand painted. At a board meeting on 18 May 1932, the decision was taken 'to complete the covering on the popular Bank'; the passageway immediately in front of the school would remain uncovered. In addition, it was resolved, at the east end of the ground, 'with local labour to step as much as possible of the popular bank and provide the necessary crush barriers'. On the issue of 'ground rights', these continued to be let to a Mr Curtis. He'd been 'Refreshment Caterer to Exeter City A.F.C.' since at least the 1910s.

By the start of the 1932–33 season, the whole of the popular side had been covered, and the Big Bank had not only been terraced but also considerably extended. 'The Chiel', saluting the club's 'enterprise', gave his impression:

Work being done on the Big Bank – perhaps the work that was carried out in the 1932 close season

Source: From the Grecian Archive, the Norman Shiel collection

[S]uch a marked advance in comfort and appearance as to enable St. James's Park to take its place amongst the cosiest as well as amongst the most compact and convenient arenas in the Third Division.

There are bigger grounds, and smaller grounds, but I doubt if there is any ground in the competition in which the spectators have a closer or better view of the proceedings, or which is so central and has such pleasing surroundings. Wet weather, for the future, then, need have no terrors for the Exeter City following. There is ample room under cover for more than ten thousand people.

For the goal of promotion to Division Two to be achieved, what the club needed was for attendances to be averaging 9,000 or 10,000. But even when League form was improving – as was the case in the 1931–32 season – gates too often were well short of that number. This contributed to a loss on the balance sheet in excess of £2,000 for the year ending 30 April 1932. Keeping players had its merits but, in the present financial position, sale income was sorely needed.

We arrive at the 1932–33 season: the most successful League campaign in the history of the club. The pinnacle was the home defeat of Torquay United (5-0) on Saturday 28 January – a sixth successive win – which resulted in City going top of Division Three South. On a 'beautifully clear, frosty Winter's day', a crowd of 11,000 saw Fred Whitlow become the most successful goal-getter in the club's history at that time. His hat-trick that day was one of his *seven* for the season – all performed at the Park; his 32 games yielded 33 goals. That said, as the run-in approached, there was a feeling the City front line needed strengthening, and to this end, two forwards from Fulham – Webb and Wrightson – were signed. 'These are days,' wrote 'The Chiel', 'when the club cannot afford to mark time.'

It's at this point – strange timing with City pushing for promotion – there's a change at the helm of the *Football Express* reporting team. Having been in post since 1919, Cyril Payne aka 'The Chiel' announced he was stepping down to take up another position at the *Express & Echo*. He'd been promoted. His successor, Lionel Wotton, adopted the pen-name 'Nomad'.

In his first column, on Saturday 1 April 1933, 'Nomad' made City the promotion favourite – only one side went up in those days – due to having 'the easiest away programme'. And under the front-page banner of 'Exeter's magnificent win [2-1] against League leaders', he reports on the atmosphere before the Norwich City game at St James' Park:

Exeter and the district for miles around had caught the football fever to-day. Quite two hours before the kick-off the trek to St. James' Park had commenced, and the stream of spectators increased with the passing of every minute. Stand accommodation was taken up nearly an hour before the start.

The period of waiting was enlivened by the efforts of the combined strength of the 4th Batt. Devonshire Regt. And the Exeter City Military Bands, under the batons of Bandmasters A.B. King and George Newman.

The scene resembled very much an Argyle match or a Cup-tie, and the packed terraces in the cheaper enclosures showed that Exeter is capable of supporting Second Division football. Before three o'clock the crowd was in the region of 15,000, and they cheered lustily after the young Devonshire Regt. Buglers had helped other musicians in the performance of stirring melodies.

Long queues still thronged the entrances and I have never seen the Duke bank so densely crowded as it was this afternoon. A full-throated roar from the nearly 20,000 spectators heralded the appearance of the Grecians, and the cheering, smaller in volume but none the less cordial, was renewed when the Canaries trotted out a few seconds later.

The official figures, 'for League purposes', were reported as a gate of 14,900 with receipts of £875. For a Saturday League match, with no 'derby' element, it was, according to 'Nomad', the biggest attendance in the club's history. But at the top of the table it was Brentford who finished the strongest, leaving City in second place, as 'Nomad' put it, to 'languish [in Division Three South] for at least another season'.

As in the 1920s, regular use was made of the Park when it was not needed by the first team or reserves; there was even a proposal to hold greyhound racing at the ground, but it was vetoed by the directors. In some cases, a nominal fee was charged, such as for the Exeter Schools sports meetings and providing the finish for a marathon organised by the Exeter Insurance Committee. Often, free use was granted. It highlights the extent of the club's involvement in and links to local organisations. One of the largest of these external events was the final of the Hospital Cup on Saturday 24 March 1934, the culmination of a day's action for hospital funds.

Later in the day, at a dinner at Deller's Café attended by civic dignitaries, players and officials, former mayor Kenneth Gatey MC gave one of the toasts, reported as follows:

> Everyone, and particularly those connected with the amateur code, was grateful to the Exeter City Club for the way they opened up St. James's Park for various fixtures. He [Gatey] was connected with the football activities of juveniles and unemployed, and never yet had application been made in vain to Mr. Sidney Thomas for use of the ground when that was convenient.

In February 1933, St James' Park had been made available for University College v Unemployed, and in April, the Unemployed Football Final, proceeds going towards the Mayor's Unemployment Fund. There was an Exeter Unemployed League organised in conjunction with the Devon FA and local Leagues. Later, in 1935, there were games at Home Park and St James' Park between teams representing the unemployed of Exeter and Plymouth.

The Park also played host to friendlies whenever there was a gap in the fixture list. In January 1933, an Army XI were the visitors, City winning 10-5; a year later, the famous amateur side the Corinthians drew a crowd of 5,000 – and in winning 6-1, City's first team avenged a 1-7 loss in 1931. There was also a number of benefit matches throughout the 1930s, beginning with one for George Purcell in May 1932. Away from games involving the City, the ground hosted its first senior representative match on Wednesday 24 February 1937, an FA Amateur XI losing 1-4 to the Universities Athletic Union.

In the mid-1930s, the club explored a novel way of communicating with the public at St James' Park. At a board meeting on 15 September 1934, a Tannoy Sound Equipment representative attended and 'placed alternative schemes for introducing sound apparatus upon the ground'. A number of other southern section clubs, including Aldershot, Brighton and Southend, had adopted the idea. A few weeks later, a test was made at the League game against Reading, before which Secretary Sid Thomas had the task of explaining to Bandmaster George Newman why, for once, his services weren't required.

While most thought the quality of the reception from the loudspeakers was excellent, one season-ticket holder wrote to the *Football Express* protesting at the band being replaced by gramophone records:

> Our band may not be the equal of the Coldstream Guards, but we have an affection for it. Many of us have been to some expense to assist in the provision of uniforms, so that we might not feel ashamed in the presence of visitors, and we object to being treated in a cavalier manner.

For 'Nomad', the system installed by 'Sound Advertisers' was 'quite effective' but he missed 'the human touch which the band's presence would have given'; if the City Military Band was to disappear altogether, a link going back to 1908 would be 'severed'. Although the directors approved the Tannoy idea, at a subsequent meeting it was resolved 'not to proceed further but to revert to the Band'.

In truth, it wasn't quite the moment to invest in a public-address system. In April 1934, a sub-committee had reported back to the board on ways of cutting expenses; recommendations were that players' wages should be cut and a cap put on the maximum wage. Sid Thomas offered to take a reduction in his salary and Manager Billy McDevitt agreed to forgo his bonus money.

In June, with 'pressing liabilities' to be met, a meeting of directors called for 'the exact financial position' of the Company to be put before a shareholders or citizens meeting. The warning was that 'unless financial support is forthcoming, the Directors will no longer take on the responsibility of carrying on the Club and it must drop out of League football'. With the club in crisis, the winning of the Division Three South Cup – the club's first trophy of significance – on 2 May 1934 provided the briefest of distractions; City had begun this competition with an 11-6 win at the Park against Crystal Palace, Whitlow scoring six.

An Emergency Committee was formed to explore potential ways to ease the financial burden. Bondholders were encouraged to convert their holdings into share capital and, in February 1935, the Supporters' Club was re-launched. Fortuitously, in place of the existing £6,000 mortgage on the ground, a local benefactor, a Mr Frederick Blandford, agreed to put up a new mortgage for £7,100 for a term of 10 years. The bank loan could at last be repaid.

In the spirit of rallying round, in a letter to Lord Mamhead, chair of the Emergency Committee, the Exeter Official Information Bureau encouraged citizens to come to the club's aid:

> In my Committee's opinion it would be a calamity if the Club was allowed to lapse, and they desire to place on record their firm conviction that the Club is a great asset to the city, and should be supported by every citizen, either by taking up shares or rendering financial and other assistance by becoming a member of the Supporters' Club.

A way forward was found at a public meeting on 28 February 1935. In a forceful speech, City Chairman Michael McGahey outlined a 'new deal' that would bring directors, shareholders, players and supporters into closer contact. 'A united pull,' according to 'Nomad', would 'lift Exeter's football prestige, whereas it would have been dragged deeper and deeper into the mire if the various interests had persisted in tugging different ways.' Before the season was out, the Emergency Committee launched an '11-pointed Appeal'. The 11 reasons for keeping first-class football in Exeter alive challenged local sportsmen to assist the club by contributing to the scheme for increasing share capital.

Exeter City players and officials at the front of the grandstand with the Division Three South Cup. City beat Torquay 1-0 in the final at Home Park

Source: © *Football Express*, 5 May 1934

On the pitch, during the decade, the good times came and went all too fleetingly. Reflecting the club's financial plight, for two seasons running – 1935–36 and 1936–37 – City had to apply for re-election to the League. Respite took the form of a Cup run to the Fifth Round in early 1937; City, having defeated top Division Two side Leicester City 3-1 at the Park, went out losing 3-5 away to Preston North End of Division One. Dido-mania and memories of the 1930–31 Cup run were a happy diversion.

Park action from November 1935 v Gillingham, with a rare image of St James' church in the background
Source: © *Football Express*, 30 November 1935

During the second half of the 1930s, as the team struggled, the Supporters' Club went from strength to strength. Having raised over £120 – over £8,000 in today's money – in their first year, the board gave them permission to have a hut put up on the popular side, close to the Supporters' Club flag; it was for use as an office and for 'propaganda purposes'. In the spring of 1938, the Supporters' Club committee decided to hand over £100 to the directors towards renovating the grandstand. Among recent fund-raising activities were two matches, one between Exeter and Yeovil Ladies, another between past City and Argyle pros. Other sources of income included a concert at the Savoy Cinema and the sale of cushions at the Park.

One note of sadness, towards the end of the 1935–36 season, on 21 March, was the tragedy at St James' Park before the League game against Clapton Orient. Arthur Chadwick, Exeter City's first manager, collapsed and died shortly after taking his seat in the stand. After recalling Chadwick's qualities as a player and a fine judge of talent, 'Nomad' reproduced an anecdote involving Chadwick and one of his biggest admirers, the late Arsenal manager Herbert Chapman:

> The two were often seen in close consultation on grounds in England and Scotland. On one occasion they were watching a Scottish junior match.
>
> Mr. Chapman asked Arthur Chadwick whom he fancied.
>
> In his broad Lancashire, 'Chaddy' replied: 'I like the reet half and t' goalkeeper.' Mr. Chapman did not agree. Those two particular players were Thomson, the Scottish international goalkeeper, who died while playing for Celtic, and Brown, another international, who is today playing for the Rangers.

It was a poignant reminiscence. Tributes to Chadwick's memory were 'sincere and impressive'. Among those at his funeral were Norman Kendall, Reg Davey, Sid Thomas and, representing the present players, Charlie Miller.

Action from City v Torquay in 1938
Source: © *Football Express*, 15 October 1938

22

Gaping wounds

'**P**ROMISE, despair, crisis and recovery', that was how 'Nomad' summed up the 1938–39 season, the last full campaign before the Second World War. Not long after an opening-day win away to Cardiff City, City lost one of their players in tragic circumstances. Bob Wallace, a 26-year-old full-back, died following unsuccessful operations for an elongated abscess of the forehead; he was, wrote 'Nomad', 'a grand sportsman, a conscientious servant of Exeter City, and a credit to his profession'. There was a fund for the player's widow – the Supporters' Club contributed £118 – and at St James' Park the club flag was flown at half-mast.

From October, League results deteriorated to the extent that re-election loomed. An FA Cup exit at the hands of Torquay added to the problems, and at the shareholders meeting in December 1938, there was criticism of the board with calls for resignations and a fresh start. So desperate was the situation that Chairman Captain Hunter warned that the club was close to having to 'put up the shutters'. Tension was eased, at least temporarily, when League results in April took the club to a position of safety.

For 'Nomad', there were three lessons to be learned. Defensive weaknesses needed to be addressed, 'youth and age were not correctly blended' – there'd been calls for some time for a 'nursery', i.e. youth team, to be set up – and the club's average of just over 6,000 for attendances at the Park was around 1,200 below the Division Three southern-section average. On the issue of support, the plain fact was that in a city such as Exeter the only way to guarantee patronage was a winning team.

Given the critical financial position, what would the club have done without the Supporters' Club? In the year up to August 1939, it had spent about £400. Ground improvements included rebuilding and repairs to refreshment huts, and the broadcasting equipment at the Park had been bought.

When a new oval type of goalpost and upright was introduced by the Football League, two sets were presented to the football club. Fund-raisers in the pipeline were a City v Argyle ex-pros game, and the visit of Billy Cotton's Band. Since the Supporters' Club had been formed, 'considerable headway' had been made.

During the 1939 close season, as the political situation in Europe unfolded, the Park played host to a variety of events – including a visit from one of the royals. In June, the Exeter Division Girl Guides, held their first-ever rally there:

> That sporting arena presented an unusual appearance with its green surface dotted with the blue and brown of Guides' and Brownies' uniforms and its terraces resembling flower gardens with the mingling hues of the colourful costumes of waiting performers – here a patch of yellow, there of scarlet, and there a broad band of blue and white. And scarcely less picturesque was the grandstand, crowded with women spectators in gay summer dresses.

With around 1,000 participating, items included a pageant – 'Guiding down the Ages' – with topical scenes such as past involvement in wartime activities and becoming familiar with Air Raid Precautions (ARP) work. In a matter of weeks, the 'sporting arena' would be harnessed for the war effort.

The purpose of the visit of Princess Mary to Exeter on Saturday 24 June was to inspect the Devon and Cornwall branches of the British Red Cross Society. Some 1,400 workers attended the ceremony. At St James' Park, despite the drizzle, as the *Express & Echo* reported:

> [T]he sight of hundreds of nurses drawn up rank upon rank was a deeply impressive one … As her Royal Highness passed in front of the bank opposite the grandstand, she was greeted by an enthusiastic burst of applause.

Later that summer, there's a further example of St James' Park being used as a community resource. It was one of the venues in the Lammas Fair Programme, featuring entertainment such as a darts competition, a novelty cricket match and al-fresco dancing. On 19 August, following the football club's annual sports meeting with foot and cycling events, there was a friendly in aid of the Football League Jubilee Fund, City v Argyle (1-2), with players wearing numbers on their backs for the first time.

On Saturday 2 September, the day before Britain declared war on Germany, 'Nomad' voiced hopes that future development at St James' Park would go ahead. But what would that entail?

> [T]he conversion of the enclosure in front of the 'Football Express' box into a decently terraced paddock. This no man's land, used chiefly by members of the band, has been allowed to become overrun and untidy. The proposal is to open it up and make it available to the public.

It was the area between the Old Grandstand and the Big Bank. It soon became clear, however, that the 'crazy times' 'Nomad' referred to at the start of his column – his last *Football Express* one for some time – meant that any improvements to the Park would have to wait.

That Saturday turned out to be the final round of Football League and Southern League matches in the 1939–40 season. While the City first team continued their unbeaten start with a 1-0 win at Port Vale, at St James' Park the reserves were held 0-0 by Hereford. Soon, the FA announced that only friendlies could be arranged in consultation with the local police headquarters. It emerged that the City management was unlikely to continue operations during the war. As a military officer, Chairman Frederick Hunter would become engaged in Home Guard activities, and the Park was wanted by local military authorities.

When a regional south-western tournament was announced at the beginning of October 1939, which included Plymouth and Torquay, 'Nomad', writing in the *Express & Echo*, appealed to the City board to go public as to why the club had opted out. Supporters had voiced 'strong disapproval'. The response was swift. Captain Hunter outlined the position of the club, giving two reasons for the decision to suspend activities. For one, wartime gates would be insufficient: 'Prospects of support would diminish … as blackout time became earlier. People then would be disinclined to attend matches and run the risk of having to scramble home in darkness.' Second, the ground had been commandeered; the Devon Regiment used it as an infantry training centre. Hunter reported that he and his fellow club officials 'may have to remove all stock from our present headquarters'. Soon, the board room was converted into an ARP post.

But Hunter's arguments seemed a trifle hollow given that, before long, an Army XI was turning out at St James' Park. On 14 October, leading amateur side Friernhay defeated their hosts 4-3; later, opposition for the soldiers included Torquay Grammar School (2-6). But despite the fact that the Army continued to play there, the East Devon Cup Final, scheduled for the Park, was transferred to another venue. 'Nomad' was perplexed:

> As to why St. James's Park is taboo, that is not a matter which I can discuss. Presumably, the authorities who now have control of the ground have a very sound reason. Yet the County Ground, which is being used for a purpose similar to St. James's during the week, continues to be available for sporting fixtures on Saturdays. Don't think I have any quarrel about that. What does strike one as unfortunate is that St. James's Park, the natural home of Association football in Exeter for upwards of 30 years, should be closed.

Not until May 1940 were competitive matches allowed to be played at the Park. There were two finals: Sidmouth v Old Haywardians, Crediton for the 'Football Express' Cup; and St Mark's v Southern Railway for the East Devon Senior Cup. Admission was 1/- for the grandstand, 6d the ground; troops in uniform were admitted half-price.

But these games were exceptions. For sport with no military connection, the Park was off limits. In June 1940, a Youth Soccer Day, originally planned for St James' Park, was held at St Luke's College ground. As for Exeter City, directors, we're told, had been holding regular meetings. 'Close contact' was being kept with the 25 players on the retained list, several local amateur clubs were receiving help with equipment, and tabs were being kept on promising youngsters. Developing links with the amateur code was a sensible strategy.

In local football, the Exeter & District League and the East Devon and 'Football Express' Cup competitions continued to run. Having been closed to the football public, in early 1941 use of the Park was sanctioned for matches in aid of the Red Cross organised by the East Devon FA; teams from the Royal Artillery and RAF were involved. There was also a game there in February between the Exeter Home Guard and an Army XI during which a collection was taken for War Weapons Week.

Perhaps the most conspicuous use of St James' Park during the war was for an Exeter Home Guard tournament on Saturday 4 October 1941. The crowd of 4,000 that watched the demonstration were mostly in the grandstand and the Cowshed terrace; an image of the Big Bank shows that it was already overgrown:

> The use of blank ammunition, imitation bombs and grenades lent a touch of realism … Displays by a bayonet squad and hand grenade throwers were given, and there were impressive performances by machine-gun teams, companies of route marchers, drill teams, etc.

Six months later, a number of those participating were on duty at the Infants School that adjoined the football ground, on the night of 4 May 1942. That was the night the city of Exeter received the greatest shock in its history.

A contemporary report in the *Devon & Exeter Gazette* described the 'gaping wounds' and 'trail of devastation' as a result of which the death toll was at least 265 with hundreds more injured:

> In the recent Exeter blitz much of the work of centuries was destroyed in less than one and a half hours. For some hours more, fire continued the work of devastation. The toll must have been infinitely heavier but for the skilful and fearless efforts of the Civil Defence services.
>
> Great gaps have been rent in the very heart of the city's thriving, vigorous life; vital sections of its principal streets have been reduced to rubble and dust; some areas adjacent to the core have been laid in ruins; nearly all the suburbs reveal in some degree the scars of a cruel mutilation.
>
> Ancient landmarks, historic shrines, noble modern buildings, many hundreds of dwellings – mansion, villa and humble home, alike – have been destroyed outright or grievously damaged by the shattering impact of high explosive or the blaze of devastating incendiaries.

At least two of the victims had links to Exeter City Football Club: Club Chairman Lieutenant-Colonel (formerly Captain) Frederick Hunter and former player Albert Potter. Hunter – Commander of the 1st Battalion (Loyal City of Exeter) of the Devon Home Guard – died from wounds received while on fire-watching duty at his home in West Avenue; Potter, an ARP warden, was hit while on his way to help one of his neighbours in Burnthouse Lane. Their deaths were remembered in 2017, the seventy-fifth anniversary of the Exeter Blitz, with football club representatives laying wreaths on their graves.

Not only did Exeter City suffer casualties, the club also lost its most distinctive landmark. One of the first buildings to be hit by incendiaries was St James' church. Despite the efforts to fight the blaze, in next to no time the roof collapsed; nothing inside survived. As the rector, Reverend Frank Lowman, put it: 'It was practically all over in half an hour.' The district's mother church, St Sidwell's, was also reduced to rubble. In the aftermath, St James' church held services at St

Anne's Chapel and later at St James' Institute Hall; eventually a new St James' church was built in the mid-1950s at the meeting of Mount Pleasant and Prince Charles roads.

The surroundings may have been different, but St James' Park remained a major venue for charity events. In August 1942, for example, a boxing meeting was held to raise funds for the Parcels Scheme for Exeter prisoners of war and the Royal Devon and Exeter Hospital. There was also, in the following summer, a reminder to the older generation of the fire-brigade competitions at the beginning of the century. The area National Fire Service held a 'Holidays-at-Home' sports at the Park, a large crowd enjoying 'fine running and athletics and with interesting and amusing demonstration of fire-fighting'.

The ground was also used by American troops, although it's not clear what form this took and whether or not they were actually billeted there. The 10th and 25th Naval Construction Battalions (Seabees) were based in Exeter from 1943–44 so it's possible that they were at St James' Park in preparation for D-Day. What we do know is that there was an American football game at the Park on 7 January 1945. The *Express & Echo* reported that the game 'had an impressive opening when the Devonshire Regiment Band played the National Anthems of the United States and Great Britain, while Service personnel of the two nations saluted the Stars and Stripes and the flag of an American Navy Unit'. The game was organised by the Americans as a way of supporting the British Merchant Navy Comfort Fund. Later in the year, in August, a crowd of 1,500 gathered at St James' Park to watch baseball: the first leg of the European Services' Championship final between the American Army and the US Navy.

During the months before VE Day, Exeter City, albeit with an improvised side, played a series of friendlies at the Park. On 2 April 1945, 3,500 – the biggest attendance of the war at St James' Park – assembled there to see City beat a weakened Argyle side 5-1. Shortly afterwards, the club launched an appeal for £5,000 to assist in preparing for League football; compensation for the loss of the ground had been 'barely sufficient' to cover current expenditure. With a new board in place, Sid Thomas returning and being elected chairman, a 'committee of local sportsmen' was formed to take on the task of fund-raising. It was known as the Grecians' Association. A fete at St James' Park was planned for the August bank holiday.

In June, 'Nomad' gave an update on the work that needed to be done to make the Park ready for League football:

St James' Park during the Second World War. The 50 is a marker for an American football game, so a likely link to American servicemen and the American football game at St James' Park on 7 January 1945

Source: © From the Grecian Archive, photographer unknown

Baseball at St James' Park

Source: © *Express & Echo*, 24 August 1945

The pitch is showing signs of wartime wear and tear. The big bank behind the far goal is overgrown with weeds. The erection of buildings on the popular side has taken away a big section of terracing. This week I saw Harry Greenaway working solo on what would be a heart-breaking task to most men. He was patching and seeding, and generally getting on with the job. If energy and enthusiasm are enough to accomplish it, then St James's will be O.K. by the autumn. But labour reinforcements would be a big help.

Groundsman Harry Greenaway did receive some support, with, for example, a member of the old Supporters' Club offering to help out on every night of the week. Volunteers were encouraged to contact Secretary Norman Foot. The volunteer-labour experiment had been successfully tried out at Swindon, 'where, following years of War Department occupation, the ground became derelict' but was rejuvenated with the help of volunteers.

As the 1945–46 season beckoned – City would be playing in a regionalised Third Division, one of 11 clubs based south of the Thames – we hear how preparations were going:

> The playing pitch at St. James's Park is now in fairly good shape, thanks to the efforts of Harry Greenaway and a few helpers. Tons of top soil have been laid down, and the ground is looking much better than could have been expected a short while ago. The next job will be to tackle the big bank.

Several weeks later, on Friday 31 August, the eve of City's first competitive home game since 1939, 'Nomad' had a request for those visiting the ground:

> St. James's Park is far from being in its normal peace-time state … It is asked, therefore, that spectators make the best of matters by avoiding congestion and crowd blocks. Properly packed, the onlookers will all get a clear and comfortable view of the game, but they must do their part to help.

The worn terracing on the Big Bank had been removed, but the buildings on the Cowshed were still there. Fifty or so German prisoners had been assisting with the task of 'putting the ground straight', according to 'Nomad'.

23

Tidy terraces

A T Exeter City's thirty-second annual shareholders meeting, on 17 October 1945, Chairman Sid Thomas declared that, despite post-war difficulties, the directors were determined to 'make the club a success'. One of the issues on the agenda was 'ground improvements'. If a covering could be provided for the Big Bank, there would be 'covered accommodation for a 20,000 gate'. It harked back to an early 1920s ambition.

Thomas thanked the Grecians' Association for the £780 they'd raised since the club had restarted in June. The appointment of a manager was announced: George Roughton, formerly on Manchester United's books, who had been guesting for City.

The *Western Morning News* report of the AGM spelt out the challenges facing Roughton:

> The players the City had signed in 1939 were 'scattered over the four quarters of the globe,' and up to last Saturday [13 October] not more than four of them had been available for any match. The club, however, had been very fortunate in having the assistance of Royal Marines and guest players, and, although early successes had not been maintained, it was not surprising having regard to the difficulties of getting together a team and the long distances to be travelled.

Back in the summer, the Football League had bowed to pressure from Third Division delegates for regionalised football, as opposed to a full peace-time programme. This avoided such journeys as Torquay to Norwich, or Southend to Port Vale; but for Exeter and Torquay, journeying to clubs south of the Thames still meant a fair bit of travelling.

During that first transitional season, for spectators at the Park the watching experience was novel. It's the one time in City's history that guest players have been fielded in competitive professional matches. There was a limit of six per team. So, for example, for the home League game against Bristol Rovers on 29 September, City's XI, according to the official programme, was scheduled to include Duke (Luton Town), Roughton (Manchester United), Haddington (Bradford Park Avenue) and Mitcheson (Ipswich Town).

The problem was the rules for guests were being flouted. In a programme article 'Club Chatter', 'Grecian', without mentioning names, had a go at the rule breakers:

A post-war crowd on the Big Bank
Source: © *Express & Echo*, 11 September 1945

All is not well in League football in these times, and some clubs are playing fast and loose with the rule which lays down emphatically that not more than six guest players must be called upon in any given match. While Exeter City are abiding strictly by the regulation – in no game have we played more than four guests – a few other clubs have been known to field more than the permitted maximum. A glaring example recently came to light when a visiting team included no fewer than ten stars from elsewhere. To make matters worse, some of them took the field under assumed names. Identity was concealed, so it rather looks as though a policy of deception was put into deliberate effect.

The culprits were Aldershot, a club with an embarrassment of riches; players serving in the forces could turn out for the nearest club to where they were based. Perhaps in Aldershot's case, there had been extenuating circumstances. But for 'Grecian' it was 'grossly unfair and cannot be tolerated'. The FA had barred guests from playing in Cup ties and, from November 1945, the quota was reduced to three, before gradually being phased out. It became easier for clubs to rely on their own resources as the number of demobilised players increased.

A word about the new-look City programme – mentioned above – priced 2d. The A5-size publication replaced the one sheet with two folds that opened out, used from the 1908–09 season until 1939. As well as the line-ups and 'Club Chatter', its four pages included adverts for the Exeter Theatre Royal and Carr & Quick Ltd, the wine, spirit and beer merchants on Queen Street. On the cover, 'Selections', it was announced, would be performed by the Southern Railway Band.

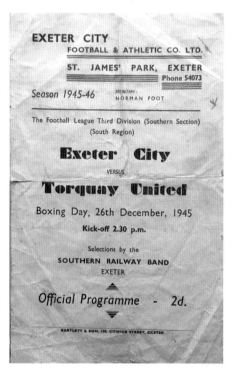

When City played their final home League game, against Torquay United on Boxing Day, 'Grecian' wrote that, given the fact that the club had not been involved in wartime competition, 'the job of reconstruction has been well tackled'. Particularly pleasing was the level of support: several gates had been around the 9,000 mark, with one exceeding 10,000. Enthusiasm such as this, it was hoped, would lead to Exeter City recapturing 'the glories of those epic seasons of Cup and League fame'. The second half of that transitional season was taken up with the Division Three South Cup (southern section), the 11 clubs playing each other twice. A City reserves team was already up and running.

As the 1945–46 season drew to a close, there was a reminder – in the City programme for a Third Division Cup match against Bournemouth on 13 April – of the rationing that remained in force. Under the heading 'Clothing Coupons', 'Grecian' anticipated close-season 're-planning' when equipment for two teams would have to be secured in exchange for coupons. The supporters' help was needed and this time the club wanted the clothes off Exeter fans' backs … literally:

An arrangement exists with the Board of Trade and the Football Association whereby **loose** coupons **collected from Club Supporters** [bold in the original] are exchanged for one voucher, so we appeal to you all to give what you can. Half coupons are better than nothing and will be most gratefully accepted at the ground. We appreciate only too well that we are touching on a very personal issue but feel that once again St. James' Park fans will rise to the occasion in the all-out combined effort to put the City Club back into the limelight.

Supporters were also made aware of the fact that there was likely to be a change of colours: it was simply not possible to get hold of the red and white vertical stripes. It might be 'one plain colour' or it might be 'squares'; it would, in fact, turn out to be red and white hoops.

In the same programme, there was reference to the fund-raising activities of the Grecians' Association. The group had arranged for a collection to be made at St James' Park in aid of the Bolton Football Disaster Fund. On Saturday 9 March 1946 at the Cup tie between Bolton and Stoke City, 33 people were crushed to death and hundreds more injured after a section of the ground was gatecrashed; inside Burnden Park there were many thousands more than the reported attendance of around 65,000. A total of £115 10s was City's contribution to the fund. It included a separate donation from the Grecians' Association, two of whose committee, past City favourites Dick Pym and Harold Blackmore, had played for Bolton.

Shortly before City embarked on a fresh Division Three South campaign, organised along pre-war lines, there was a public meeting at the Guildhall to galvanise support. Convened by the Grecians' Association, the packed attendance heard Sid Thomas pay tribute to the efforts of Norman Kendall in getting the Association off the ground: the birth of the organisation had been 'a wonderful thing'. Besides boosting club finances, interest was being stimulated in the surrounding area. With the club's expenditure for the coming year likely to reach £12,000, an average home-gate receipt of £600 was needed. That would only be achieved if support from outside Exeter could be harnessed.

Action from a public trial at the Park

Source: © *Express & Echo*, 23 August 1946

In his *Football Express* column of 31 August 1946 – his first since 1939 – 'Nomad' outlined the transformation that had taken place at the Park in the 12 months since the end of the war:

The big bank behind the far goal has been terraced in concrete to bring about the best improvement that has taken place for the spectators' comfort in my experience. The re-stepping of the covered-in popular side is nearly finished at the time of writing, and the amount of work done is almost incredible having regard to the derelict look the ground wore a twelve-month ago. Tidy terraces have replaced overgrown slopes, which might have been a section of jungle country. Guns, ammunition dumps and other legacies of wartime occupation have been removed. The playing pitch, used as a drill ground for the troops early in the war, and then as a park for heavy military vehicles until more sensible counsels put an end to that, is in surprisingly good trim. Perfect, no, but a lot better than could have been expected, having regard to the rough usage to which it was subjected over the war years.

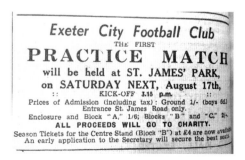

Advert for a practice match at St James' Park

Source: © *Express & Echo*, 16 August 1946

Exeter City Football Club
THE FIRST
PRACTICE MATCH
will be held at ST. JAMES' PARK,
on SATURDAY NEXT, August 17th,
KICK-OFF **3.15** p.m.
Prices of Admission (including tax): Ground 1/- (boys 6d)
Entrance St. James Road only.
Enclosure and Block "A," 1/6; Blocks "B" and "C," 2/-
ALL PROCEEDS WILL GO TO CHARITY.
Season Tickets for the Centre Stand (Block "B") at £4 are now available
An early application to the Secretary will secure the best seats

|| There is a neatness about St James's Park which has transformed this compact ground into one
|| of the best in the Southern Section. Definitely the ground is first-class.

In the pressure to get the ground ready, the players had volunteered to do a couple of hours' work each afternoon. Tasks included the job of 'laying sleepers and getting the covered popular side terracing in shape'. There'd also be a new Well Street entrance to the Big Bank.

Ground safety, following the Bolton tragedy, was a priority. Clubs were advised to refer to the report on the disaster. Admission to any enclosure ought to be 'scientifically calculated'. True, the main focus was on far bigger grounds than St James' Park but even for City's two practice games in August 1946, with parts of the ground resembling a building site, special crowd arrangements were announced. Later, in a programme article for City's home game against Bournemouth on 28 September, 'Grecian' informed readers that in the event of City drawing one of the big clubs in the

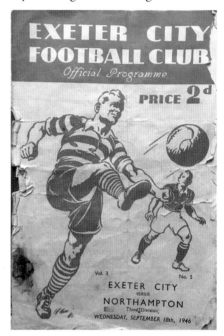

Cup, for the first time in the club's history, admission would be all ticket. The directors had discussed this with the police, ahead of the FA announcing that a ticket-only policy might be enforced for local derbies and Cup ties. Around this time, to avoid congestion at the turnstiles, 'change' boxes were provided at the St James Road and Well Street entrances.

In the same issue of the programme for the Bournemouth game, there's a whole page devoted to the Grecians' Association – 'for the support of Exeter City FC'. We learn that a public-address system at the Park, paid for entirely by the Association, was in operation: 'We do not intend to use the equipment for the diffusion of music but solely for announcements concerning crowd control, team changes, etc.' It was the safety issue, again. As well as a report of the fortnightly whist drives held at the Polsloe and Priory Conservative club, the winner of the regular '2d. on the Ball' draw was announced.

To add to the fund-raising, away support was being encouraged, with details of train fares and itineraries provided. Many of today's programme items were already in place back then.

In November 1946, 'Nomad' reported that plans had been drawn up to terrace the St James Road end. Once the necessary licence had been received, the work would be done in sections. The terracing cost of £600 was met by the Grecians' Association. Besides providing money for ground improvements and broadcasting equipment, the Association purchased training appliances for the club. What's more, its gift of £1,000 in 1948 enabled the club to buy a house in Old Tiverton Road and the land adjoining it. This meant accommodation would be available for players who needed it and an entrance could be constructed behind the Big Bank end. By June 1948, the Association had donated £2,400 to the club.

All in all, in manager George Roughton's six post-war seasons with City, while the average League placing was just below mid-table, League gates at the Park averaged over 9,000. The lowest point was a record 0-9 League loss away to Notts County, in October 1948, followed, several weeks later, by trouble on the pitch at a home match against Watford (2-1). Objects – apple cores and orange peel – were thrown at the referee after an Exeter player had been dismissed. The FA ordered warning notices to be posted at the Park, and the player, Johnston, was suspended for a week. 'The warning,' said Sid Thomas, 'must be taken seriously, because a repetition of what occurred might lead to a closure of the ground.'

Away from Division Three South, in those six seasons there were two Cup runs of note, both to the Fourth Round. The best of these was in the 1950–51 season.

24

By ticket only

O N Thursday 11 January 1951, the day after City had beaten Grimsby Town 4-2 in a Third Round Cup replay at the Park, 'Nomad', writing in the *Express & Echo*, memorably put the achievement into perspective:

This was Exeter City's greatest day for years. The biggest attendance since the Sunderland replay 20 years ago acclaimed the victory, and so loud was the roar which went up when the City scored their first goal that a Whipton resident heard it nearly two miles away.

Some 18,000 had crammed into the ground. With kick-off approaching, 'there was hardly an inch of room beneath the covered shed [perhaps this is where the name Cowshed originated] on the popular side, and the Big Bank behind the far end goal was also filling rapidly'. In the stand, there was a good number of managers on scouting missions.

No sooner had the game ended than the City directors were meeting to discuss arrangements for the prize: a Fourth Round tie against First Division Chelsea at St James' Park. The match, it was decided, would be all ticket – the first in the club's history. Prices would be raised to match those for Argyle's recent tie against Wolves: 10s for the grandstand, 4s for the enclosure, 3s the ground. The directors, after initial euphoria, found themselves in a quandary. Given the gate for Grimsby, how could demand for tickets best be met?

'Operation All Ticket' didn't start well. The following week, on Wednesday, there were 'angry scenes' at the Park. Hundreds of supporters had gone there having read in the *Express & Echo* that tickets would be on sale but a notice had been put up saying none would be sold. The reason was that the night before, Chelsea had decided to take up part of their allocation; consequently, the 2,500 tickets due to be sold at St James' Park were forwarded to them. Secretary George Gilbert explained that it had been too late to reallocate tickets from the other selling centres in Exeter. At these places, in the snaking queues, there were complaints about the way in which ticketing was being organised.

Queueing for tickets at St James' Park, 1951
Source: © *Express & Echo*, 23 January 1951

During the forthcoming distribution, thousands were left disappointed. Many, counting themselves as 'regular supporters', had particular reason to feel aggrieved. In a letter to the *Express & Echo*, a group of 'Disgruntled Supporters' protested at the way in which tickets had been allocated. A voucher system, they felt, would have meant fairer treatment for regular matchgoers. At City's home League game against Leyton Orient, on the Saturday after the Grimsby Cup tie, vouchers could have been distributed unannounced. Tickets could also have been made available at the reserve match on the following Saturday. As for the timing of the sales, workers were effectively debarred from queuing.

The last tickets – returned ones – went on sale at the Park on the evening of Tuesday 23 January. Determined not to miss out, some had been queuing for as long as nine hours. 'Nomad' witnessed the event:

> Postman George French is Exeter's luckiest football fan. This member of the G.P.O. team which plays in the Mid-Week League is the holder of the last ticket sold for the City and Chelsea Cup-tie.
>
> His wife bought it for him, last night, and she waited four hours in a queue which stretched from the Well-street entrance to the City football ground to the top of St. James's-road.
>
> Nearly 2,000 people were in the line, and all were after the 500 tickets which were on sale.
>
> 'My husband will be delighted,' said Mrs. French. 'He has tried over and over to get a ticket. No one likes his football more, and he will be playing for the Post Office team to-day.'
>
> The final sale began at 7 p.m. Thirty-six minutes later every ticket had been sold. The fortunate went away happy. The unlucky went disappointedly on their homeward way. But there were no demonstrations.
>
> First in the queue, Mrs. E.R. Verner and her 13-year-old son Trevor, arrived at 10.15 in the morning. 'Was it worth it?' he was asked. 'You bet,' said the smiling Trevor.
>
> In orderly batches, the Cup-tie customers were admitted into the ground. Each paid his or her 3s. Mr. Cyril Bartlett [member of the Grecians' Association executive committee] handed out the ticket. Exeter City director Mr. Leslie Seward took the cash. Manager George Roughton and Mr. Alfred Wills marshalled the ticket seekers.
>
> Busmen, soldiers, airmen and schoolboys were represented. There were industrial workers and clerks, but the majority in the queue were women.
>
> The tickets were strictly on the ration of one to each person. Another rule was that no child under 12 years would be served, and every schoolboy was closely questioned on that score. 'How old are you, son?' was the stock question. 'Thirteen, sir,' was the common reply. Those lads certainly had the answers.
>
> Before and after the sale there were other queues. A nearby fish and chip shop did record business, and satisfied the appetites of hundreds whose main concern was with Chelsea buns.

Chelsea had been entitled to 25 per cent of the ground capacity – and of their 5,000 allocation, as well as 2,500 ground tickets, they had taken 500 tickets for the enclosure and 350 for the stand. According to 'Nomad', a 'substantial portion' of that allotment had 'filtered back to Devon'. Some City supporters had managed to get tickets by writing to Stamford Bridge.

As the tie approached, 'Nomad' offered three 'hints' for those lucky enough to have a ticket. With a crowd of 20,000, everyone would get a good view and there'd be no need for trouble if the requests were obeyed:

> Spectators must enter by the gate indicated on their ticket, and leave by the same exit. Onlookers are asked to respond to the directions of the police and stewards, who will supervise crowd-packing. Finally, be at the ground as early as possible.

It was five years after the Bolton disaster, and City were in the spotlight. Police officers had made inspections of the Park; 'walkie-talkie apparatus' would be used. After Bolton, the Home Office had recommended allowing 15 square inches per person; at St James' Park, the capacity was based on 18. No chances were being taken.

(Left) Exeter City
official programme
for the Chelsea Cup
tie, 27 January 1951

Source: Dave Fisher collection,
Westcountry Studies Library,
Devon Heritage Centre

(Right) Action from
the City v Chelsea
Cup tie

Source: © *Express & Echo*, 27
January 1951

A section of the
crowd at the
Chelsea Cup tie

Source: © *Express & Echo*, 29
January 1951

What follows is an extract from Nomad's *Football Express* report on the day of the game, Saturday 27 January:

Six hours before the great kick-off, a small queue of enthusiasts was waiting outside St. James's Park to-day. They were the first arrivals of the advance guard of the 20,000 crowd which later packed into the ground for the City and Chelsea Cup-tie.

Men, women and children from every town, village and hamlet in Devon were joined by hundreds more from Somerset, Cornwall and Wiltshire.

The Chelsea contingent, numbering 2,000-odd, travelled by rail and road and most of them were inside the ground in plenty of time.

Relieved of beat work by members of the Special Constabulary, regular members of the City Police Force were drafted for special duty in and around St. James's Park. Under the charge of the Chief Constable (Mr. A.E. Rowsell), more than eighty police officers, reinforced by scores of voluntary stewards, saw that the crowd was properly packed.

Quiet, Then –

Cup-tie fans responded to the request to 'Come early,' so that at 2 o'clock more than 15,000 were on the terraces. There were no signs of disorder.

It was a quiet crowd. There was a strange absence of pre-Cup-tie excitement until the main body of the Chelsea contingent arrived. They marched to the ground and were headed by two stalwarts who carried a chromium banner on which the word 'Chelsea' was surmounted by a beautifully-modelled Chelsea Pensioner.

With the consent of the police, a running commentary was broadcast by Mr. Leslie Seward, an Exeter City director. The commentary was relayed by wires to loud-speakers in Powderham-crescent, and several thousand City supporters, unable to get a Cup-tie ticket, appreciated the service.

Selections by the British Railways Southern Region Band, and community singing under the direction of Mr. Billy Wheeler, were enjoyed by those inside the ground.

On the following Monday, summing up the 'thrill-packed' tie (1-1), 'Nomad' discussed the two inconsistent decisions that went against City. The first was when centre-forward Archie Smith was flagged for offside. He'd gone on to score. Having allowed play to go on, referee Carter, after 'many seconds', agreed with his linesman – and curiously then gave the free-kick where Smith had scored from:

Although there appeared nothing wrong with the goal, the linesman was better positioned than any of the critics in the Press row. His decision was definite and promptly made.

But so was another which came soon afterwards. A City forward was impeded from behind, and the offence occurred a yard or more inside the penalty area. Persistent flagging eventually attracted the attention of the referee, who this time shook his head and allowed play to continue.

Why, Mr. Carter, support the linesman on the first occasion, and ignore him the next time?

A third unlucky break came to the City when Angus Mackay, their best forward while he remained sound, was the victim of an ankle injury which inevitably curbed his effectiveness for more than half of this keenly-contested tie in which First Division Chelsea had little in hand of their Southern Section opponents.

For the gallant City strove valiantly to match by dogged determination the superior craft of the men in blue. Exeter merited the right to the replay, which became theirs when Duggie Regan, four minutes from time, equalised the goal which Williams had scored in the 32nd minute.

Gate receipts were a record £3,760. In the replay, on the following Wednesday, City were beaten 2-0 in front of over 46,000.

Early in the season, League rivalry had been renewed with Argyle after a lapse of 21 years. City had won 1-0 at Home Park. Now, one week after the Chelsea tie, there was another all-ticket crowd of 20,000 at St James' Park for the return Devon derby. It was estimated that almost half of the attendance came from outside Exeter.

'Nomad' was in no doubt that the City–Argyle game on Saturday 3 February 'eclipsed City's latest Cup battles' at the Park:

All the ingredients were blended into this feast of football entertainment at St. James's Park. Exeter City's doggedness, Plymouth Argyle's poise, several dramatic goalmouth incidents, and many pleasing constructive movements made Saturday's Devon 'derby' one of the best in the long series of meetings between these county rivals.

It was a thrill-a-minute contest, with the City 3-2 winners of the best game seen at Exeter this season. Better than the Chelsea Cup-tie because the tempo was faster, superior to the Grimsby match because fewer mistakes were made, this City-Argyle clash was rightly praised by members of both clubs.

Supporting Manager George Roughton's tribute that the game would have done credit to First Division sides was Argyle director Archie Cload's comment that he never wished to see a better match.

City had come back from 0-2 down. Perhaps there'd been a hint of offside about the winning goal but no one, with the exception of Plymouth supporters, could begrudge City that break. In both of the Chelsea games, decisions had gone against them.

The Norman Kendall
Gate on Old Tiverton
Road, *c.*1965
Source: Dave Fisher collection,
Westcountry Studies Library,
Devon Heritage Centre

Later in the day there'd been a 'Devon derby dance' at the Civic Hall, with dancing to
Norman Pincott and his orchestra until 11.30 p.m. Admission was 3s at the door. The City
players were invited to attend. It was the latest fund-raising initiative organised by the Grecians'
Association.

The Association continued to offer practical support to the 'City Club'. Membership had
reached a high of 1,130, and there was a balance of over £400. Branches had been established
outside Exeter, such as the one at Exmouth.

In October 1951, in his *Football Express* 'Soccer Survey' column, 'Nomad' listed the annual
amounts the Association had handed over to the club. Since the war, Exeter City FC's overall
profit of £3,921 was almost entirely due to the Association's contributions. A 'substantial part'
of the payments was used for ground improvements. The latest of these was an entrance in
Old Tiverton Road, opened in January 1951; the 'Norman Kendall Gate' was named after the
Association's president. In a separate project, funding was provided for a 'Grecian Gate' in Well
Street. In the 1952 close season, financed by the Association, a treatment room 'equipped with
the most modern machines' was constructed adjacent to the home dressing room.

Inevitably, when a new phase in the Park's development was launched in 1953, it was the
Grecians' Association that provided the all-important backing.

25

Under the lights

ITH Christmas 1952 just around the corner, 'Nomad' had a scoop for City followers. He was able to reveal that it wouldn't be long before they'd be watching 'floodlit Soccer' at the Park. 'City board favourable to floodlit idea game' ran the banner headline to his *Football Express* column of 20 December.

Player-manager Norman Kirkman had seen how popular football under lights was while at Southampton; he'd played in the club's first floodlit exhibition in October 1950. An increasing number of clubs were installing the necessary equipment and there was a feeling that it could work well in Exeter. While taking for granted the question of funding, 'Nomad' outlined why it was important for the club to act:

> If, and when, it is decided to install the necessary apparatus, the directors will no doubt receive the full backing of the Grecians' Association, whose executive committee would see in a floodlit St James's Park a lasting memorial to the Association's work.
>
> Matches under the light would provide additional entertainment for supporters. Club finances would benefit. Trade would receive a boost. Players would be able to earn extra money.
>
> For the signs are that a Floodlight League of Southern Clubs is nearer at hand than most people imagine.

But before that ever got off the ground, it was floodlight friendlies that were pulling the crowds in. Later in the column, opportunely, 'Nomad' announced that City had received an offer to play a representative side from Trinidad.

St Luke's College alumnus, now FA secretary, Sir Stanley Rous had contacted the club. The request was for City to put out a side against the Trinidadians at the start of the following season. The City board replied they'd do all they could to keep the midweek date free. The prospect of such a fixture provided impetus for the lights scheme. When it finally took off, the floodlight fixtures at the Park against overseas teams were an added attraction. It's these fixtures, in the 1950s and 1960s, that are the focus of this chapter.

Lights were used for the first time at St James' Park not long after the war. On the evening of Thursday 31 October 1946 part-time pros and amateurs trained under arc lights supplied by the Grecians' Association. The experiment was reportedly 'a big success'. Presumably these training sessions were repeated. But it wasn't until the early 1950s that clubs, taking the lead from Southampton, began investing in lights.

In February 1953, the City directors, having kept a close watch on tests with lights at Home Park back in the autumn, were already making plans for the opening floodlit match at St James' Park. As 'Nomad' had anticipated, the Grecians' Association was sponsoring the installation. What better than a Devon derby to introduce football under lights in Exeter?

On Monday 2 March, the eve of the game, 'Nomad' gave details of the 40 1,000-watt lights that comprised the installation. Final tests were taking place that evening:

> There are seven lights on each side of the ground focussed directly on to the touch lines. Twenty-six more lights will floodlight the pitch, and are so synchronised that there are unlikely to be any shadows. ...

The lights are little over 30 feet above ground level. Two separate mains from the South-Western Electricity Board's supply will feed each side of the ground.

A member of the firm Messrs Hucklebridge and Son, who carried out the installation, said to-day that the work began in mid-January. The installation was of galvanised steel conduit, and an additional advantage was that every two lights would be controlled independently by a switch and fuse.

Those in charge of the work commented that the view would be perfect from anywhere in the ground. But 24 hours later, not for the first time that season, a big occasion ended in disappointment. Fog in the hours before kick-off meant the game had to be postponed. The hundreds of rival supporters didn't even make it into the ground.

Image of the first floodlit game at St James' Park played on Monday 9 March 1953

Source: © *Football Express*, 14 March 1953

The all-ticket match finally went ahead on the following Monday, 9 March, with a 7.30 kick-off. Anyone wanting to buy a ticket before the game could do so from one of the kiosks outside St James' Park – 'and enter through special turnstiles'. It was the first Football League ground in Devon to be permanently floodlit. 'Nomad' in his 'Floodlit Commentary' enjoyed the opportunity to pun:

The lights were brilliant. Plymouth Argyle dazzled. Exeter City were eclipsed. Three sentences tell the story of last night's first floodlight football match at St. James's Park, when 8,130 customers paid £908, and saw Argyle win by three goals to nil.

No fault could be found with the installation. Play could be followed easily from all parts of the ground, and the onlookers delighted in the many rhythmic movements that Argyle produced against opposition of inferior quality.

The result was correct. Argyle were the complete Soccer machine, compact in defence and constructive elsewhere. Exeter rarely possessed a spark of ability.

The clash between the Devon rivals was illuminating in that it spotlighted the difference between good Second Division football and poor Third Division Soccer.

The Mayor of Exeter was there to switch on the lights, and the installation was formally handed over to Exeter City Football Club by the chairman of the Grecians' Association. Sid Thomas spoke about the friendship between City and Argyle over the years, and said he hoped one day City would be joining Argyle in Division Two.

Before the season was out, the issue of clashes between sports played on the same night was raised. In his column of Saturday 18 April, 'Nomad' referred to the previous Monday when darts, football and speedway were competing for spectators. The attendance at the County Ground for the Falcons' fixture was much greater than at the Park where Fred Davey and Angus Mackay had a joint testimonial game. City's preferred day for floodlit games was a Tuesday but due to the end-of-season fixture overload, the club had no option but to use Mondays.

And so to the Trinidad Touring XI. They were not the first group of foreign footballers to visit St James' Park. In August 1945, a Norwegian Air Force XI had played there, followed in November 1947 by a team from the Polish Navy. In the past, in the decades before the Second World War, it was more a case of British clubs – both amateur and professional – doing the travelling, as a way of stimulating the development of the game abroad, as Exeter City had done in Argentina and Brazil (1914), and in Holland (1925). Now, as 'Nomad' pointed out: 'under expert teaching of British coaches, the foreigners have caught up with and, in some cases, overtaken our own sides'.

On Wednesday 16 September 1953, Trinidad surprised many in the crowd of just under 2,000 at St James' Park. City, playing in blue and white, had taken the lead after just 15 seconds; the

visitors drew level ten minutes after the break. And 1-1 was how it finished. For 'Nomad', in the *Express & Echo*, honours had been 'rightly shared':

> Speed, intelligence, ball-craft and the will to work – the touring side had all these qualities. The crowd's prolonged applause at the end of an entertaining struggle was a fitting tribute to a team whose members played and enjoyed their football.

The headline in the *Express & Echo* was: 'Well Played Trinidad!' The attendance figure, however, was disappointing. A measure of the unpredictability of a gate at the Park was the figure for a Southern League game a few weeks before: 4,428 were there to see the reserves play Yeovil on Saturday 22 August. There can't have been many bigger home gates for City's second string.

On 30 January 1954, 'Nomad' reported on a 'floodlit double' at the Park; his *Football Express* column had become 'Soccer by Lionel Wotton'. First, an Army XI, on tour in the West Country, would visit on Wednesday 10 February; a week later there'd be 'world famous' opponents in the shape of Vienna FC. The Austrians were known as the 'football factory' on account of the number of internationals they produced. For 'Nomad', it was a chance for local fans to see 'all that is best in Continental Soccer'.

The visit of 'FC Wien' was advertised in the official programme for City's game against the Army FA XI as a 'Grand Floodlit Attraction'; prices were stand 4s, enclosure 3s, ground 1s 9d, boys 9d. Season-ticket holders were able to reserve their usual seat. A record crowd for a match under the lights was anticipated.

There was one folded sheet for the 'FC Wien' programme. In the 'Club Chatter' notes, reference was made to the pioneers who launched Exeter City as a professional organisation in 1908: could those 'stalwarts' ever have imagined City would be meeting Continental opponents under lights in 1954? One of them, Sid Thomas, was almost certainly at the game; as for 90-year-old Norman Kendall … perhaps he made it along. The 6,050 who were at St James' Park saw a goalless draw. 'A fitting result,' lamented 'Nomad', 'it emphasised the finishing ineptitude of the rival forward lines.'

One year later, two more Austrian sides visited the Park. First up, on Monday 14 February 1955, was Grazer Sportklub. 'Nomad' described the conditions as 'wholly unsuited to football. … Pools of water lay on the surface. The ball played all manner of unexpected tricks, and the game was a travesty of Soccer.'

BLINDED WITH SCIENCE!

'Blinded with Science!' A Stil cartoon

Source: © *Football Express*, 23 October 1954

It was also a flop financially: an attendance of 1,430 produced receipts of £140 4s. For the record, City won 4-1. While victory was 'richly deserved', 'Nomad' 'felt sorry for the Grazer side, unused as they are at home to the sort of pitch they had to play on last evening'.

On the following Monday, 21 February, there was adverse weather of a different kind. City's opponents were FC Colombia from Vienna. This is how 'Nomad' described it:

> Watching floodlit football on the snow is a he-man's pastime, and well the thousand spectators knew it at St. James's Park, last night. They shivered as they looked on, Spartans who paid to endure discomfort.
>
> Two inches of snow covered the playing pitch when the City and Colombia game began. More fell during the play, and the miracle is that this soccer-cum-ice hockey show ran its scheduled course.

The headline above Nomad's *Echo* report: 'Exeter City won this ballet on ice 4-2.'

The previous October, 'Nomad' had commented on the difficulties in arranging floodlight matches in the 1954–55 season. Nineteen clubs had been approached by City, almost all had declined. They'd either received too many offers, or the guarantee they wanted was too large. Of the overseas ones, Racing Club de Paris had agreed to play two games in England and no more; Simmering from Vienna wanted a £400 guarantee, or 50 per cent of the gate. Reportedly, matches under lights at St James' Park had already produced gross receipts of £5,200 but then there were the guarantees and other expenses to be deducted.

'Nomad' made a contrast between two games in the autumn of 1954 to illustrate that football under lights was 'a chancey business'. A crowd of 6,945 had paid to see Torquay's friendly against Birmingham, while at Aldershot, there were 646 for the visit of Bury.

It was just as well Exeter City had rejected Bury's offer to come to Devon; Bury had wanted a guarantee of £300.

At St James' Park, in the early 1960s, there was another flurry of floodlit games that featured foreign sides. In the 1961–62 season, the opposition came from

EXETER CITY FOOTBALL CLUB

Floodlight Match

EXETER CITY

versus

GRAZER SPORTKLUB
AUSTRIA

ST. JAMES' PARK
EXETER

Monday, February 14th, 1955
Kick-off 7.30 p.m.

★

OFFICIAL PROGRAMME 2d.

Programme v Grazer Sportklub, 14 February 1955

Source: © ECFC. From Dave Fisher collection, Westcountry Studies Library, Devon Heritage Centre

Bolivia, Yugoslavia and West Germany. Against Bolivian champions CAR – Club Always Ready – from La Paz, on Thursday 26 October, City won an 'attractive' encounter 3-1. The report in the *Express & Echo* was penned by Tony Court; he'd taken over from Lionel Wotton ('Nomad') following Wotton's death in May 1955. City by now were playing in Division Four:

> It was a triumph for the Fourth Division side against glamorous South American opposition who have wiped the board with some European clubs in the past few weeks.
>
> C.A.R. pulled out most of the Continental tricks – right down to shirt-pulling – but though they were often faster and sharper to the tackle than the City, they were nowhere as direct or effective in front of goal.
>
> They used several substitutes to keep their team as fresh as possible, while the City pulled in two – Arnold Mitchell and Peter Rutley [a 15-year-old apprentice].

The attendance was 5,004. One month later, Wednesday 22 November, OFK Belgrade, showing 'speed and sting', defeated City 4-2 in front of 3,548. OFK, after all, had included six internationals in their line-up. In the official programme, in 'Club Chatter', Maurice Golesworthy wrote authoritatively and extensively about football in Yugoslavia; he had an impressive knowledge of the game, both at home and abroad:

> If what we have seen of Yugoslavian football in their two post-war internationals at Wembley is a fair reflection of the style of football adopted by most of their senior clubs, then, in one respect, our opponents this evening will probably resemble our South American visitors. I refer to the Yugoslavians' liking for the close-passing game.

This, he went on to say, was combined with 'a reluctance to shoot'. Usually, too many passes were taken inside the penalty area. Golesworthy then offered another possibility: 'if they do pack shooting strength then we may be sure that they will present much keener opposition than did our friends from South America'. And so it proved.

Finally, on Thursday 1 March 1962, there was a visit from FC Kickers Offenbach. The crowd, we're told, 'got their money's worth'; if only more had turned up. For Tony Court, the figure of 2,498 was 'a pitifully poor attendance and response for a match like this'. Drawing 1-1, the visitors had struggled to impose themselves:

> Not that the Germans were a poor team by any strength of the imagination. But they didn't quite turn out to be the world-beaters that everyone expected – and though the City had to play up to their standard, they rose to the style and the occasion very well.
>
> Some of the Kickers' midfield football was delicate and delightful; some of their attacks sharp and dangerous. They worked a close-packing defensive system, and they had a great goalkeeper in Ottamar Groh – but at the end the City had given as good as they had received.

Gate-wise, in the 1950s and 1960s, by far the best-attended floodlight game at St James' Park was on Wednesday 2 December 1964 for the visit of Arsenal.

The FA had insisted that City improve the quality of their lights after complaints from visiting clubs and match officials. The friendly against Arsenal marked the turning on of a new £8,000 floodlighting system. Maurice Golesworthy began his programme notes reverentially, by referring to the pride City could take in Arsenal honouring them by putting out their First Division XI. He went on to say how fitting it was that the Gunners were there that evening given that one of their stars of the 1930s was 'the greatest player ever produced by Exeter'. That player, Cliff Bastin, was guest of honour at the match.

Before the action, the crowd of 11,507 was entertained by the band of the Royal Marines, 'those graceful keep-fit ladies' and 'a beat group'. For the 'City Club', the result (1-4) was immaterial; the encouraging turnout was what mattered. Towards the end of his notes, Golesworthy made a plea to the fans:

> We now have a first-class floodlighting installation (for those who are interested, there are 90 lamps totalling 180 kilowatts) and providing that you show by your support this evening that you really want to see top-class football in Exeter, then the club are prepared to embark on a programme of such matches, inviting many of the biggest clubs from this country and abroad to show their paces at St. James Park. It's up to you and your friends.

Six months before the 1966 World Cup, City Secretary Dick Miller – son of former City skipper Charlie – succeeded in bringing a leading Czechoslovak side to the Park.

Slovan Bratislava came to Exeter with two players who'd represented Czechoslovakia in the 1962 World Cup Final in Chile: centre-half Popluhar and goalkeeper Schrojf. Along with these, there were four other internationals in the side that took on City on Monday 6 December 1965. That proved to be the spur for City to raise their game. Tony Court, in his *Echo* write-up, explained why they were able to beat their 'star-studded' opponents 4-1:

> Slovan showed their class in their intricate inter-passing and running off the ball.
>
> But their style also meant plenty of space and opportunity for the City to play some football themselves – and they took great advantage of it.

Off the field, however, not for the first time, the turnstiles needed to be busier for the match to be profitable.

Dick Miller's reaction to the 5,000 gate was reported in the *Express & Echo*. Receipts barely covered the £650 guarantee that had been agreed with Slovan:

> We were pleased with the game, but not the attendance. I know that the weather was against us, but we really need a little better support than this if we are to consider any more matches like this.

Floodlit football, as 'Nomad' had noted in 1954, was a gamble. By the 1970s, the novelty of games against foreign teams at the Park, it appears, had worn off.

Perhaps pre-season was a more preferable slot for these games? And that's what Exeter City tried by organising a friendly against Dutch side DVV Go-Ahead from Deventer on 7 August 1970. The result was a 4-0 defeat for the Grecians, and just 3,334 were there to see it.

26

The European champions

NEW floodlights were not the only reason for a celebration at St James' Park in 1964. On Saturday 25 April, for the first time in City's history, promotion was achieved. The point at Workington in the final game of the 1963–64 Division Four season was, according to Tony Court, 'probably the most valuable point gained in the history of the club'.

'Hurrah, City Are Promoted!'

Source: © *Express & Echo*, 25 April 1964

Exeter City had finally shaken off the tag of having a 'near-triumph' League history. Twice promotion had fractionally eluded the Grecians, in the 1932–33 and 1958–59 seasons. Mostly though, since becoming a founder member of the Third Division in 1920, the focus had often been on fighting for League survival. On seven occasions City had had to seek re-election; the latest being in the 1960–61 season.

Emotion got the better of skipper Arnold Mitchell when he was asked to give a speech after a special dinner at the Carlisle hotel where the team had been staying. He later paid tribute to manager Jack Edwards and to the fans:

Speaking for the players, I think Mr. Edwards must get most of the credit. He has built the team up by using each man to the best advantage and kept us going all the time when we needed encouragement most.

Next comes the tremendous team spirit which has come from the most experienced players and the newest professionals – and the 100 per cent effort which all the lads have put into every game.

And the away support?

After travelling 400 miles, they gave us a great reception. It really made the lads feel good to see them there, and when we heard them shouting it really did something for us on the pitch.

Those fans were cheering as they and the team boarded a train at Carlisle at 9.30 p.m. And they cheered at Crewe three hours later as the connection to Exeter was made.

On Sunday morning, 26 April, the scenes at St David's were reminiscent of those that greeted the players on their return from Sunderland in 1931. The fans who'd travelled back with the team were joined in Exeter by hundreds more:

> Wearing scarves and rosettes; waving rattles and banners, cheering and shouting, the waiting crowd surged towards the train as it pulled in. They surrounded the players inside and outside the station for about half an hour, cheering for one and then another and carrying placards that read: 'Thanks Banks and all the Ranks' and 'Grand show Exeter, Now Division Two.'

In the *Express & Echo*'s last Football Final edition of the season, Tony Court – before the Workington result was known – singled out the impact made by Alan Banks since his arrival from Cambridge City in October 1963. Banks' 18 goals in 28 games was the sixth fastest scoring rate in City's history. For Court, he was the club's player of the year:

> Not only is he doing the all-important things – getting goals – but he has shown all the qualities that people expect from professional footballers but don't always get.
>
> When Banks gives 100 per cent – and he always does – you can SEE it. You don't have to be told that he was doing his best.
>
> He gives no displays of tantrums, temper, or temperamental exhibitions – yet he still manages to be a personality on the field, and this in itself is a rare enough thing in the Fourth Division.

Along with Banks, three other members of the promotion side – Dermot Curtis, Arnold Mitchell and Graham Rees – have been inducted into Exeter City's Hall of Fame.

During the 1963–64 campaign, a number of season 'bests' included two that were St James' Park related. The record for the fewest home defeats – two – was equalled; and the double had been done over five clubs, a post-war record. More significantly, the average League gate at St James' Park over the course of a season had gone from 4,444 to 7,300.

The home fixtures had been completed with a 6-1 win over Chesterfield watched by 9,449. In the preceding game at the Park, just to add to the suspense, City had lost 3-2 to Bradford Park Avenue. And in the run-in, there'd also been added local interest with two games against Torquay United, who themselves were near the top of the table. On Good Friday, 27 March, there'd been 16,141 at St James' Park for 'a typical 'derby' match that was full of 'petty fouls and misdemeanours'; it was the largest League gate at the ground since the Plymouth game in 1951. The draw, 0-0, was replicated on Easter Monday (1-1) at Plainmoor.

(Left) City fans at the Park at the game v Bradford Park Avenue (2-3) during the promotion run-in
Source: © *Express & Echo,*, 20 April 1964

(Right) 'Perchance?' A cartoon by Stil before the promotion-clincher at Workington
Source: © *Express & Echo*, 25 April 1964

* * *

Four years later, back again in Division Four and struggling, memories of City's Cup history were stirred when the club landed a home tie against Manchester United in Round Three. They'd got there after a 'glorious' Alan Banks goal away to Colchester in the previous round. The 1-0 win took the club further in the competition than they'd been for nine years. It was also the first time two away ties had been won in the same season since the giant-killing run of 1930–31.

As the visit of Manchester United approached, Maurice Golesworthy's programme article on 14 December 1968 caught the mood of expectation, placing the tie in a historical context:

What a fine reward for our efforts – the plum draw of the 3rd Round. Not since the mighty Sunderland came here nearly 38 years ago have we had such a star attraction at St. James Park as Manchester United; indeed, considering that United are the current holders of the European Cup there is no doubt that January 4th will be the most momentous day in the history of Exeter City Football Club.

Way back in 1914 we had Aston Villa here the season after they had won the F.A. Cup and finished runners-up in the First Division, and they came again the following season [in fact it was City who went to Villa Park]. In 1928 we had a visit from Blackburn Rovers when that famous club was on the way to winning the Cup the same season; and in the following year Leeds United were held to a draw on this ground. There have been several other more recent visits from leading First Division clubs, but none of these sides can have included so many world-famous players as the galaxy of stars we shall see here in only three weeks' time.

It would be United's second visit to the Park. In October 1960, a team that included former Grecian Maurice Setters was held to a draw (1-1) there in Round One of the inaugural edition of the Football League Cup. Graham Rees netted first early on for Exeter; the equaliser came late in the game. The replay was 4-1 to United.

On Saturday 4 January 1969, it was the presence of fans from Manchester that provided the theme for the *Express & Echo's* front-page headline: 'Cup Rowdies Roam City'. The report described the scenes at St James' Park:

More than 4,000 Manchester football fans swarmed into Exeter today for the City's biggest sporting occasion for years – the Exeter City v. Manchester United F.A. Cup-tie at St. James's Park this afternoon.

Some, however, jumped on a bus for a free ride on the platform, others followed passers-by, mimicking their walk, and one smashed a bottle on the pavement in Sidwell Street. Girls walking to work came in for plenty of remarks.

The young Manchester fans who roamed the city streets contented themselves mainly with chanting and wandering aimlessly.

The White Ensign outside the Royal Marines' recruiting office in Sidwell Street was hauled down by fans and carried away.

Long before the 3 p.m. kick-off, it was possible to sense the excitement in the air, as the chanting, rattle-waving fans filled the city streets – and the cafes and public houses, where there were ample stocks ready for the 'invasion'.

… Only by their accents and their chants was it possible to tell who were the 'foreigners' among the fans – the regular colours of the two sides are red and white, and so are the scarves and favours of their fans.

EXETER CITY FOOTBALL CLUB

Saturday, 4th January, 1969
F.A. Cup—Third Round
EXETER CITY
Versus
MANCHESTER UNITED
Kick-off 3.00 p.m.

Souvenir Programme   1/-

Programme v Manchester United, Saturday 4 January 1969

Source: © ECFC, from the Grecian Archive, Lewis Jones collection

The police, who had recalled the leave of some of their men, introduced their special traffic arrangements during the morning. Parking was banned within a radius of about 500 yards of the ground. Strictly-controlled parking was allowed further away.

Part of Old Tiverton Road was closed for part of the day to all traffic except buses and the only traffic allowed in St. James's Road, Oxford Road, and Well Street was that calling at houses there.

As well as unruly behaviour, the big game also brought ticket touts or 'spivs' to St James' Park:

> The luck of the draw brought to Exeter not only such soccer immortals as Manchester's Bobby Charlton, George Best, Denis Law, and Nobby Stiles, but unwelcome Manchester spivs with fistfuls of tickets for sale at inflated prices.
>
> And the tickets were in demand – shortly after the spivs arrived yesterday the word went around that they were in town, and ticketless fans were looking for them.
>
> For the City fans among the all-ticket capacity crowd of 18,500 this was the match of the decade [it was the biggest gate at the Park since the 20,193 at the Luton Cup tie in the 59–60 season].
>
> Many of them were optimistic about how Division IV Exeter would fare against Manchester, European champions and World Club Championship runners-up.
>
> … Early in the morning, queues began to form at the main and St. James's road entrances to the ground.
>
> In the streets nearby, Manchester ticket touts were stopping passers-by and offering them tickets.

City fans who'd attended the previous home game – against Southend on 14 December – received a voucher, guaranteeing them a ticket for the match. No wonder over 12,000 turned up, many of whom, having pocketed the voucher, promptly went home. But importantly, unlike the Chelsea tie in 1951, it meant the regular supporters didn't miss out.

Decades later, Alan Banks recalled the hours before the game – and noticing some original vantage points supporters had found at the Park:

> We had a pre-match meal – which was very unusual – at the Imperial Hotel, now Wetherspoons. Arriving at the ground, the crowds were so dense we had difficulty getting to the stadium entrance. The dressing room was quite calm and jolly, all of us getting to grips with the fact that we were going out to play the European champions. Once out on the pitch, we could see the trees at both ends of the Big Bank were laden with supporters hanging on to the branches.

One or two of the older supporters present might have brought to mind images of the Argyle games in the 1920s when fans took up some precarious positions overlooking the ground.

A 16-page souvenir programme cost 1s. Pen pictures of the Exeter players were followed by Maurice Golesworthy's feature. It began by underlining exactly what the presence of the opposing XI meant for Exeter City and their fans:

> This is without doubt the most notable event ever to take place at St. James Park. In the past we have seen 10 First Division sides in Cup games on this ground, but never before have we had the privilege of welcoming such an illustrious team as Manchester United – current holders of the European Cup.
>
> We have no wish to embarrass Manchester United by piling on the superlatives, although there is nothing we could say here that has not been said many times over when ringing the praises of this the most dedicated of all football clubs. But I wonder if the United and the supporters who are with them today appreciate what the visit of such a team means to the football fans in this part of the country, the majority of whom so seldom have the opportunity of watching top-class players in action except on television.

Later in the publication, the Cup games against Sunderland and Chelsea were recalled. Finally, among the United pen pictures there were reminders of the calibre of the opposition: Best, 'a player with exceptional skill'; Charlton, 'can be rated amongst the all-time greats of World football'; Law, 'has scored more F.A. Cup goals than any post-war player'.

The *Express & Echo*'s reporter at St James' Park was Tony Phillips. His write-up of the first half was headed 'Banks shocks United with goal in 16 minutes'; Fitzpatrick equalised just before the interval. There was brief reference to the atmosphere – and those touting tickets:

Within 15 minutes of the gates being opened, something like 2,000 people were in the ground. They were chanting and it was a fantastic sight for St. James's Park.

Outside, the ticket spivs were asking £3 for ground tickets.

Both teams received a reception when they arrived at the ground about an hour before the kick-off.

The capacity crowd were entertained by the Devon band and drums of the Wessex Volunteers.

The black market for tickets collapsed outside the ground, well before the start of the game. Spivs suddenly found themselves out of business.

What follows are Alan Banks' memories of the game and what the players did afterwards to unwind:

I am sure we all enjoyed the game. I know I did, especially after scoring the first goal. I feel we all raised our game to match our opponents. My personal feelings were of wonder and joy at being on the same pitch as Best, Charlton, Law and Stiles etc. I cannot remember being over impressed with them that day. They were the opposition and we were trying to play the best football we could in an effort to beat them.

I do remember after I scored Bobby Charlton gave his fellow players a rollicking using some very choice language. I cannot remember any banter between City and United players, and we did not speak after the game. But Matt Busby came into our dressing room after the game and said 'Well played lads', which was a nice thing to do.

In those days, there was no after-the-game hospitality and we just took ourselves off to the Greyhound Pub in Sidwell Street which was full of our supporters who were very surprised to see us and would not let us buy a drink.

On the Monday after the game, which United went on to win 3-1 with a Newman own goal and a goal from Kidd, Tony Phillips reflected on City's 'brave show':

Exeter gave United a fight and a fright. The First Division club were a worried side for a time – they admitted this afterwards in the dressing room.

Manager Sir Matt Busby said: 'I thought Exeter did very well. They had us frightened for a little while. These are always nasty matches for us.'

Skipper Bobby Charlton: 'As we expected, Exeter played hard early on. We could easily have come unstuck, and Exeter had us worried for a time. But we just kept pegging away, and it came right for us.'

Perhaps the outcome would have been different had City not had a goal disallowed for hand ball after 26 minutes. From the press box, Phillips thought it 'looked legal enough' and the linesman appeared to agree. The result apart, for City Chairman Leslie Kerslake, in a tribute to the spectators, 'overall … everything went satisfactorily'. There'd been no crowd segregation.

On the fiftieth anniversary, the game was remembered in various ways. In December 2018, Alan Banks attended a meeting of the Senior Reds for an afternoon of reminiscing.

Alan Banks with a cutting from 1969
Source: Photograph by Martin Weiler at ECFC Senior Reds meeting, December 2018

The following month, there was a special feature in the match programme. Then, after an appeal to fans, items of memorabilia were collected for future display in the new Exeter City Football Club Museum room.

27

Keep off the pitch

TWO seasons after the Manchester United game, one of the first editions of a revamped City official matchday programme – costing 5p – featured none other than the club's head groundsman on the cover. For the Aldershot League game, on a Wednesday evening in November 1970, there was a photo, framed by a red rosette, of Sonny Clarke.

Inside, a new feature – 'Front Cover Story' – focused on Sonny's '18 years' at the club. He was described as being 'part of the fixtures and fittings at St James' Park'. In the past, as many as seven apprentices had assisted him; in the absence of a roller, he'd get them to pull a railway sleeper across the pitch. Later, cost-cutting left Sonny with one helper. The fact that the players trained away from St James' Park meant that he had 'every opportunity of producing the goods for match days'. Back in 1956, one of his tasks had been to level the orchard behind the Big Bank terracing to produce an area where the players could train.

If the '18 years' service is correct, Sonny was already working at the Park when he was appointed groundsman in the 1955 close season, perhaps on an unofficial basis or in a different role. A note in the first programme of the 1955–56 season stated that there'd been 'much work' done on the playing pitch; the club was grateful for the assistance provided by volunteers. And while welcoming 'Mr. L. (Sonny) Clarke' to his new post, it was reported that City's Irish full-back, Theo Foley, would be his assistant.

Often, throughout the history of Exeter City, ground development and improving on existing facilities have taken a back seat. In the past, funds were pressingly needed elsewhere. Sometimes only if a sufficient number of supporters demanded it was action taken. A typical example was reported by 'Nomad' in October 1953:

> City supporters who stood in discomfort on the broken terraces at the far end of the covered popular bank were justified in grousing. Grumbles reached the board room. The directors are acting. A load of old railway sleepers has been delivered, and repair work is in course of operation.

Occasionally, there were some jobs that couldn't be put off. In August 1955, the programme's 'City Chatter' included the following:

> The payment of transfer fees and the purchase of additional houses for our married players has meant that ground improvements during the close season have been restricted to a minimum. A very essential job, the renewal of the fence dividing the approach to the big bank turnstiles from the railway embankment, has, however, been carried out.

Today, in the railway corner of the Big Bank, remnants of a red-painted corrugated iron fence look as if they go back decades. It's a unique reminder of the changing face of the Park.

When it came to work on the ground, in the post-war period, right through to the 1960s, the City management – as we've seen with the floodlights – relied heavily on the fruits of fund-raising by the Grecians' Association. And there was the generosity too of others, such as the individual who bore the cost of having the grandstand roof repainted. By the mid-1950s, the Association had raised £9,100 since its formation in 1945. At the beginning of the 1955–56 season, this supporters' group had an office at the back of the stand, '2d on the Ball' ticket sellers were on the lookout for new members, and a 'Devon derby' dance was being planned for the evening of the Torquay game on 3 September. At the back of the official programme, we learn that it was the Grecians' Association who 'supplied and operated' the half-time scores; with each letter from A to T representing a game, numbers were displayed on boards at either end of the ground. Looking up the scores in the programme at half-time is a ritual that went out in the late 1970s.

That 1955–56 season felt like the start of a new era in more ways than one. Links with the past were being severed: the death of Lionel Wotton ('Nomad') in May 1955 coincided with the end of the *Football Express*; Norman Kendall's passing soon afterwards meant links to the first City professional XI of 1908 were being lost; and Sid Thomas' tenure as chairman would last for just two more seasons. Looking ahead, for the first time, the club was promoting itself as being not only at the heart of Exeter, but also at the very heart of Devon.

An eye-catching matchday programme cover included a photograph of Exeter cathedral and a map of the region with lines radiating from Exeter to all major places. The idea came from the Exeter Information and Publicity Bureau, which saw in the programme 'tremendous potential advertising power'. The new cover design, it was felt, would serve as a publicity vehicle for the city. Exeter City Council, however, refused permission for the city coat of arms to be included.

Later that season, a novelty: the FA Cup tie against Stoke at the Park, on 7 January, was filmed. A cine camera and projector had been given to the club by director and future chairman Albert Line. Footage of games could now be studied in order to address tactical failings; it was a different purpose to the filming at the Villa Cup game in 1914, where Rover's report mentions a 'cinema operator' being present. Four years later, in September 1960, the BBC was at St James' Park to film the League game versus Peterborough United. Some of the action was broadcast later the same day on 'Sports Special', with former footballer Maurice Edelston commentating.

But attendances, as always, were what mattered, and whenever those dwindled it was ground upkeep that suffered. In March 1957, the City board requested that the Grecians' Association transfer the £1,100 they'd earmarked for ground improvements to the club's account to cover working expenses. Four years later, the situation became so critical that the City Council were approached: they could buy St James' Park for £60,000 as long as they rented it back to the club. The proposal was flatly rejected.

Despite the financial crisis, there *were* ground improvements in the early 1960s. They included renovation work on the Cowshed terrace: repairing the roof and replacing railway sleepers. Another area that was targeted was the terracing between the grandstand and the Big Bank that was known as 'The Transport Men's Enclosure'. Before the start of the 1963–64 season, action was finally taken to re-roof the grandstand after guttering had fallen off. There was always something that needed doing.

In September 1966, one supporter bypassed the club by writing to the *Express & Echo* to complain about the state of amenities at St James' Park. He'd been watching games from terracing near the grandstand:

> I renewed my visits to St. James's Park hoping that there might have been some improvement in the amenities.
>
> Not likely! At the Grecians' terrace ancient and rotting sleepers led to the toilets, unlit, and unbolted, and quite filthy … and, of course, there is no toilet for the women at all.
>
> Having to leave ten minutes before time, I went to the exit, to find the doors locked. This meant clambering through the stand customers before emerging at the end of Well Street.
>
> These conditions spoilt what I thought was a fairly good game, but if the directors want support they must consider the ordinary 4s fan.

One week later came a reply from City secretary Dick Miller. He regretted that the supporter had not contacted the club first:

[W]hile we realise that the facilities we have to offer do not compare with First Division clubs, we none the less endeavour to give the best we can.

The state of the toilet in question is very much regretted, but, being in an open position, it is comparatively easy for anyone to make things dirty.

Indeed, last week hooligans smashed a toilet basin in this particular block. Needless to say, this costs the club money, and one wonders whether some of the people deserve facilities of any standard.

It was a defensive response to a genuine concern, more an expression of exasperation at mindless behaviour. A year earlier, in a message to supporters in the City programme, Dick Miller had called for life bans for football hooligans, as well as for supporters at the Park to refrain from throwing toilet rolls onto the pitch – anyone who did would be removed from the ground by the police – and slow hand-clapping. The supporter who chose to write to the *Express & Echo* had unwittingly touched a nerve.

Close-season preparation
Source: © ECFC, Sonny Clarke testimonial programme, 13 October 1980, from the Grecian Archive

For some, the pitch was sacred. The feature on Sonny Clarke in the 1970–71 programme referred to his various tasks, such as the re-seeding and re-cultivating that was done at St James' Park during the close season. By the 1970s, the time between the end of one season and the beginning of another was getting shorter. Whenever Sonny was doing work on the pitch, he made sure people kept off it. For City legend Alan Banks, there was a special rapport between Sonny and the players:

He was the first person I met when I joined the club in 1963. He had just finished cutting the pitch which was his pride and joy. Sonny was one of the great characters at the ground. The players would say to him: 'the pitch is looking great'. And he would answer: 'yes, it is, considering the shit that plays on it!' He would not let the manager or the players on it after he had just cut it. Remember, he had no help, and he didn't have the equipment the groundsmen have today. He got on very well with the players, who had a lot of respect for him. Sometimes, after training, we would join him for a cup of tea in his little cubby hole under the stairs of the main stand where he would have lunch.

His 'greatest pride' was to have prepared the pitch for the Manchester United Cup tie, the game in which Banks opened the scoring, even though 'the weather conditions were against him'.

At the end of the programme feature, we hear briefly from Sonny Clarke himself:

Sonny with his dog
Source: © ECFC, Sonny Clarke testimonial programme, 13 October 1980, from the Grecian Archive

It is no easy job keeping a football pitch up to scratch, but we try to produce a good pitch here for every match, and the fact that not very often do we have to abandon matches here at the Park, the record speaks for itself.

Ten years later, in 1980, Sonny was granted a testimonial in recognition of his 25 years as groundsman.

In the 1971 close season, work was done to different parts of St James' Park. At the old Grecian Gate on Well Street a new players' entrance was built, and above the turnstiles leading to the grandstand the façade was improved. The Cowshed received new roofing, the refreshment huts were painted and the guest area under the main stand was redecorated. The following September, there was a reference in the programme to the work that had started at the top of the Big Bank. This was the site of the new Exeter City Supporters' Social Club. Opened in August 1973, it was relocated to behind the Big Bank in 1979.

In the story of St James' Park, one of the tragic incidents that has occurred there was in 1972. During the League game against Stockport County on 16 September, referee Jim Finn from Essex collapsed in the sixty-eighth minute, after suffering a heart attack. He died soon after being carried off on a stretcher. The game continued with one of the linesmen in charge.

In happier times in the 1970s, by far the most memorable event at the Park was the celebration of promotion from Division Four. For the final game of the season against Aldershot (3-0) on 14 May 1977, a souvenir edition of the programme was produced; on the cover were the words 'We're Up! Doncaster Rovers 0, Exeter City 3'. The *Express & Echo*'s Tony Phillips described the scenes at St James' Park where a season-high crowd of 10,750 had assembled:

> It was a nostalgic, carnival occasion at St. James's Park. The sun-drenched supporters rarely stopped cheering and chanting, particularly from the 'cowshed' stand where hundreds of young fans spent most of the match either sitting or standing on the banking.
>
> Three times they invaded the pitch during the game, but they immediately returned to their positions to celebrate the victorious goals from Bobby Hodge, Alan Beer, and Nicky Jennings.
>
> It was certainly a bonanza occasion emphasised by the atmosphere before the kick-off. The big sun-drenched crowd were entertained by Devon and Cornwall Police Band; and supporters were flooding into the ground.

And at the end of Phillips' report?

> At least two people needed medical attention in the crowd as they were carried out on stretchers.
>
> Hundreds of Exeter supporters swarmed on to the pitch at the end of the game chanting 'We want Saxton, we want Saxton.'
>
> Up went the cries, the scarves, the banners, and just about everything as the Exeter players came out into the directors' box to wave their tribute to the fans to finalise what has been an outstanding season.
>
> One banner even said: 'Alan Beer reaches parts other beers cannot.' Another said: 'Grecian Magic.'

Later in the day, more than 2,000 supporters gathered outside the Guildhall where the Mayor of Exeter had laid on a reception for the players. City finished runners-up with a then-club-record points tally of 62.

Away from the League, there was humiliation in the FA Cup. Among City's early exits, in November 1973 there was the infamous home defeat to Alvechurch (0-1), an amateur club from the Premier Division of the West Midlands Regional League. On 2 May 1978, there was a first-ever international match at the Park, 'England Ladies' v 'Eire Ladies'; in November 2006, England Women's Under-21s played their French counterparts here. Testimonials in the late 1970s included one for a member of the promotion side, Nicky Jennings. Luckily for him, the visit of League Champions Nottingham Forest (0-5) in February 1979 coincided with a first appearance for their new signing Trevor Francis, England's first £1 million player. Some 9,479 were there to see it, with receipts amounting to £12,000.

Finally, we come to Sonny Clarke's benefit game. Second Division Derby County were the visitors to the Park (3-2) on 13 October 1980; so it meant a return to Exeter for their assistant manager John Newman. Among the many tributes to Sonny in the programme was one from former FIFA President Sir Stanley Rous:

(Left) Sonny and a team of volunteers
Source: © ECFC, Sonny Clarke testimonial programme, 13 October 1980, from the Grecian Archive

(Right) Surveying a waterlogged St James' Park pitch
Source: © ECFC, Sonny Clarke testimonial programme, 13 October 1980, from the Grecian Archive

There is no substitute for skill. Exeter City football players know that they can only practise and demonstrate the skills of the game on well-prepared pitches. For twenty-five years Sonny Clarke has maintained with care and pride a playing surface enjoyed by the Exeter City players and visitors to St. James Park. When I have been privileged to attend matches there I have heard them say: 'if we cannot play football on a pitch as good as this we ought not to be in the team. It is a beautiful playing surface.'

The praise is due to Sonny. Good luck to him at his benefit match. I hope it will help to compensate for all his devotion and pride in his work.

'From the Terraces' was penned by Richard Knight, someone who, like Sonny, would go on to give long service to the club. While questioning the frequency of benefits and the merits of some of them, he was in no doubt that the award of a testimonial to Sonny was 'genuine, justified and thoroughly deserved':

In his twenty-five years at the Park he has seen it all. Two re-election uncertainties, the jubilation of both promotion campaigns and the stigma of relegation. He's seen the City giant-kill and giant-killed. Nothing seems to move him. He knows his job and does it so few can complain. Whether City win or lose, are pathetic or brilliant, he is always the same. Even when the occasional 'star' puts his boot through the dressing room door in frustration he just dismisses it as youthful exuberance with a shrug of his shoulders.

Nothing influences Sonny. He's just as meticulous preparing a pitch for the youth team as he was for either of Manchester United's Cup visits. Every match is the same whether it be for immortals such as Charlton, Best, Law or the boys from a local club.

Yes, Sonny's achieved a lot more than produce nearly 600 League pitches and umpteen Cup, reserve and other match surfaces. I know. I've had the privilege of helping him. With school friends I assisted Sonny after a first-team game – sweep the terraces, fork out the divots and cut and prepare the playing surface. Old Son does all that and much more. He does it all with pride. Right down to raising the club standard on match days. All of it thankless tasks for which we are all very grateful.

Knight feared the turnout might not be what Sonny deserved. And he was right. The gate was a disappointing 1,504.

Ironically, in the following months, the ground would be packed to the rafters during another of the club's famed FA Cup runs.

28

Fortress St James' Park

I N the 1980s, Grecians' fans had precious little to cheer about and this was reflected in consistently low gates. At the same time, from 1985, the club was forced to make major structural changes to St James' Park. But the decade, nonetheless, was bookended by two of the biggest triumphs in the club's history. One was the FA Cup run to the quarter-finals; the other, the League Division Four title.

On 28 January 1981, there were over 15,000 at St James' Park to see Exeter City defeat First Division Leicester City 3-1, having drawn 1-1 away four days earlier. They'd reached the Fourth Round of the FA Cup after wins against Leatherhead, Millwall and Maidstone. Tony Kellow's hat-trick against Leicester was the first in the Cup by a City player since Dick Smart's in 1949; in the League, the Grecian legend was on his way to winning a Golden Boot for his tally of 25 goals in 46 appearances, the highest in the four divisions during the 1980–81 season.

In Round Five, City were paired with Newcastle United of Division Two. In front of 37,420 at the Tyneside St James' Park, Exeter conjured up a late equaliser to earn a replay. Manager Brian Godfrey called it 'a gritty performance'. The Magpies had a recent habit of Cup exits by Third Division sides, and in his programme notes for the replay in Exeter on Wednesday 18 February, Tony Pullein wondered whether there'd be another of Newcastle's 'now-familiar Cup experiences'.

Programme for the Cup game v Newcastle United, 18 February 1981

Source: © ECFC, from the Grecian Archive

In his own programme notes, Godfrey made it clear what he wanted from the crowd at 'our own St. James' Park … whatever the number swells to, I want to hear the same sort of noise which greeted us at Newcastle and please keep it going throughout the entire game'. Under these notes, there was a 'Police Notice' in bold: 'In the interest of safety, spectators are requested not to exchange ends during the half-time interval.' With the need to respond to the problems of hooliganism, the Cowshed custom of changing ends freely had had to stop.

City not only won through to the Sixth Round, they did it with a 4-0 victory in front of TV cameras. The 17,668 inside the Park included a reported 3,000 supporters from the north-east. The *Express & Echo* celebrated the significance of the feat:

This was no act of traditional giant-killing, but a ruthlessly professional performance by a head and shoulders better side that enabled Exeter City to turf Second Division Newcastle United unceremoniously out of the F.A. Cup and reach the quarter-final for the first time in fifty years.

City's tremendous triumph was created by a first half of champagne football mixed with ice cool finishing. They lashed in three goals in that opening 45 minutes that rocked the Geordies to their very foundations.

And then their total determination and will to win was enough to contain Newcastle in a second half spell in which they threw everything they had in trying to get back into the game.

For City's Peter Hatch, it was a personal triumph, scoring from a corner and helping to create two of the goals. Both he and Tony Kellow are now members of Exeter City's Hall of Fame.

In the quarter-final, City's opponents were Tottenham Hotspur, the tie to be played in London. When the ticket allocation was announced, Brian Godfrey made an appeal to supporters 'to have patience with the administration staff who find themselves in an impossible situation'. Needless to say, there were angry scenes at the Park when some who had queued for hours found that the 3,500 allocation had sold out. As a precautionary measure, the police were called in.

Later, in losing 2-0, City were unable to extend the tie to a game at St James' Park, as they'd done in 1931 against First Division opposition but they'd earned a civic reception at the Guildhall – and, as Brian Godfrey pointed out, 'made many new friends as a result of our success'. Then there was the age-old challenge: 'Time will tell whether in fact we can hold them.' For the three home games following the Spurs match, attendances hovered around the 4,000 mark.

Three seasons later Exeter City finished bottom of the Third Division. After that, with the side struggling in Division Four, crowds declined correspondingly. Gates at the Park in the mid-1980s averaged between 1,500 and 3,000. It was one of the leanest periods for home support in the club's history.

An illustration of this was the 1985–86 season. New manager Colin Appleton, assisted by former City favourite Fred Binney, was unable to prevent the club from having to apply for re-election; two clubs finishing with the same number of points as City had better goal differences. In the programme for the final home game, against Crewe Alexandra (1-2), there was a reference to crowd figures in the column 'Out and About':

It will not come as a shock to you to learn that attendances are again down for the 4th time in 5 seasons. The previous 22 home games have attracted 43648 for an average of 1984 which represents a drop of 354 on last year and down 1392 on 1983–4. The highest gate (2868) was recorded against Port Vale on the opening day of the season and only 8 crowds have passed the 2000 mark. The gate of only 1369 for the visit of Cambridge was the club's lowest at St James Park.

Back in November 1985, addressing the decline in gates, Appleton had called for club officials and supporters to meet in the Centre Spot Social Club in an effort 'to understand each other's needs and problems'.

If attracting people to the Park was difficult enough at this time, it became even more so when the image of association football was tarnished by a series of stadium tragedies. First, there was the Bradford City fire on 11 May 1985, followed soon after by the Heysel disaster on 29 May; then, on 15 April 1989, there was Hillsborough. After Bradford, a Safety of Sports Grounds Order required safety standards at Third and Fourth Division grounds to be brought up to those at First and Second Division clubs.

Following consultation between Exeter City, the local authority, police and fire officers, and the County Engineers Department in the summer of 1985, capacity at the Park was limited to 8,569. On becoming a 'designated ground' on 9 August, extensive work needed to be done to all parts of the stadium, with the wooden grandstand, put up in 1926, the main target. As well as fireproofing the structure, there were alterations to exits and seating. Funding in part was available through the Football Grounds Improvement Trust.

As the transformation of the Park intensified, there was reflection on the old days. At the beginning of the 1986–87 season, City's official programme had a nostalgic look about it. The cover featuring Exeter cathedral was a replica of the one used in the 1955–56 season. And before the game against Orient on 23 August, an old friend of the club was remembered: there was a minute's silence in memory of Sir Stanley Rous, 'football's most respected elder statesman'.

In the programme column 'City Desk', there was an update on ongoing improvements to the ground:

During the close season, St. James' Park has been closer to resembling a building site rather than a football ground – largely due to the work being carried out by the contractors in the Cowshed to comply with the Ground Safety Certificate, but nevertheless the opportunity has been taken to smarten up the ground with a coat of paint and the Club would like to thank all those volunteers who have assisted with this work – a large proportion of the workforce comprising of members of the Centre Spot Social Club and the Junior Grecians Committee.

Volunteering has always been a hallmark of how things are done at Exeter City. Just over a month later, the renovated Cowshed was re-opened.

A packed Cowshed for a friendly v Tottenham Hotspur, 1987

Source: © Martin Weiler

On Wednesday 1 October, a commemorative plaque was unveiled by England Manager Bobby Robson to mark the completion of the conversion work, which had reportedly cost £100,000. That evening in the programme for the game against Southend, there was a notice to 'spectators' in the Cowshed about a new safety feature: 'The walkway area at the front of the Cowshed is provided for safety reasons and must not be entered. Your co-operation in this matter will be appreciated and those who do encroach into this area will be asked to leave it.' Ground improvements at the Park were only just starting.

In 1987–88, there was another bottom-four finish in the Fourth Division; and then, finally, a turn in fortunes after the appointment of Terry Cooper as manager in May 1988. Two years later, Exeter City won the first title in their history as a professional club. It all came to a rousing finale over three home games in the space of a week.

City had guaranteed promotion by beating Southend (2-1) on Wednesday 25 April 1990; 'the final whistle,' wrote the *Express & Echo*'s Trina Lake, 'was greeted with a lusty cheer and a good-natured pitch invasion with players chaired shoulder-high back to the dressing room.' The Division Four title was secured with a 3-2 win against Scarborough on 28 April. Trina Lake again:

> Tears of joy mixed with broad smiles of delight as the celebrations began in earnest when the final whistle blew.
>
> The triumphant City players were engulfed in a sea of supporters, each fan determined to mark a moment in history with their own personal tribute to the red and white shirted heroes.
>
> Carried shoulder high and savouring every last moment was skipper Shaun Taylor who will have the honour of collecting the championship trophy before tomorrow night's final home game against Burnley. The look of sheer ecstasy on his face captured the atmosphere to perfection.

During 1989–90, Exeter City set a club record in being unbeaten at 'Fortress' St James' Park for the entire season, with gates averaging just under 5,000. Lake described the scenes at the Park before the game against Burnley (2-1) on Tuesday 1 May:

> Cheers of 'Champions' rang out over the ground.
>
> The players understandably lingered over their lap of honour, soaking up adulation from terraces and grandstand.
>
> There was a particularly special moment when team acknowledged manager and Terry Cooper was hoisted high to receive the warm applause of the fans.
>
> He was rightly feted for steering City to their first major honour.

Previously, post-1908, the club's first-team trophy wins were the Division Three (South) Cup in 1934 and Devon Professional Bowls. Terry Cooper summed up the extent of the achievement: 'We couldn't have written the script any better. This season has had everything – we've sold a player to a top club [Chris Vinnicombe to Glasgow Rangers], we've had money-spinning cup

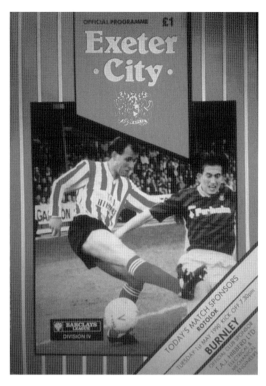

(Left) Barclays
League Division
Four Champions
Trophy 1989–90
Source: © ECFC, from the
Grecian Archive

(Right)
Programme v
Burnley, 1 May
1990
Source: © ECFC, from
Martin Weiler's collection

runs and now we're champions of Division Four.' Cooper acknowledged the part played by the 'magnificent' supporters: 'They have remained patient and lifted us whenever we have needed them. They could be fickle and critical when I first came here, but now they stick by us through thick and thin. They're superb.'

The Exe Directory's Simon Carter felt 'particularly pleased for the supporters who have stuck with the side throughout the lean years and who are now being rewarded for their loyalty'.

In the programme for the Scarborough game on 28 April 1990, there's a reminder of the serious challenges association football was facing. It was just over a year after the Hillsborough disaster in which 96 supporters lost their lives and hundreds more were injured. The inquiry that followed, led by Lord Justice Taylor, exposed the over-emphasis that had been put on dealing with spectator disorder to the detriment of ensuring that the environment for watching games was safe. A chief recommendation of the Taylor Report was that terracing at major sporting venues be phased out and that stadiums become all seater.

The Exeter City Supporters' Association surveyed its members on the issue of all-seater stadiums and potential locations in Exeter should the club be forced to act. Committee member Mike Paxton reported back on the findings:

> From the results it was noted that 70% of supporters were against the principle of all-seater stadiums. However, given that such a stadium was chosen as a viable proposition, or was required to be built by legislation, 57% expressed their preference for it to be purpose-built away from St James' Park, and in many cases on the outskirts of the city.
>
> Understandably, there would always be a strong feeling of tradition towards keeping football at St James' Park. Nevertheless, the potential of constructing a modern-purpose stadium at a convenient, more spacious location could be considerable. Whatever the decision, there is a strong argument to improve both football and other sports facilities within a society which is putting greater emphasis on leisure pursuits.

Later, the requirement to convert to an all-seater model was limited to the top two divisions. Even so, in 1994, when – not for the first time – the 'City Club' was threatened with extinction, a move to a multi-purpose stadium was seen as the solution.

Chairman Ivor Doble appealed to supporters and the local business community for help. He termed the possibility of moving 'one glimmer of hope'. Earlier in the year, plans for turning the Big Bank into an all-seater grandstand had been rejected by the City Council.

The last time a move away from the Park was seriously considered was in 1907 when a site in the Barnfield area was identified. In October 1994, talks started between Exeter City and the Council about relocating the club to the southern fringes of Exeter. There were two preferred sites: Matford Marshes and Old Rydon Lane. One month later, the club went into administration. The administrators supported a move to a 10,000-seater stadium at Matford, and on 9 February 1995 one of them made a plea to the planners: 'If planning is not granted, closing the club down and selling the ground is the only option I will have from that point.' The Matford proposal was rejected by the Council.

Other locations for a new stadium were put forward, and in March the Matford scheme was revived. The site at Old Rydon Lane was eventually withdrawn. With time running out, the black edges to the programme for the final home game of the 1994–95 season against Fulham (0-1) on 29 April signalled the distinct possibility of this edition being the last one ever. That afternoon 83-year-old Hedley Boyce was a special guest at the Park. He'd been following City since he was seven and had only stopped attending games four seasons before. 'It will be such a great shame if Exeter City fold,' he told the *Express & Echo*. 'Many of my happiest memories are about following the Grecians.'

29

Saved!

A S bleak as the situation was – and it was far bleaker than the crises in the mid-1930s and early 1960s – Exeter City, by the skin of its teeth, managed to survive. But before that happened, there were several twists and turns.

A fortnight after the Fulham game, the football club thought it had a rescue package in place but it fell short of the figure of £390,000 the administrators needed. Nevertheless, the club was granted a stay of execution by the Football League: eight working days to raise the necessary funds. It's at this juncture, on 22 May 1995, that the Exeter City Football Trust was formed.

Trustees were chiefly made up of local councillors and supporters of the club; later, members of the business community lent a hand. Profits from fund-raising would be controlled by the Trustees and kept separate from funds held by the administrators or directors. Citizens were encouraged to support one of a variety of collections that had been organised in workplaces, schools and commercial outlets; to spur the process, the *Express & Echo* set up a 'Save The Grecians' hotline. The objective, through a bond scheme, was to raise £200,000 to buy the club out of administration. Suddenly, there was an urgency, and the local community had become involved.

At the launch of the Trust, Councillor John Lloyd called on all parties to pull together:

> We have spent a lot of time blaming others in recent times for the club's problems. The club's board of directors have been blamed, the administrators have been blamed, the council has been blamed, the developers have been blamed. Now it's time to bury our differences and forget our quarrels for the sake of the club.

Linked to efforts to raise money independently of the football club were calls for there to be supporter representation on the club board. This had happened briefly at the start of the 1994–95 season – before the administrators arrived.

The idea of supporter directors was not new. During Exeter City's first decade as a professional organisation, there had been attempts by the City Supporters' Club to have the club board agree to it sending a representative to meetings. These had invariably been thwarted by the diplomacy of Chairman Michael McGahey. The activities of the Exeter City Football Trust, in 1995, sowing the idea of increased supporter involvement in the running of the club, culminated in the formation of the Exeter City Supporters' Trust in 2000 and, finally, majority ownership of the club in 2003.

On 1 June 1995, a last-minute rescue package was approved by the Football League, thus lifting the club's transfer embargo and covering predicted weekly losses of £5,000 over the next 12 months. A deal had been struck with developers Beazer Homes; it entailed the club handing over the deeds to St James' Park. The future of the Park was uncertain, depending as it did on the decisions of property developers and planners. There was the distinct possibility that the ground might be developed for housing, and the possibility of City moving to an out-of-town stadium remained. For City fans, the new era in Exeter's history meant contemplating a home game against Darlington on 12 August, and, for the first time in 38 years, League derbies against Plymouth and Torquay.

Two seasons before, City had been relegated from Division Two – with Terry Cooper returning to the club in January 1994 in place of another former England international Alan Ball. In the following season, 1994–95, to add to the threat of extinction, the Grecians finished bottom, the first time since 1958. Had the ground of Conference winners Macclesfield Town met League requirements, City would have been relegated out of the Football League.

In June 1995, Peter Fox succeeded Cooper and, for the rest of the decade, assisted by Noel Blake, he restored some stability to the club's League standing. Early in his tenure, the sale of Martin Phillips to Manchester City raised a then club record £500,000. It contributed greatly to City being able to come out of administration in August 1996.

Soon afterwards, the future of football at St James' Park was secured. The City Council bought the land from Beazer Homes in the summer, and the club took out a 25-year lease on the ground. Talks about redevelopment and how this could be achieved could now be resumed. On the question of whether remaining at the Park was the right decision, Chris Whiffin, writing in the City fanzine *There's a Good Time Coming (Be It Ever so Far Away)*, in September 1996, argued for a future at St James' Park, as opposed to a move:

> Weighing up the cons of the … state of the ground and the lack of room for expansion with the pros of the excellent location near the city centre with plenty of pubs and shops as well as that oft-underestimated factor tradition, I feel that this [staying] is probably for the best. If this is to be the case, though, work needs to be started on improving St James Park which has been allowed, albeit understandably, to fall into an appalling state of disrepair. This, combined with improvements at other grounds, means our home is now amongst the worst in the League.

In the editorial comment that followed the article, the football club was berated for failing to consult supporters in 1994 over the planned Big Bank redevelopment and the proposed out-of-town move. For these fans, it was 'a missed opportunity' to canvass the views of the City faithful.

In the distant past, it was often the fans, through the Supporters' Club, who led the calls for structural changes to the Park, and who ended up funding those changes. Immediately after the First World War, there were plans to build a stand – part seating, part standing – on the side opposite the grandstand, the popular bank; and in place of the Big Bank a new 'popular' bank was to be built. There was even talk of covering the whole ground. But when it came to actual change, covering the Cowshed was as far as it went.

Over 75 years later, in March 1999, ambitious plans to redevelop two sides of St James' Park were approved by the City Council. First, the Big Bank would be replaced by a new covered terrace; then, a new all-seater stand would take the place of the Cowshed. This scheduling meant that during the rebuild, there'd always be a covered standing area available for City fans.

In the spring of 1999, as change was contemplated, the primroses on the grass bank that fronted the Cowshed were out. Supporters were concerned about what would happen to this unique feature among League grounds. In the 'Histories of St James Park' film, club Operations Manager Andy Gillard refers fondly to the primroses as 'another one of our little unique foibles'.

It was groundsman Sonny Clarke who did the original planting 30 years before. In the programme for the game against Rotherham (3-0) on 13 April, the then groundsman Colin Wheatcroft explained what the flowers meant to him and his staff – as well as the players:

> Sonny told me that he planted three primroses on the bank all those years ago, and they have since spread and spread into what is now a carpet of flowers. Even players who use the bank to launch a long throw-in, carefully avoid treading on the primroses!
>
> The ground staff always take great pride in the display at this time of year and we try to look after the primroses. It's certainly not something I expected to do after becoming groundsman at Exeter City! But it is an enjoyable aside to the usual cutting of the St James' Park pitch.

Before the rebuilding of the Cowshed, a home was found for the primroses. The flowers were offered to supporters, and some were later replanted in what became known as the Memorial Garden, situated directly behind the stand that replaced the Cowshed. The garden – the brainchild of volunteer Andy Holloway – is where the club remembers players who were killed during two world wars as well as other fellow much-missed Grecians.

(Left) Programme v Halifax Town, 8 May 1999, just before redevelopment work started on the Big Bank
Source: © ECFC, from the Grecian Archive

(Right) The modern-day Big Bank
Source: © ECFC, 2018

By early February 2000, work on the new Big Bank terracing was complete. In December, with three sides of the ground open, City had held Everton 0-0 in the FA Cup Third Round; with capacity reduced, the gate was just over 6,000. Given the fact they had to use a replacement keeper, Jason Matthews, following Stuart Naylor's concussion, City received a deserved standing ovation at the end. In the replay at Goodison Park, Everton scraped through 1-0.

The opening of the new stand, which was named after Cliff Bastin, took place on Saturday 12 February, with Darlington visiting the Park in Division Three. On the cover of matchday programme *The Grecian*, there was a reminder of what the Big Bank used to look like, under an image of its handsome replacement. Noel Blake, who'd recently taken over from Peter Fox as manager, admitted an empty Cowshed would be 'strange' but he hoped the old atmosphere there could be recreated: 'The choir and the noisy support will now be even better under the roof of the Big Bank!' Off the pitch, the official opening; on it, City were beaten 4-1.

Work on the Cowshed could now begin. It had been used for the last time on Saturday 29 January 2000 for the League visit of Rochdale (2-0). On the programme cover that day: two splendid images of how the stand had looked since the 1930s – one with the later addition of the primroses. Inside the 'farewell' issue, one of the 'Cowshed Memories' is Mark Hooper's, recalling the sensation of watching a game from a packed Cowshed:

> [I]n the pre-Hillsborough days, the side-splitting crush on a big match day like the Football League cup matches against Bolton Wanderers and Blackburn Rovers, and FA Cup ties versus Wolverhampton Wanderers, Leicester City and Newcastle United – with considerably fewer crush barriers than there are now – meant that on big goal celebrations you could leap up at the top of the Shed landing about half way down, sometimes on your feet, sometimes not. But always starting the next chorus of 'C'mon you Reds …' or some such like. Those were the days: the noise, the press of the crowd, the atmosphere, losing at home 1-0 to Halifax … the walk back to St Thomas, standing outside the telly shop for Final Score.

(Left) Redevelopment of the old Cowshed into the Doble Stand, *c.*2000
Source: © ECFC, from the Grecian Archive

(Right) How the Main Stand looks today
Source: © ECFC, 2018

For another contributor, David Morgan, 'the departure of the railway sleepers was the beginning of the end'.

ECFC Museum
exhibits

Source: © ECFC, from the
Grecian Archive

'The Doble Stand', as it was named (after Chairman Ivor Doble), received supporters for the first time on Saturday 27 January 2001. The League game against Brighton drew a crowd of 4,490 to the Park, City winning 1-0 with a goal from Steve Flack. As well as a designated area for families and one for disabled supporters, the new 2,200 all-seater stand provided an opportunity for the club to offer hospitality to potential sponsors in corporate boxes. The redevelopment also included the conversion of the adjacent building that had housed St James' School. After refurbishment, it would provide space for the club's offices, a social club, corporate hospitality and, more recently, the Exeter City Football Club Museum room.

Two years later, Exeter City were midway through a season that turned out to be the most turbulent in the club's history. It's a period described by Neil Le Milliere – founder member of the Exeter City Supporters' Trust – as 'a madcap twelve months'. In the 2002 close season, the then chairman and majority shareholder, Ivor Doble, brought in John Russell and Mike Lewis to run the club; both had had experience in football administration, at Scarborough and Swansea respectively.

The pair announced their arrival with a bizarre publicity stunt aimed at putting St James' Park on the map. On 15 June 2002, pop star Michael Jackson paid a brief visit to the stadium, invited by illusionist and TV celebrity Uri Geller, newly appointed to the City board. A smaller than expected crowd turned up. Children's charities were supposed to benefit from the event. Later, it emerged that not only had these charities not received a penny, but also firms who'd provided services for the event had not been paid; the football club reportedly lost as much as £70,000.

In September, after the club had posted record losses of £500,000 in the year up to June 2002, the co-chairmen revealed plans to reduce debts of almost £2 million. These, according to Neil Le Milliere, included 'knocking down the old grandstand, replacing it with a shallower stand and earmarking surrounding land and the old Centre Spot clubhouse for housing development'. The City Council, who owned the land, was against the idea. By early December, according to Supporters Direct, 'nine companies had lodged county court judgments against the club, and the Sheriff of Devon had even taken "walking possession" of the floodlights at St James' Park'. Before the end of the season, six directors resigned after an FA report into the club's finances.

With the club also struggling on the field, it wasn't surprising that in February 2003 a third manager was appointed since the season began. Gary Peters replaced Neil McNab. Results did improve over the final two months, and for the last home game at the Park, on 3 May, City needed to beat Southend. They did, 1-0, but with Swansea winning too, City were the ones who were relegated to the Conference. Having staved off relegation in the past by winning re-election appeals, City's 83-year Football League status had come to an end. In a first for the Park, Neil Le Milliere and partner Julie Rangeley were married on the pitch in front of the crowd of 9,000.

Russell and Lewis were eventually forced to leave the club in May 2003 after being questioned by fraud-squad officers during an investigation into alleged financial irregularities at the club; both were later convicted of fraudulent trading. In an article for the *Guardian* (19/01/2005), Neil Le Milliere explains what happened next:

When the Trust was invited to save Exeter [City Football Club] by Ivor Doble, the majority shareholder, roughly £4.5m was owed and people were issuing notices against the club to get it closed down, including the Inland Revenue, ground improvements authority, local businesses and national breweries. It was all hands to the pump, making people aware that without a strong

'Fans in Charge' headline

Source: © *Express & Echo*, 5 September 2003

Trust the club would fold. Overnight our membership went from about 50 to 450, with everyone paying at least £2 a month.

Without the Supporters' Trust, Exeter City would not have survived.

Former club director Frances Farley remembers how the club managed to pull through during the 2003 close season:

Like many others, I became one of the many volunteers who spent that summer at St James' Park weeding, painting, cleaning toilets, answering phones and anything else needed in order to get the ground and club ready for, what we hoped would be, our first season in the Conference.

What should be remembered is that there was no certainty that ECFC would ever play another game. Would we be able to find sufficient funds to operate during the close season? Would we be allowed to join the Conference and, if so, would we have enough players to field a team? Talk that summer was not about new signings or possible League position for the coming season; it was all about the likelihood of survival and whether or not we would still exist to play Premier League Portsmouth in the first home friendly. There were many people involved behind the scenes, too numerous to mention, who worked tirelessly to secure the club's future. How many people remember Terry Pavey's temporary home in what is now Red Square, for example?

Players' wages had to be paid, and to address the huge amount of debt a Company Voluntary Arrangement was successfully negotiated. Helped by Supporters Direct and local MP Ben Bradshaw, creditors were persuaded to accept 10 pence in the pound (in reality, it was 7 pence). Among the debts was the £500,000 still owed to builders Mowlem for work on the Doble Stand, the interior of which had been left unfinished.

In the 2003–04 season, Exeter City narrowly missed out on the play-offs. Attendances at St James' Park averaged 3,665, and for the final game against Accrington Stanley a crowd of 8,256 was present. Not long afterwards, in May 2004, nearly two years after the Jackson fiasco, there were stars of a different kind at St James' Park.

With the club celebrating one hundred years as Exeter City, a Brazilian Masters XI came to town. Ninety years before, the Grecians, on a tour to Argentina, made history on the return journey. Stopping briefly in Rio de Janeiro, Exeter City played a Rio–São Paulo XI in a game that marked the start of the 'seleção', the Brazilian national side. It seemed appropriate that Brazil was returning the favour.

The 'Centenary Friendly' on 30 May 2004 drew 6,000 to St James' Park. On the pitch, there were 1994 World Cup winners such as Dunga, Jorginho and Branco; off it, a samba-style carnival atmosphere. For City manager Eamonn Dolan, it was 'astonishing' that his players were taking on the Brazilian veterans: 'Football is about entertainment; it's about glory, and it's about adventure. And this list of players is simply awesome.'

Just over six months later, in another memorable chapter in the club's history, City fans had the chance to acquaint Manchester United with the chant 'Have you ever played Brazil?'.

ECFC v Brazilian Masters programme, 30 May 2004. The Brazilians won 1-0

Source: © ECFC, from the Grecian Archive

30

A community club

Looking back on FA Cup ties in Exeter, certain feats naturally stand out. The 14-0 win against Weymouth in 1908, in City's first-ever tie, is one. The 1931 FA Cup run is another, including two victories at the Park against First Division opposition – Derby and Leeds – before the quarter-final loss to Sunderland of Division One. And, more recently, there was the ruthless manner of the defeat of Newcastle United, 4-0, in 1981.

The FA Cup third-round tie in early 2005, however, is something apart; it was far more than a triumph in a purely footballing sense. Conference-side Exeter City had caused a sensation when they held Manchester United to a 0-0 draw at Old Trafford on 8 January.

Some 9,000 Grecians were among the total attendance of 67,551; a figure, which incidentally, was 16,000 more than the number at Roker Park in 1931 – so a new record for an Exeter City fixture. In the context of City's situation at the time, the game in Manchester, as well as being a lifesaver financially, signalled the beginning of a new era for the club. Frances Farley, who attended the match as a City director, recalls the practical impact the tie had:

> That was the game that gave us the money to come out of the CVA. So it paid off the debts; it gave us that breathing space – it just took all of the pressure away. I'm not saying that without it we wouldn't have managed; I think we probably would [have], because we had the Red or Dead pledges. That money was there, and I think that that would have grown as we got closer to the end. So we had a substantial amount of money in that anyway.

For the replay at St James' Park on Wednesday 19 January 2005, prices were kept at the normal level. It was the club's way of thanking fans and volunteers who had helped it to survive. That evening, in the edition of *The Grecian*, as well as celebration of the achievement in Manchester, there was comment in 'Grecian Chatter' on how the games against United had enabled the club to move on. It prompted reflection on how much the football club had changed:

> Whatever the outcome, it seems that at long last we have managed to shake off the short-lived and many will say disastrous 'showbiz' image that City had – we will always recall the likes of Michael Jackson, David Blaine and Uri Geller etc. – but that period of time has been confined to the history books months ago. Now, Exeter City FC are a true community club, owned and administered by the fans for the fans. We really have taken giant steps forward on all fronts since then, and long may it continue.

Since May 2003, membership of the City Supporters' Trust had reached almost 1,700. In the programme, there was mention of some of the fund-raising schemes: the Exeter City Bond, Red or Dead, and Grecian Goal Plus. Funds raised by the Trust to the end of June 2004 totalled £355,750.

Towards the back of *The Grecian*, Pete Bishop gave an update on work parties. On the following day – Thursday 20 – there was to be 'a post-match tidy-up'. Anyone with a free morning was encouraged to come along to the Park. The appeal in particular was aimed at 'all the extra supporters here tonight':

> There should be people here by about nine a.m., so just walk into the ground and you should see some of us out and about on the terraces, armed with brushes and bags. You won't need to bring anything with you, although a pair of gloves can be handy.

The informal way in which St James' Park was being opened up like this typified the extent to which the relationship of the 'City Club' with its supporters had been transformed. Work parties were, and still are, vital to the club.

Before the game, volunteer Stadium Manager Dacre Holloway commented that, as the previous home game had been on Boxing Day, there had been no rush in getting things ready: 'There has been a fair bit to do, but we get a lot of people helping out.' Following Dacre's untimely death in 2008, a tree was planted at the training ground in memory of this popular figure, one whose fund-raising activities included creating Grecian Goal. On the wall outside the Doble Stand, there's a plaque dedicated to him, alongside plaques for other individuals and plaques commemorating those who died in the world wars.

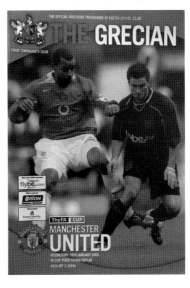

Exeter City v Manchester United matchday programme, 18 January 2005

Source: © ECFC, from the Grecian Archive/Aidan Hamilton

Elsewhere in the Exeter City v Manchester United programme, there are *Express & Echo* accounts of City's two previous meetings with Manchester United at the Park, in 1960 and 1969, and a picture of Alan Banks participating in the Brazilian Masters event. In his *Echo* report of the game, Nicholas Randall – one hundred years after Rover's first *Football Express* column – gives a flavour of the atmosphere and the action:

> Banners, scarves, flags and *Echo* foam cups adorned shop and house windows. And for days before, in shops and pubs, this match was the topic of conversation as the Grecians suddenly gained the frenzied support in Exeter that United have in Manchester.
>
> Last night, pubs were packed with fervent fans and with people who could barely distinguish Wayne Rooney from Paul Scholes, let alone Sean Devine from Steve Flack.
>
> But all of them were partisan and cheerful and proud of their city's team.
>
> At kick-off, 7.45pm, the whole city held its breath, hoping against hope City would be giantkillers against one of the world's top teams – 97 League places above them.
>
> The dream looked over after Cristiano Ronaldo's early goal, but then seemed possible again when for 80 minutes an array of international stars were held at bay by a determined non-League defence.
>
> It was only when Rooney hit the target in the dying minutes that many fans in a crowd that included Flybe-sponsored Birmingham City manager Steve Bruce, accepted it was finally over.
>
> However, while City had been beaten, this match was part of a larger triumph for Exeter, both footballing and financial. And the fans who packed into the St James's Park social club knew it.
>
> Perhaps, immediately after the final whistle, before the full magnitude of what had been achieved kicked in, there was slight disappointment that Sean Devine and the boys had played so well over two legs and yet this was it – the end of the Cup run.
>
> But soon the celebrations were beginning – the singing, the chanting and the dancing.

Several hundred yards from the Park, fans had packed the Odeon cinema on Sidwell Street to watch the game live. Back in 1931, after the famous City versus Sunderland replay, there had been a screening at the King's Hall Picture House in St Thomas.

What the Manchester United games did were to instil a belief and purpose into the plans for a return to the Football League. After the arrival of Paul Tisdale in June 2006, City reached Wembley via the Conference play-offs in the next two seasons, 2006–07 and 2007–08. By winning the second one of these finals – 1-0 against Cambridge – the club regained its League status. Average attendances at the Park had reached 3,700.

In League Two, gates at St James' Park continued to rise – to almost 4,000 on average – and come the end of the 2008–09 campaign, there was an automatic promotion place up for grabs on the final day of the season. City made sure it was theirs by winning 1-0 win away to Rotherham. It was the fifth promotion in the club's history; of the five, just the one in 1990 was achieved at St James' Park. More recently, there have been two League Two play-off semi-finals at the Park – pulsating successes against Carlisle and Lincoln, in 2017 and 2018 respectively.

Three seasons in League One followed, the first ending in dramatic circumstances at St James' Park. On 8 May 2010, City, playing Huddersfield Town, were rescued from relegation by a winning goal – a 'classy volley' – from Ryan Harley. The *Express & Echo*'s Matt Bamsey described the scene:

> St James's Park erupted – Tisdale and his management team leapt out of the dugout and the players mobbed their saviour.
>
> This was a big goal in a big football match, not just saving the club from the drop but laying firm foundations for the future.
>
> City can look forward to next season with renewed optimism.
>
> Tisdale will avoid a budget cut, fans will get to see Sheffield Wednesday and Southampton instead of Stevenage and Burton and the players will have another chance to showcase their talents on the big stage again.

The crowd for the 2-1 win was over 8,000.

Ten days later, work began on the St James' Park pitch – the most thorough renewal of the surface in the club's history. The installing of under-soil drainage and sprinklers was funded by a £150,000 campaign called 'Pitch in for City' led by Tony Badcott; it was hoped it would be a lasting solution to the drainage problems that went back to the late 1900s. The next season, 2010–11, despite City finishing eighth in League One, average gates at the Park dropped several hundred to around 5,400. In 2012, the club returned to League Two.

During the League One period, in 2010, tragedy hit Exeter City Football Club. On 10 August, Adam Stansfield, a real fans' favourite, lost his battle with cancer. On the day after his death, hundreds gathered at St James' Park, with the ground, as the *Express & Echo* headline ran, becoming 'a shrine to football hero': 'In an outpouring of grief, supporters left huge photos, bunches of flowers, messages, banners, posters and red and white City flags as well as number nine shirts on the Big Bank.'

The club, as it had done in 1938 after Bob Wallace's death, gave support to the player's family. As a mark of respect, Stansfield's number-nine shirt was retired for nine seasons. Today he's immortalised in a huge flag and in the chant 'Sing a song for our Stanno'.

During the 2010s, with the centenary of the First World War being commemorated, two events were held in the Memorial Garden at St James' Park. On 11 November 2014, City players and staff assembled there to remember former players who lost their lives, several of whom lived a stone's throw from the ground – Bailey, Stoneman, Turner and Worner. Then, on 1 July 2016, there was a Somme memorial service in partnership with the Royal British Legion: four City players died in the bloodiest of battles.

Finally, to mark one hundred years since Armistice Day, before the Blackpool FA Cup tie – 10 November 2018 – the Park fell silent and wreaths were laid on the pitch. In the Centre Spot, the City Supporters' Club produced a commemorative display. It was based on a trip to the battlefields of northern France made by a group of City supporters, during which visits were made to the graves of City players.

In July 2015, there was another reminder of Exeter's proud link to Brazil when City played a pre-season friendly at the Park against Fluminense's Under-19s (0-2); the Brazilians were on their way to tournaments on the Continent. One year before, the City first team and a sizeable group of fans had made a trip to Rio de Janeiro for a centenary game at Fluminense FC. It had been 45 years since City's last home match under lights against foreign opponents – Dutch side DVV Go-Ahead.

In the mid-2010s, capacity at St James' Park was around 8,500. It was reached on Friday 8 January 2016 for the visit of Liverpool in the third round of the FA Cup. That evening, in a game shown live on BBC1, City produced vintage cup form in drawing 2-2. It was one of those occasions when, as Alan Banks puts it, 'the place was jumping and the atmosphere was electric'; just as he'd experienced in 1969. Memorably, Jurgen Klopp did a pre-match interview in the tiny tea room in the Old Grandstand. The game proved to be the last big occasion at a packed Park before this grandstand, the stand that was built in 1926, was pulled down and a modern one put up in its place.

Development plans for St James' Park had been announced in June 2015. As well as building a replacement for the Old Grandstand, the land behind the Big Bank would be developed for a block of student flats, not completed at the time of writing but due to be named after Lady Anne Clifford, featured in Chapter 1. For Exeter City, working in conjunction with the City Council, who owned the land, and developers Yelverton, it was an 'exceptional' arrangement. 'One of the starting points,' said City Chairman Julian Tagg, 'was at no risk and at no cost to the club.' After a consultation process lasting almost a year, the go-ahead for the redevelopment project was given.

In October 2016, one year before work on the development began, Chris Gosling of City fanzine *Some Sunny Day* produced a 'User's Guide' for the Old Grandstand (OG), 'unquestionably the most distinctive part of the ground'. Anyone who hadn't experienced the stand was encouraged to 'give it a try':

> [F]or a while longer at least, the OG is truly the beating heart of Exeter City. I doubt that it will ever have the iconic status of the Cowshed, but some of us will miss it nonetheless. I urge you to make your pilgrimage before the JCBs close in. Its replacement may be modern and shiny, but it cannot possibly have as much character: the OG is a tobacconist's or a sweet shop in a world of shopping malls. I am prepared to accept its drawbacks: the exterior green paint; the cramped toilets; all those OAP-unfriendly steps; and, above all, the view of the pitch, but my biggest issue with the view is how seldom it is of a home victory. You can't blame the OG for that.
>
> So often with facilities used by the public, these days it is a case of 'use it or lose it'. With the Old Grandstand it is more a case of 'use it and lose it'. Use it you should. It won't be there for ever.

Following a period of preparation work, demolition of the historic stand began on Monday 30 October 2017. The dressing rooms were moved opposite, to what had been called the Doble Stand, which has taken various sponsor names since. Also, as part of the project, there were plans for new toilets and refreshment facilities at the Big Bank end; and the away end would be covered, with a stand bought from Barnet FC.

View across St James' Park after the demolition of the Old Grandstand
Source: © Aidan Hamilton, 2018

Before the Old Grandstand was taken down, efforts were made to remove items of interest, such as an 'A Block' sign. Bolts and seats were also sold to fans. Workers were then asked to look out for historical items that might have been concealed. What they discovered astounded the club's History Group. Items included a framed photograph from the 1930s of Supporters' Club President Lord Mamhead and a framed hand-written list of Supporters' Club members from the 1938–39 season. One mystery, which has yet to be cleared up, is the date and context for a damaged photograph that features City Manager Billy McDevitt and Sid Thomas. The group in the image are holding a horseshoe, so perhaps it's tied to one of the games in the 1930–31 Cup run.

On Thursday 25 October 2018, the 'New Old Grandstand', as it had been dubbed, was officially unveiled, the official opening being performed by City Council Leader Peter Edwards. The official name chosen served to commemorate fans' favourite Adam Stansfield: The Stagecoach Adam Stansfield Stand. The fact that naming rights were shared, between a loyal sponsor and a player who represented everything fans like to see in a footballer, was symbolic of the way in which the project had been successfully concluded with the different parties working in tandem. The covered away end was used for the first time on 10 November by Blackpool supporters. As Julian Tagg summed it up, what had been achieved was 'a stadium to reflect the values of our club, our city and our community'.

Today, as well as the new stands, a distinctive characteristic of St James' Park are the stadium-wide displays of heritage. It's become an Exeter City Football Club Museum project supported by the Heritage Lottery Fund.

On the railway side of the ground, there are three exhibits: a timeline recording key moments in City's history; Hall of Fame banners; and a Walk of Fame featuring murals of some of the most popular City strikers of recent years. On the Old Tiverton Road side, in Stadium Way, there's a display of images entitled 'Grecians through the years'; an exhibit dedicated to the loyal supporters who have witnessed changes to the Park from the Edwardian period to the present day. These are some of the many displays around the stadium.

Since the mid-nineteenth century, St James' Park has been a resource for the local community and beyond: from the political demonstration in the 1880s to military training during two world wars; from menageries and circuses to fetes and dances. It has always been much more than a sports ground. In 1902, the Co-operative Society exhibition was held there. More recently, there have been festivals and concerts, and a sleep-out to raise awareness and funds for a homeless charity. The Park is also where Exeter City Football Club's charity, the City Community Trust, is based. The award-winning organisation is widely recognised as Exeter's foremost sport, health and well-being charity.

In 2016, as one part of the 'History of St James Park' project, a film was produced documenting the history of the ground from its origins. It ends with a personal view of the Park from Paul Tisdale, Exeter City's longest-serving and most successful manager. What he said, before the latest

development phase got underway, is a reminder of what the club, the city and the community almost lost, 20 years before:

> You've got an old-fashioned stadium that's quirky, that's odd-looking. If you stand in the directors' box, you can look out and you can see terraced streets behind the Old Grandstand … Then you've got this very imposing terrace, the Big Bank, behind one goal, which holds thousands of people, and when it's packed it's fantastic – you could be in a Championship ground.
>
> You're not talking about a symmetrical stereotypical stadium that we see so often now, that's characterless, and you turn round and it looks the same one to the other. This is a unique place.

Bibliography

Books

Blackstone, M. (1992) *Exeter City: A Fascinating File of Football Facts.* Exeter: Obelisk Publications.

Blackstone, M. (1992) *Exeter City: Down the Years.* Fife: Rel8 Media.

Blackstone, M. (2008) *Exeter City F.C.: A Grecian Anthology.* Exeter: Exeter City Football Club.

Fisher, D. & Gosling, G. (1998) *Exeter City Football Club 1904–1994.* Stroud: Tempus.

Fisher, D. & Gosling, G. (2000) *Grecian Voices.* Stroud: Tempus.

Fuller, F.A. (1967) *Century of Soccer 1866–1966: St Luke's College AFC.* Exeter: St Luke's College.

Golesworthy, M., Dykes, G. & Wilson, A. (1990) *Exeter City: A Complete Record 1904–1990.* Derby: Breedon Books.

Hamilton, A. (2014) *Have You Ever Played Brazil?: The Story of Exeter City's 1914 Tour to South America.* Exeter: Exeter City Supporters' Trust.

Harvey. H. (1986) *Sidwell Street.* Exeter: Exeter Civic Society.

Harvey, H. (2003) *A History of St Sidwell's School.* Exeter: Woodward Press.

Harvey, H. (2011) *The Story of Exeter.* Andover: Phillimore.

Jenkins, A. (1806) *The History and Description of the City of Exeter.* Exeter: P. Hedgeland.

Juson, D. & Bull, D. (2001) *Full-Time at the Dell: From Watty to Matty 1898–2001.* Bristol: Hagiology.

Walters, R. (2011) *The History of Argyle* [online]. Available from: www.greensonscreen.co.uk.

Young, P. (1968) *A History of British Football.* London: Stanley Paul.

Newspapers

Athletic News
Devon & Exeter Gazette
Devon Evening Express
Exeter & Plymouth Gazette
Exeter Flying Post
Express & Echo
Football Express
The Guardian
Southern Daily Echo
The Sportsman
Western Evening Herald
Western Morning News
Western Times

Documents

Bill of Complaint: Lady Anne Clifford to the Lord Chancellor, 4 February 1664. The National Archives.

Bundle of Clifford Charity apprenticeship indentures, 1659–1805. Devon Heritage Centre.

Exeter City Football Club Directors' Minute Book, 1930–35. Devon Heritage Centre.

Indenture between Clifford Charity Trustees and Exeter City Football Club for lease of St James' Park, 26 August 1908. Devon Heritage Centre.

Miscellaneous

Collections of Dave Fisher, Norman Shiel and Lewis Jones
'Hall of Fame' brochure (ECFC)
'The History of St James Park' programme (ECFC)

Websites

www.bl.uk
www.britishnewspaperarchive.co.uk
www.cwgc.org
www.exetercityfc.co.uk
www.exetermemories.co.uk
www.findmypast.co.uk
www.forces-war-records.co.uk
www.grecianarchive.com
www.greensonscreen.co.uk
www.weownexetercityfc.co.uk

DVDs

Grecian Voices (ECFC and ECFCST)
Grecians Remember (ECFC and ECFCST with the University of Exeter)

Index

'Artful' Thomas 72, 85, 95, 98

American football 113

Appleton, Colin 141

Armistice 85–6, 89, 152

Arsenal FC 38, 97, 109, 128

Bailey, Fred 83, 87, 152

Ball, Alan 145

Banks, Alan 7, 8, 131, 133–4, 137, 151, 153

Banks, Jack 43–5, 47, 49, 60

Barnes, Phil aka 'Rover' 9, 32, 42–7, 49, 50–7, 59–67, 69, 71, 73, 76, 82–3, 86–8, 92, 136, 151

Barnfield 37, 43, 45, 56, 144

baseball 113

Bastin, Cliff 56, 97, 128, 147

Bell, James 'Daisy' 53

Big Bank/popular bank 54, 60, 80, 87, 88, 90–3, 95, 97, 103, 105, 111–15, 117–19, 133, 135–6, 138, 143, 146–7, 152–3, 155

Blaine, David 150

Blake, Noel 146, 147

Blitz 14, 112

boxing 27, 75, 85, 113

Bradford, Elizabeth and Thomas (Tom) 15–18, 20, 30–1

Brazil 9, 125, 149, 151–2

CAR – Club Always Ready (La Paz) 128

Chadwick, Arthur 48–9, 51–3, 55–6, 61–2, 65, 69, 86–90, 94, 109

Chaplin, Charlie 55

Chelsea FC 103–4, 119–22, 133

circus 15, 17, 20, 30–1, 55, 154

City Community Trust (formerly FITC) 16, 154

Clarke, Sonny 135, 137–9, 146

Clifford, Lady Anne 7, 11–13, 16, 153

Clifford Charity/Trust 12–13, 15–16, 18, 21, 40, 42, 46–8, 82, 92

Collingwood House (school) 27–8

Cooper, Terry 142–3, 145–6

Co-operative Congress/Society 36–8, 40, 154

County Ground 21, 27, 30–1, 36, 38, 42, 45–6, 49–50, 57, 60–1, 70, 95–6, 111, 125

Court, Tony 128–31

Cowie, Stan 82

Cowshed/popular enclosure 105, 112, 114, 119, 136, 138, 140, 142, 146, 147, 153

cricket 19–25, 27, 47, 55, 61, 81, 85, 111

Curtis, Dermot 131

cycling 22, 30, 50, 85, 111

Devon County Football Association (Devon FA) 24–6, 38, 107

Devonshire Regiment 24, 30, 56, 60, 113

Dick-a-Dick 20

Dido 99–104, 109

Doble, Ivor 143, 148

Doble Stand 147, 149, 151

Dolan, Eamonn 149

Duke MP, Sir Henry 61–2, 92,

DVV Go-Ahead 129, 152

East Devon FA 41–2, 46–7, 51, 112

Evans, Arthur 82, 86, 87

Exeter City Supporters' Club 75–8, 86¬–90, 92–5, 97, 108–110, 114, 145–6, 152, 154

Exeter City Supporters' Trust 7, 9, 10, 145, 148–50

Exeter Rugby Club 24, 30–1, 38, 46, 61

Exeter United AFC 31–41, 50

Exeter Wesleyan United 33–5

Farley, Frances 149–50

FC Colombia (Vienna) 127

FC Kickers Offenbach 128

First World War (Great War) 42, 56, 78, 86, 147, 151–2

floodlight 124–5, 127–30, 135, 148

Fluminense FC 152

Football Association (FA) 23, 38, 60–1, 79, 84, 97, 111, 116

Footballers' Battalion 82

Fox, Peter 146–7

Geller, Uri 148, 150

Godfrey, Brian 140–1

Golesworthy, Maurice 128, 132–3

Goodwin, Fred 82

Goodwin, William 92

Grazer Sportklub 126–7

Grecians' Association 113, 115, 117–18, 120, 123–5, 135–6

Harding, Gus 86–7

Harvey, Frederick 32, 38, 41–2, 47, 51, 56

Hatch, Peter 141

Holloway, Dacre 151
Houghton, Harry 101–2, 104
Hunter, Frederick 110–12

Jackson, Michael 148–50

Karno, Fred 55
Kellow, Tony 140–1
Kendall, Norman 32–3, 45–7, 51, 53, 57, 62–3, 65, 76, 85, 92, 109, 117, 123, 126, 136
Kirkman, Norman 124

Lake, Trina 142
Line, Albert 136
Lion's Holt railway halt 14
Liverpool FC 8, 153

Manchester United FC 8, 44, 92, 115, 131–3, 135, 137, 139, 149–51
McDevitt, William (Billy) 100, 104, 107, 154
McGahey, Michael 55–6, 61, 76–7, 84, 88, 90, 92–3, 103, 105, 108, 145
Memorial Garden 146, 152
Minehead AFC 22, 30
Mitchell, Arnold 18, 130–1
Museum, ECFC 9, 91, 134, 148, 154

OFK Belgrade 128
(Old) Grandstand 9, 50–1, 60, 67, 75, 82, 92, 95–6, 105, 108–9, 110–12, 119, 135–6, 138, 146, 148, 153–5

Park House School 25, 27–8, 30
Payne, Cyril aka 'The Chiel' 9, 88, 90–2, 94–8, 100–1, 103, 105–6
Pitch in for City 152
Plymouth Argyle FC 44–5, 53, 57, 63–5, 70, 72, 78, 87, 91, 97–8, 106, 109–11, 113, 119, 122, 125, 133
Potter, Albert 112
Pym, Dick 'Pincher' 56, 73, 83, 89, 91–2, 94, 117

Red Lion Hotel, Exeter 38, 42, 44, 55–6, 96
Red or Dead 150
Rees, Graham 131–2
Roughton, George 115, 118, 120, 122
Rous, Sir Stanley 124, 138, 141
rugby 21–2, 24, 26, 27–33, 40, 43, 46, 50, 60, 95, 126

St Anne's Chapel 13, 23, 112–13,
St James' church 7, 13–14, 17–18, 20, 22, 33, 40, 54, 60, 109, 112–13
St James' (Institute) Cricket Club 20, 27, 55
St James' School 16, 148
St Luke's Training College 21, 24–5, 28, 31, 35, 38, 41, 46, 65, 112, 124
St Matthew AFC 27–8, 30, 32
St Sidwell's church 11, 13, 23, 31
St Sidwell's School 20, 33
St Sidwell's United 18, 34–5, 37, 39–41, 43, 52, 59
Second World War 110, 113–14, 125, 146, 151
Senghenydd Colliery disaster 76
Slovan Bratislava 129

Smith, Billy 73, 86, 88–9
Sportsmen's Battalion 82
Stagecoach Adam Stansfield Stand 154–5
Stansfield, Adam 152, 154
Stuart, Alexander 26–9
Sunderland FC 99–104, 119, 131–3, 150–1

Tagg, Julian 153–4
Taylor Report 143
Thomas, Sidney 32, 34–5, 39, 41–6, 51, 55, 64, 79, 80–1, 85, 90, 94–5, 97, 107, 109, 113, 115, 117–18, 125–6, 136, 154
Tisdale, Paul 151–2, 154
Titanic disaster 66–7, 76
Torquay United FC 24, 41, 54, 68, 106, 109–115–16, 127, 131, 136, 145
Trinidad 124–6
Tucker, Henry 25–8

Victoria Hall 17, 36–7
Vienna FC 126–7

Wallace, Bob 110, 152
Watson, Bob 48, 52–3, 56, 60, 62, 65
West Bromwich Albion FC 38–9, 44, 104
White, George 'Cadie' 60, 81, 83, 87
women's football 109, 138
Wotton, Lionel aka 'Nomad' 9, 106–11, 113–14, 117–29, 135–6
wrestling 19

Subscribers

Abbott family, Curry Mallet, Somerset

Timothy Adkin, New Zealand

Mark A. Alford

Anne Allen (née Thomas), Leicester

Ian Andrews

Ian, Jane and James Aplin, Tiverton

Rod Ash

Giles E. L. Ashman, Alphington, Exeter, Devon

Martyn Ashmead, New Forest, Hampshire

Lucy Ashton, Painscastle, Powys

Adrian Autton, London Exile

David T. Ayre, West Down, Ilfracombe, Devon

Tony, Tom, Chris and Daniel Badcott

Graham Baker, Sidmouth, Devon

John Baker, Exmouth, Devon

John Baker, Cannington, Somerset

Andrew R. Barclay

Paul Barnard, Poole, Dorset

Phil Bater, Exmouth

Paul Beckett, Brentwood, Essex

Andrew, Julen and Jon Beer

Mark Bendell

Eric Berry, Cramlington, Northumberland

Hugh Betteridge

Bigcol, Exeter, Devon

Chris Binstead

Jon Bint, Rushford, Chagford, Devon

Barry Blackmore, Rydon Park, Exeter, Devon

Harold Blackmore, Walton Road, Exeter, Devon

Mike Blackstone, Morecambe

Claire Blaker

Mrs Margaret Blomley, Glastonbury

Julian Bostock, Tottenham, London

Terry and Hazel Bound

Richard Bovey, Nottingham

David Bradford, Exmouth

Damien Bragoli

Andy Bratt, Talaton, Nr Exeter

Nick Bray, Deanshanger, Northamptonshire

Ken Brimacombe, Dawlish

Darren R. Brooks, Cullompton, Devon

Phil Broom

Mike Brown, Stoke Canon, Devon

Richard W. Brown, Exeter, Devon

Mike Butler, Minehead

Andy Butt, Billericay

Jonathan Cale, Canberra, Australia

Matt Capel, Exeter, Devon

Simon Carnall

Brian C. Carpenter, Barnstaple, Devon

Brian Carpenter, Devon Archives and Local Studies Service

Jon Carr

Josh Carr, Exeter

David W. Chapman, Bere Ferrers, Devon

Maisy Chapman, Sidmouth, Devon

Graham Chudley, Crediton

Steve Church, St Ives, Cornwall

Michael Clark

Greg Clemett, Bristol

Norman Clinnick, Southampton

David Clough, Commercial Director, Kingsbridge, Devon

Bernadette Coates and Kate Searle, Exeter

Adam Cocking, Exeter, Devon

Peter Cole, Exeter

Pete Cousins

Gary Cox, Moretonhampstead, Devon

Mike Craddock, Dawlish, Devon

Trevor Craddock, Exeter

Andy and Meera, Craddock, London

Trevor Craddock, Devon

Russell Cram, in memory of Stanley Challis

Dr Ian Cumming, Lyme Regis

Steve Darke

Stephen Dart (aka Grecian in Guzz)

Richard Davey

Elaine and Clive Davis, Topsham, Exeter

M. P. Davison, Exeter

Leonard Dennis, aka BIG LD

The Dienes Family of Cullompton

Robin Doble, Cornwall

Matthew Dominey, Ottery St Mary, Devon

Mark Donsford, Exeter

Matthew Donsford, Guatemala

Jonathan Down

Thomas Down

Nigel Down

Darren, Ali and Elena Drew, Harrogate, North Yorkshire

Jane, Julie and Jilly Dunlop, remembering their Dad, William Dunlop

Shaun Dyer

Garry Dyer, Norton, Worcestershire

Nigel Edwards

Quinn George Elliott

Morris Henry George Elliott

Jon Elliott, Folkestone, Kent

Grant England, Exmouth

Paul John England, City 'til he dies

Roy Everett, Burch Gardens, Dawlish, Devon

Janice L. Everett, Exeter, Devon

Simon Faircloth, Melbourne, Australia

Arthur, Brian, Mike and Adrian Farley

Paul and Frances Farley, Devon

Thomas Farley, London

David Field, Thornton Hill, Exeter

Greg Finch, Northumberland

Stuart Fishleigh, Exeter, Devon

Rachael Gammon, Tiverton, Devon

Mike Garrick, East Devon

Marilyn and John Germon, Exmouth

Peter Gibbs, Braunton, Devon

Andy Gillard

Pam Goodrich, St Albans (formerly of Exeter)

Harry A. Gozna, Oak Drive, Cullompton, Devon

Angus Graham, Halberton, Tiverton, Devon

Derek C. Grandin, Wimple, Devon

Martyn, Bev, Sammie, Abbey and Matthew Gray, Exeter, Devon

Alex Grogan

John Guest, Exmouth, Devon

Kate and Dan Hall, Coventry

Nick Hamilton, London

Mark Hammett, Payhembury

Rosalind Hardwick, Southampton

Peter Hardy, Sandys, Bermuda

Clive Harrison, Clyst St Mary, Devon

Trevor and Sue Harwood, Dorchester

Nick Hawker, ECFCST Chairman

Marcus Heap, Stockport County AFC

Chris Henley, Honiton

Michael Thomas Higgins, Exeter

David Hill, Kington, Herefordshire

Spencer House

Michael J. Howard, Feniton, Devon

Bernard Hughes OBE, Exmouth, Devon

Paul Hunkin, Exeter, Devon

Brian Hutchings, Pitney, Somerset

Richard Jarman, Exeter 1974

Richard and Karen Jarvis, El Paso, Texas, USA

Alexia Jewers, Cramlington, Northumberland

Finley Jewers, Cramlington, Northumberland

Lewis Jones

Tim Jones, Trowbridge, Wiltshire

Ian Jubb, Exeter and Edinburgh

Kamran Keenan

Jonathan Kellaway, Exeter

Colin Knight, Exmouth

Paul Knowles

David Knowles, High Bickington, Devon

Ken Lamacraft, Ashstead, Surrey

Paul Lamacraft, Exeter, Devon

Lammie R. Appreciation Society

Richard Lane, Norwell, Notts

Keith Le Milliere, Bideford, Devon

David Lee, Director ECFC

Peter Loader (Former student, Exeter University)

Tim Long

Paul Luscombe, Marchwood, Southampton

Neal Luxton, Lyme Regis, Dorset

Dave Luxton, Julie Moore, Exeter, Devon

Charlie and Alfie Mabey

Andrew P. Marchant

Paul Trevor Marks, Exeter

Sue McQueenie

Mikael and Tone, Oslo, Norway

Peter Minhinnett, Leicester

Mick Mitcham, Barnstaple

Pete Moore

Nathan Moore, Exeter

Dave Moore, Wexford, Ireland

Brian and Helen Moore, Exeter

David H. W. Morgan, Sergy, France

Rodney Morgan, Axminster, Devon

Stephen James Morris CTID

Ivor Morrish

Paul Morrish

Edward Morton

Penelope Mountain, London

Rob Mulholland

Charles Neary, Staunton, Virginia, USA

Graham Needs

Gary Nelson

Boucar Ngom and Sarah Lawson, London

Richard Norris, Bishopsteignton, Devon

Max Oliver, Exeter, Devon

Nigel Parton, Huddersfield

Michael J. Paxton, Chestnut Close, Exmouth, Devon

Brian Peeke, Topsham, Exeter

David J. Phillips, Tiverton, Devon

John A. Pitts, Plympton, Devon

Stuart Price, Exeter

David Price, Exmouth, Devon

George Edward Prouse, Barnstaple, Devon

Phil Radmore

Nick Rendle, Braunton

John Revell, Exeter, RIP

David Robinson, Exeter

Oliver J. Rooney, Draycott, Somerset

Steve Rudawski, London

Russell Sadler

David Salter, Exeter

Mark A. Selley, Oxford, Oxfordshire

Andrew Sharp, Exeter, Devon

Jim Shepherd

Alderman Norman Shiel, Exeter

Mike Shotter, Bristol

Ray Silcox, Green Lane, Exeter

Sittaford Strollers

Rupert Smith, St Thomas, Exeter

Michael Smith, Exeter, Devon

The Soper Family, Luton, Bedfordshire

Pete Southwell, Exminster, Exeter

Colin Stanley, Nottingham

Phil Stemp, Chelmsford, Essex

Steve, M. J. and David (Leeds Grecians)

Graham Stone, Rustington, West Sussex

Frances and Paul Stoneman, Tiverton, Devon

Martyn Stoneman, Tiverton, Devon

Theunis Stortenbeker, Ashill

Robin Stowell, Cardiff

David Stowell, Manchester

John Summers, Lincoln, Lincolnshire

Chris Sumner, Exeter

Paul Sussex, Aldershot

Myles Sutherland, Exeter, Devon

Peter H. Taylor

Malcolm Tipper, Teignmouth

John Tolliday, Exeter, Devon

Ian Totterdell, Exeter

John Treleven, Jersey

James Trevelyan, Bradninch, Devon

Adrian Tripp, Exeter

Adam Tripp, London E20

Mark Turner

Phil Uzzell, Herne Bay, Kent

Gerald Uzzell, Herne Bay, Kent

Devon Uzzell, Herne Bay, Kent

Ian Webber, Coldridge, Devon

Graham J. Webster, Hatfield Peverel, Essex

Barry Wedlake and Family, Exeter, Devon

Francis Welland, Uffculme

Stephen Richard Weston

Ron White, Liverpool Exile

Neil Williams

Ken Williams, Folly Gate, Devon

Colin Williams-Hawkes

Sarah, Chloe and Harry Willis

Barry Wilson, Exeter

Allan Philip Woodland

Chris Woodley Pincott, Exeter

Gary Woollacott, Northam, Devon

Jacob Woollacott, Northam, Devon

Phil Dan Wright, Exeter